Stephen Gorard
Beng Huat See
Rebecca Morris

The most effective approaches to teaching in primary schools

Rigorous evidence on effective teaching

LAP LAMBERT Academic Publishing

Impressum / Imprint
Bibliografische Information der Deutschen Nationalbibliothek: Die Deutsche Nationalbibliothek verzeichnet diese Publikation in der Deutschen Nationalbibliografie; detaillierte bibliografische Daten sind im Internet über http://dnb.d-nb.de abrufbar.

Bibliographic information published by the Deutsche Nationalbibliothek: The Deutsche Nationalbibliothek lists this publication in the Deutsche Nationalbibliografie; detailed bibliographic data are available in the Internet at http://dnb.d-nb.de.

Coverbild / Cover image: www.ingimage.com

Verlag / Publisher:
LAP LAMBERT Academic Publishing
ist ein Imprint der / is a trademark of
OmniScriptum GmbH & Co. KG
Bahnhofstraße 28, 66111 Saarbrücken, Deutschland / Germany
Email: info@omniscriptum.com

Herstellung: siehe letzte Seite /
Printed at: see last page
ISBN: 978-3-659-95669-0

Contents

The most effective approaches to teaching in primary schools

Part 1 - Overview

1. Introduction

The first part of the book is a summary of the findings of the detailed review of evidence that follows. It addresses the following question, and sub-questions:

- What are currently the most effective approaches for teaching primary school children?

And, as far as it is possible to tell:

  - Do the effective approaches differ for different sub-groups of pupils, and if so, how?
  - Do the effective approaches differ for particular ages or phases within education to age 11?

The book does so by summarising and synthesising a wide range of relevant international research reports and evidence. The research questions are causal in nature and so the review only considers evidence that is potentially capable of addressing this causal question – most notably this includes randomised controlled trials and similar. Each study included is assessed in terms of quality (how trustworthy the results are judged to be) and its outcomes (whether it works and how effective it is), and the most promising approaches are described in more detail. This overview summarises the evidence in each over-lapping area through use of a summary table. The columns in each table show whether the approach is deemed effective and beneficial or ineffective and/or possibly harmful. The rows given an indication of the quality of each study – ranging from higher quality meaning that the study is about as good as could be expected in real-life, to lower quality meaning that the study is not to be trusted on its own as evidence that an approach works. A lot of further 'research' on the relevant topics has simply been ignored because it is not capable of uncovering causal influences. The lower quality work in the tables has been retained because it was capable of providing useful evidence – but was perhaps too small in scale, had very high numbers of missing cases, or unreliable measurements.

It is important to distinguish between approaches that do not work in terms of raising attainment, those that have either not been tested or have mixed or unclear results, and those that have evidence of beneficial impact. The focus here is more on the latter, although the first two groups are also summarised briefly. The importance of knowing about approaches that are not evidence-informed is that they may be widespread and so harming individuals' lives either directly or at best by not permitting better approaches to use the same time and resources.

2. Summary of the findings

The full report notes a small number of specific interventions that *have* been trialled with success – such as "My Reading Coach" and "Grammar for Writing". Other than these, and where work has been replicated in some way so that the results are more secure, the following are probably worth pursuing:

- **A range of literacy interventions including phonics and similar approaches, with programmes like Reading Recovery and Accelerated Reader, all giving an 'effect' size of 0.2 or more**
- **Tiered individual and small group programmes, including Response to Intervention, all giving an 'effect' size of 0.2 or more**

However, all of these are mostly tested and successful with pupils struggling with literacy or maths. Few have been shown to be successful with mixed ability whole classes.

On the other hand, **appropriate and targeted work for small groups in heterogeneous classes has an 'effect' size of around 0.1**. All of the above provide a role for TAs. They also provide disguised examples of teachers using research evidence in practice – disguised because the evidence is built into the protocol.

Although these interventions can be used at almost any primary age when a problem surfaces, other studies in the main report suggest that early-years interventions are most effective. Early literacy is important to allow pupils to access the wider curriculum. However, there is barely enough good evidence overall. It is hard to find solid evidence about the differential age effectiveness of different pedagogical approaches (i.e. studies that compare the impact of an approach for different age groups).

For whole classes, the evidence is that the following are probably worth pursuing:

- Greater pupil autonomy such as occurs in circle discussion time, and teaching reasoning skills, giving an 'effect' size of around 0.2.
- Maths Mastery, giving an 'effect' size of around 0.1.

There is not enough evidence on interventions related to mindfulness, focusing on developing pupil content knowledge, teacher content knowledge, explicit teaching, pupil:teacher interactions and raising teacher expectations. However, many of these are not looking promising.

There is considerable evidence on peer-tutoring, collaborative learning, quizzes and practice, self-regulation and enhancing formative feedback. Unfortunately, the evidence is mixed and therefore unclear. These approaches have not been found to be harmful and are relatively inexpensive.

The following are probably not worth pursuing if the aim is solely to improve attainment – grade retention, setting and streaming, improving attitudes, aspirations or motivation alone, teacher's direct use of evidence (as opposed to teachers using evidence based protocols, approaches or resources), participation in arts, drama or music for improvement in other subjects, behavioural interventions, and the generic use of ICT/CAL in the classroom. It follows then that these issues should not be promoted in literature, courses, resources or initial training for primary teachers. The full report also notes a range of specific interventions that have been trialled without success. Given the number and range of possible interventions, unsuccessful ones should be avoided.

3. Approaches currently deemed effective

Beginning with the important areas where there is good or at least promising evidence of effectiveness, this section considers approaches for individuals and small groups before turning to whole class issues.

3.1 Individual/small group approaches

Table 1 - Quality and impact summary: studies of phonics/phonological approaches

	Effective	Ineffective/unknown
Higher quality	1	0
Medium quality	1	1
Lower quality	12	3

Phonics

Unlike the kinds of literacy interventions described above, there is a wide range of specific interventions and protocols that have been used successfully with small groups or even individual pupils to help overcome problems in literacy (and to a lesser extent maths). The evidence for teaching via phonics approaches is not as strong as some commentators envisage but suggests that the approach is successful - at least for struggling readers (Table 1). The scoping review discusses 18 evaluations, as well as the results of a number of prior reviews. On balance it appears that **phonics does work for young children who are not readers from an early age.** This is not proposed as a whole class intervention, and the evidence base is largely about individual or small group teaching. The direct cost is minimal but the approach does mean having another trained staff member for each class so that work is in parallel (this scoping review does not address extra classes or outside school activities).

Reading Recovery

There is slightly more secure evidence for **Reading Recovery/Switch-on, which has about the same impact as phonics interventions for the sub-set of pupils who are struggling to read** (Table 2). The scoping review presents eight trials, of which most are positive including the strongest. Again this is not a whole class treatment, but has the advantage over phonics that the precise formal nature of the protocols for the related approaches of Reading Recovery and Switch-on Reading can be conducted in or out of class by teaching assistants (TAs). As with technology and other resources, merely having TAs present is not effective. But if deployed appropriately it is clear that TAs can contribute to class outcomes, and are cheaper than extra trained teachers. As discussed in relation to teachers' use of research evidence below, such evidence is most easily digested and used when engineered into a simple observable protocol like this that appears to work, and which teachers and TAs can follow.

Different approaches to improving literacy may have similar 'effects' in terms of size (see below) but in somewhat different tests of literacy. For example, a phonics approach will tend to improve word sounding more than fluency, decoding or spelling.

Table 2 - Quality and impact summary: studies of Reading Recovery/Switch-On

	Effective	Ineffective/unknown
Higher quality	1	0
Lower quality	1	1
Minimal quality	4	1

Accelerated Reader

The evidence is almost as secure for Accelerated Reader, which can be used as a whole class intervention or with individuals and small groups of struggling readers. Again the benefits are relatively small, but the overall evidence including that from the two strongest evaluations is that it works, especially for the lowest attainers (Table 3).

Table 3 - Quality and impact summary: studies of Accelerated Reader

	Effective	Ineffective
Higher quality	2	0
Medium quality	0	0
Lower quality	12	6

There must be a larger number of specific interventions in literacy and in other subject areas that could be deployed as evidence-informed, and could be implemented with the help of TAs (but which the scoping review has not picked up or which have not been evaluated at scale). And given that the named approaches discussed here all have a similar impact, it is very possible that the precise protocol does not matter as much as might appear.

Response to Intervention

Indeed there are some indications from other evidence that within limits it is not the precise nature of the protocol that is being effective in any of these approaches. Rather, **many coherent approaches to overcoming low attainment based on small group or individual attention or deployment of TAs are equally effective.** And (as above) each could address different aspects of low attainment. This is different to reducing class sizes. Altering class sizes within traditional limits, such as from 30 to 24, is not particularly helpful. The successful interventions of the kind being discussed here involve groups of only one to four pupils, while the same approaches used with whole classes, even small classes, may be only weakly effective or even ineffective. Similarly **there is reasonably good evidence that within class groupings for specific activities and events can be beneficial.** The tiered approaches of Response to Intervention (RTI) are an example (Table 4). RTI or similar has been assessed in many subject areas across the primary age range. The effective elements are Tier 3 (individual or very small group) and Tier 2 (small group) work. Other than that, a wide range of suggested interventions and approaches are labelled here as RTI, because the idea is deliberately vague. It involves breaking the class down so that pupils can be given targeted and appropriate attention. The scoping review found 25 studies of which the strongest and the majority suggested that the idea has considerable promise.

Table 4 - Quality and impact summary: studies of RTI

	Effective	Ineffective/unknown
Higher quality	3	0
Medium quality	3	0
Low quality	15	4

Within class grouping

A lot of the studies in this area are focussed on the lowest attainers. There is less evidence on gifted children, and almost nothing directly focussed on average attainers. There are studies of within-class grouping. **As with grouping *into* classes, the indication is that within-class groups should be of mixed ability** (except where a short-term intervention such as those above is targeted). It is the scale and level of attention that seems to matter more than having pupils at the same level of progress. In general, **small group work is effective, although the evidence base is not large** (Table 5).

Table 5 - Quality and impact summary: studies of class grouping

	Effective	Ineffective/unknown
Higher quality	2	1
Medium quality	0	0
Lower quality	1	0

Other than those addressed elsewhere the scoping review found only four studies on this, and one of the better ones found grouping to be ineffective.

Individualised instruction

A similar picture emerges from studies of individualised instruction (Table 6). There is a weak set of evidence pointing weakly towards benefits for individual attention. The scoping review outlines a further 7 studies on this. In summary, **combining evaluations of specific interventions, more generic tiered teaching, and studies of grouping and individual attention there is a clear message that small is good**. If the resources are available, then within-class tiers or groups given suitable tasks would form part of the work of the evidence-informed primary teacher. It is not the purpose of the scoping review to suggest or promote specific commercially available products, and any examples given are only illustrations.

Table 6 - Quality and impact summary: studies of individualised instruction

	Effective	Ineffective/unknown
Higher quality	0	0
Medium quality	1	1
Lower quality	5	0

However, whatever small group or individual protocol is to be used must itself be evidence-informed. As the previous section showed, there are small group and targeted interventions promoted and currently in use that do not appear to work. It is important to distinguish between approaches with no promise (and to avoid them), some promise (and test them rigorously at scale), and considerable promise (our best 'bets' at present).

3.2 Whole-class approaches

This section moves from interventions for individuals and small groups to whole class approaches.

Reasoning skills

In contrast to an emphasis on subject knowledge (above) and basic skills, it is possible to **emphasise the reasoning skills of pupils. There is a reasonable body of evidence now that such a focus has a small benefit for literacy and numeracy** (as well as any possible intrinsic merits). There is also **some promise from studies of the linked idea of teaching pupils strategies for meta-cognition (and self-regulation).** The scoping review describes 16 evaluations of which the majority, including all of the most robust studies, show at least small benefits for general attainment (Table 7).

Table 7 - Quality and impact summary: studies of teaching reasoning skills

	Effective	Ineffective/unknown
Higher quality	3	0
Medium quality	0	1
Lower quality	10	2

This has to be seen by schools as a promising, cheap, and currently evidence-informed way forward. Although several of these interventions involve a change to the layout and structure of classes, most of them are best undertaken in whole class groups with the teacher ensuring that all pupils can contribute, while passing considerable control to the pupils themselves.

Maths Mastery

There is a **growing body of evidence that Singapore Maths/Maths Mastery may be effective (for maths attainment).** The overall impact (if it is an 'impact') is small. The scoping review found 7 studies of which only three are medium and higher in quality, and one of these suggests no benefit (Table 8). **Similar mastery learning approaches may be effective in other subject areas (such as science) as well but the evidence here is weaker**.

Table 8 - Quality and impact summary: studies of Singapore Maths/Maths Mastery

	Effective	Ineffective/unknown
Higher quality	1	0
Medium quality	1	1
Lower quality	3	0

4. Approaches currently untested or with mixed evidence

There are many approaches that offer some promise but either have not been robustly tested at an appropriate scale, or where they have been tested the aggregated results are mixed. The first four summaries address evidence specifically related to literacy, science, maths and arts (including music), other than studies (such as feedback) that might have been successful in any one of these areas, but where the subject area is not intrinsic to the approach. What links the studies in these four summaries is that even though a few have shown promise, they are stand-alone without replication.

Interventions to improve literacy

Where there are a number of studies on a specific approach, such as for Accelerated Reader or READ180, these have their own summaries. Other than these, and the very poor studies mentioned in the first section, the scoping review came across a relatively large number of one-off lower quality studies purporting to test a specific approach to improving literacy outcomes (Table 9). One study of poor quality or small scale cannot be anything like definitive. The scoping review describes a total of **seven medium or higher quality evaluations, only a few of which address the same specific approach.** These include Project CRISS, and Writing Wings. **None are found to be effective.** There is **one robust study suggesting that teaching young children more about formal grammar has a small benefit for later tests of literacy**, and this might be worth pursuing.

Table 9 - Quality and impact summary: approaches to improve literacy

	Effective	Ineffective/unknown
Higher quality	1	0
Medium quality	4	2
Lower quality	23	4

Interventions to improve science

As with literacy, so also with measures to improve science (Table 10). Other than more general approaches applied to science and covered elsewhere in this overview, the safest evidence comes from a study of the use of school gardens for biology which does not provide general evidence about pedagogy. Otherwise, **the picture is very mixed. Four of the studies looked at inquiry approaches and showed no benefit.**

Table 10 - Quality and impact summary: studies of improving science

	Effective	Ineffective/unknown
Higher quality	1	0
Medium quality	1	1
Lower quality	2	1

Interventions to improve maths

As with literacy (above), and other than more promising approaches covered separately, such as Maths Mastery, there is a large number of studies trying a range of approaches to improve maths (Table 11). **The evidence of benefit is slightly stronger, but there is still not enough weight of evidence to draw clear pedagogical implications of a general nature.** The strongest study reported an effect size of only 0.05 for maths improvement.

Table 11 - Quality and impact summary: studies of improving maths

	Effective	Ineffective/unknown
Higher quality	1	0
Medium quality	1	0
Lower quality	19	4

Arts interventions

Participation in the arts, drama and music has been used as a means of increasing attainment in core subjects and skills (Table 12). The scoping review describes 9 studies in this area, and the **balance is currently that arts interventions are not known to work**. However, given that a large number of weak or medium quality studies do suggest positive effects, it seems that more work in this area, taking into account some of the most promising avenues (e.g. music), would be justified.

Table 12 - Quality and impact summary: use of Arts to improve attainment

	Effective	Ineffective/unknown
Higher quality	0	1
Medium quality	1	0
Lower quality	5	2

4.1 Individual/small group approaches

Peer tutoring/mentoring

Table 13 - Quality and impact summary: studies of peer tutoring

	Effective	Ineffective/unknown
Higher quality	1	1
Medium quality	1	1
Lower quality	4	3

A similar picture emerges for **peer mentoring**. There has been considerable research on the impact of peer-tutoring and mentoring, especially cross-age mentoring, and some of it is of higher quality. However, **the results are mixed**. It may be that peer collaborative work is less effective, and cross-age tutoring more so, but the overall picture is that the evidence is evenly divided (Table 13). The scoping review discusses 12 studies, of which some of the better ones report a benefit and some do not.

Behavioural interventions

Most of the studies involving behavioural interventions do not consider attainment or pupil progress as outcomes (and so are largely ignored in this review). The scoping review presents results from five trials, and again the evidence is evenly split (Table 14). **At present, behavioural, social and emotional interventions in order to improve general attainment are not indicated as promising**. They may, of course, have other advantages or work for specific individuals in a way that does not show up in larger datasets.

Table 14 - Quality and impact summary: Behavioural interventions

	Effective	Ineffective
Higher quality	0	0
Medium quality	2	2
Lower quality	1	0

4.2 Whole class approaches

Explicit teaching

Other than covered elsewhere in terms of specific subjects, the scoping review found only 4 evaluations of explicit teaching (an instructional strategy used by teachers to meet the needs of their students and engage them in unambiguous, clearly articulated teaching), of which only one was medium or higher quality (Table 15). **The evidence from this is sparse but promising, and several other interventions claimed to use explicit teaching as part of a package or other changes making it hard to decide on the causal model.** Any description of explicit teaching also tends to be a list that includes other approaches such as prompt feedback and frequent quizzes that can (or not) be effective in their own right.

Table 15 - Quality and impact summary: explicit teaching

	Effective	Ineffective
Higher quality	1	0
Medium quality	0	0
Lower quality	2	1

Teacher knowledge

There has been considerable research on the value of teacher pedagogical and content knowledge. The aggregate result is mixed. It is **not clear that intervening to make teachers themselves know more about their subject areas, or about theories on how to teach, makes much difference to pupil attainment**. This may be because it is hard to alter teaching knowledge in a feasible way in an intervention. There is evidence from this review that teacher 'quality' is related to pupil results (Section 4), but the picture for teacher initial qualification is not so clear.

Several studies have attempted to enhance **teachers' use of research evidence directly. This does not seem to work**, and suggests that evidence-informed teaching needs a conduit that translates the research into something more practical that teachers (and support staff) can use. It is probable that this must be more than access to information, like the EEF's Teaching and Learning Toolkit (but that may be more suitable for policy-makers and school leaders than class teachers). The current evidence on what works could be built into initial teacher preparation, texts, resources, and lesson plans – these are what need to be evidence-informed. Examples appear in the next section. The scoping review discusses 20 mixed studies in this area (Table 16). On balance, these suggest that directly seeking to increase teacher knowledge, as such, may not work to improve pupil attainment.

Table 16 - Quality and impact summary: studies of teacher knowledge

	Effective	Ineffective
Higher quality	1	3
Medium quality	4	6
Lower quality	4	3

Teacher interaction

The evidence in general on the **impact of how teachers interact with pupils in classes is weak but perhaps promising** (Table 17). This includes work on teaching styles, facilitating pupil autonomy, and how teachers handle expectations of their pupils.

Table 17 - Quality and impact summary: studies of teacher interactions

	Effective	Ineffective/unknown
Higher quality	0	0
Medium quality	0	0
Lower quality	4	2

Feedback and enhancing self-regulation

The evidence for **enhanced immediate formative feedback in the classroom is still relatively weak.** Correlational evidence shows that it is clearly an approach that 'good' teachers use but it is not so clear that the approach can be easily taught to others for them to use effectively such that it translates into better pupil attainment. Enhancing feedback has the intention of assisting pupils to be self-regulated learners, and so studies of self-regulation are also included here. The scoping review presents 19 studies of mixed quality, and these are reasonably evenly split between those presenting successful outcomes and those where the intervention had no impact (Table 18).

Table 18 - Quality and impact summary: studies of feedback/self-regulation

	Effective	Ineffective/unknown
Higher quality	1	1
Medium quality	1	2
Lower quality	11	3

Mindfulness

The evidence on mindfulness interventions is sparse and weak, and the approach should probably be treated as ineffective in the same way as improving attitudes and aspirations until better studies emerge. As with all approaches there may be intrinsic or other benefits – the studies are all judged here only in terms of pupil learning and attainment. The scoping review only found two small trials with the relevant age group (Table 19).

Table 19 - Quality and impact summary: mindfulness

	Effective	Ineffective/unknown
Higher quality	0	0
Medium quality	0	0
Lower quality	2	0

Content knowledge

There is currently **very little robust work on the impact of emphasising wider content knowledge in teaching primary age children, and overall the current conclusion has to be that it is not known to be effective** in terms of attainment in maths and literacy. Emphasising cultural, historical, geographical or other knowledge may have so far unknown intrinsic or long-terms benefits however. The scoping review describes 6 relevant studies of which the most robust is of only medium quality, all of which test the "Core Knowledge curriculum" or approaches based directly, and suggests that this approach does not work (Table 20).

Table 20 - Quality and impact summary: studies of Core Knowledge

	Effective	Ineffective/unknown
Higher quality	0	0
Medium quality	0	1
Lower quality	4	1

5. Approaches currently deemed ineffective or harmful

Grade retention and ability grouping

It is reasonably clear from evidence prior to this review that **grade retention, and setting and streaming of young children so that each class includes a narrower range of ability or prior attainment** (and teaching is largely traditional and in whole classes), **are not effective**. It may even be harmful for attainment (and wider socialisation). This is very different from saying that specific interventions and activities should not be targeted at groups and individuals within mixed ability groups (see below).

Motivation and attitudes

It is also reasonably clear from previous robust reviews that **intervening to increase children's motivation to attain, their aspiration to succeed or attitudes related to education does not, in itself, improve attainment**. Attitudinal change either needs to be tied to specific behaviour changes that may then be rewarded and build towards better attainment (such as attendance in class or completion of homework), or accompanied by tuition to improve competence as well (which may then be sufficient in its own right). Motivation is more about whether any other interventions work rather than being the basis for an appropriate intervention in its own right.

Use of technology

There is now a **considerable body of evidence that simply using commercial software or replacing teacher roles with Information Technology (IT) and Computer Assisted Learning (CAL) is not effective**. There are approaches that have been successful that do involve technology (and some are described above) but it appears as though each approach works (or not) and may involve technology (or not). Simply having and using interactive boards, tablets, clickers and so on is not sufficient. The scoping review describes 35 studies using IT/CAL that are not otherwise covered elsewhere (Table 21). The better studies are clearly negative in the sense of showing no benefit (or worse) for learning. There are some studies suggesting that use of technology instead of teachers is actually harmful. The weak studies are mixed in their reported outcomes, which is unusual compared to other approaches where poor studies are well-known to report overly positive outcomes.

Table 21 - Quality and impact summary: studies of ICT/CAL

	Effective	Ineffective/unknown
Higher quality	0	3
Medium quality	1	3
Lower quality	19	9

<u>READ180</u>

There are a small number of specific interventions that have been trialled more than once with no obvious benefit for outcomes, including READ180 (Table 22). This shows that READ180 does not work, with the bulk of evidence including the most powerful studies showing no benefit.

Table 22 - Quality and impact summary: READ180

	Effective	Ineffective/unknown
Higher quality	0	2
Medium quality	1	0
Lower quality	1	3

6. Conclusion

We can only provide summary evidence here for the approaches that been evaluated, and there may be many more that have not been. There are interesting questions raised by the pattern of approaches with evidence of effectiveness - whether it is about structured (evidence-informed) protocols where evidence most easily informs teaching, or teachers organising lessons to provide opportunities for pupils to reason and debate. Perhaps then this is less about making less effective teachers behave like the more successful ones, but more about being able to provide structures and successful protocols for the less effective ones. This would have to be investigated further.

Part 2 - The full review of evidence

1. Introduction

1.1 Background

Comparisons of school outcomes both nationally (school 'league tables') and internationally (PISA PIRLS and TIMSS) have spurred a body of research on school effectiveness and improvement since the 1980s, looking at school level variables such as school leadership, structure, organisation and policy. After decades of research it is still unclear within a national system how much difference individual schools make to pupils' school outcomes. The causal influence of attending specific schools is difficult to determine without actually randomly allocating pupils and teachers to different types of schools. More recently, attention has turned to processes within the classroom - what happens in the classroom, what is taught, and how it is taught (Harris and Ratcliffe. 2005). Comparisons have been made with schools in the Pacific Rim countries (deemed more effective) where the focus appears to be more on whole-class teaching, focused group work, and collaborative learning with clearly defined learning objectives.

Several theories of learning and instruction have been put forward to explain differential teacher effectiveness (e.g. Creemers 1994, Scheerens 1992, 1999). The Hay McBer report suggested that teacher characteristics, teaching skills and classroom climate contribute as much as 30% of the variance in pupil progress (DfEE 2000), although this work has been widely criticised (Gorard 2002). The Pearson Report identified seven effective pedagogical strategies (Siraj-Blatchford and Taggart 2014). A longitudinal study by the same team looking at Year 5 classroom pedagogies identified 11 effective strategies (Siraj-Blatchford et al. 2011). These included good classroom climate, behavioural management, making clear the learning objectives, making links explicit, and assessment for learning.

Marzano (Marzano et al. 2001, p.7, Marzano, 2003, p.80) listed the following nine categories of instructional strategies that affect student achievement: identifying similarities and differences; summarising and note taking; reinforcing effort and providing recognition; homework and practice; non-linguistic representations; cooperative learning; setting objectives and providing feedback; generating and testing hypotheses, questions, and cues; and advance organisers.

Coe et al. (2014) noted in their summary of teaching practices that many commonly used classroom strategies widely thought to be effective do not work. Examples of these included unearned praise, ability grouping, and individualised teaching tailored to meet pupils' learning styles. According to Coe teaching must include imparting knowledge and critical thinking (Economist 2016). The review summarised effective teaching as having six key components (content knowledge, classroom climate, classroom management, teacher expectations and professional behaviour).

In the US the quality-plus teaching strategies which set the benchmark for effective practice listed 13 strategies:

- Frequent assessment to provide feedback to parents and pupils
- Modelling and practice
- Use non-verbal or visual representations of content and skills
- Collaborative learning
- Content and explicit teaching
- Summarising – explicitly teach students to summarise their learning
- Improve literacy – explicitly teach literacy skills
- Questioning –teach questioning and cueing/prompting techniques
- Build basic background knowledge
- Use technology to plan, teach and assess
- Set goals – teach students to set personal goals for improving achievement
- Teach children skills to compare and contrast concepts and content.

There is some observational evidence that the quality of teaching practice may be associated with student achievement (Cantrell et al. 2008). It is generally agreed that to be effective teachers, be it in maths, science or literacy, a good grounding in the subject knowledge is necessary. But this alone is not enough. Equally important is the skill to convey that knowledge to learners in a way that can be easily assimilated. Pedagogical skills are therefore a component of being an effective teacher. In the last two decades a wide range of technology, gadgets, commercial software, interventions and scripted curricula have become available to teachers. Examples of technology include the interactive whiteboard, mobile phone devices and ipads. Besides these, computer software for teaching, such as Accelerated Reader, Star Maths as well as scripted curricula like RTI and feedback strategies have also been employed to support teaching and learning.

There is a wide range of strategies currently tested and implemented in primary schools to improve the learning of children. These include:

- Whole class teaching
- Effective questioning
- Explicit teaching/direct instruction
- Small group learning
- Collaborative or cooperative learning
- One-to-one
- Individualised instruction
- Differentiated instruction
- Use of feedback
- Blended learning
- Game-based learning
- Student engagement (behavioural management)
- Technology/computer
- Teacher knowledge and skill
- Modelling
- Inquiry learning
- Flipped learning
- Identifying needs
- Student-centred
- Mastery through repetition

- Learning/improving academic skills through behaviour modification
- Project-based instruction
- Phonological awareness training
- Use of data

A number of these strategies have elements of one or more of the others. For example, self-regulation training involves feedback strategies, explicit instruction, developing positive attitude and self-efficacy, and computer software programmes may be used to train self-regulation or improve teacher-student relationships.

However, the studies cited in the reviews cited above (and the recommendations made based on them) have been largely passive in design (looking at existing patterns rather than actually trying the ideas out as part of robustly evaluated interventions). Reviews have tended to define teaching approaches as' effective' by comparing schools having good results with those with poor results (however defined), and attempting to summarise strategies merely associated with such 'effective' schools as effective strategies. This is what Ouston (1998) described as the 'potted plant theory' of educational effectiveness. The next step is not to identify what 'good' schools and teachers do, but to **test whether these ideas and other like them lead to practical interventions that can, for example, make 'bad' teachers better, and satisfactory teachers good.**

Therefore, this new review will robustly evaluate all relevant empirical research to look for evidence of a *causal* effect of teaching strategies or classroom processes on academic attainment at primary level, over and above mere association (Gorard 2013). It will then blend this with knowledge about other research and theories in this area, and come up with a judgement of trustworthiness of the results in each field. As far as we know no such analysis has been conducted in England, hence the call for this new review.

1.2 Aims and procedures

The review will:

- map the current international research on effective teaching pedagogies in primary schools (children aged 4 to 11 years)
- identify the most effective teaching practices in primary schools that have an impact on children's academic attainment
- critically evaluate the quality of studies using pre-set criteria to determine the security of the findings
- where possible, synthesize the relevant studies and categorise the approaches or strategies by phase of schooling (pre-school, KS1 and KS2) and for different groups of children (FSM eligible, SEN and ethnic minority)
- consider different teaching strategies for different subjects, where these are found.

1.3 Research questions

- What are currently the most effective approaches for teaching primary school children?

And insofar as it is possible to tell,

- Do the effective approaches differ for different sub-groups of pupils, and if so, how?
- Do the effective approaches differ for particular ages or phases within education to age 11?

1.4 Definition of terms

For the purpose of this project, we adopt the definition of pedagogy as the 'science of the art of teaching' (Gage 1985) and an 'effective' pedagogy as a set of classroom practices that lead to progress or improvements over some baseline measures.

The outcome of interest as specified in the call for this review is academic achievement. This covers any measures of academic attainment (e.g. standardised tests, KS or SATs, teacher assessments, and later educational progression).

The review also discusses possible outcomes such as on-task behaviour (for children with emotional and behavioural difficulties), attention in class, learning motivation/interest, and so on. But these are only included to the extent that they lead to better attainment outcomes.

2. Methods used in the scoping review

The review undertook several overlapping steps.

Stage 1	Identify the databases and develop the keywords for the search
Stage 2	Perform the electronic searches
Stage 3	Screen the title and abstracts for relevance, then export to EndNote
Stage 4	Remove duplicates and retrieve full text
Stage 5	Screen full texts for more details (sometimes it is not clear from the abstracts what the age of the participants were or what the intervention is about)
Stage 5	Data extract and assess quality of studies
Stage 6	Summarise the findings

2.1 The search

Our search involved systematically searching electronic databases, searching the internet using Google and Google Scholar to capture studies that may have been missed in our electronic searches, and adding literature known to us from our previous studies.

The electronic databases searched included:
WebofScience (Science Citation Index; Social Sciences Citation Index; Arts and Humanities Citation Index; Conference Proceedings Science Citation Index; Conference Proceedings Social Science and Humanities Citation Index; Book Citation Index - science, Book Citation Index - Social Science and Humanities, Emerging Sources Citation Index) and

Ebscohost (American doctoral dissertations, BEI, Child development and adolescent studies, eBook collection, Educational abstracts, Educational admin abstracts, ERIC, Library, information science and technology abstracts, MathSciNet via Ebscohost, Medline, PsyARTICLES, PSYCINFO)

The focus was on interventions and empirical research that included academic achievement as one of the outcome measures. The main outcome measures included improvement in a child's cognitive development, performance on standardised tests (such as Key Stage assessments) and teacher assessments.

The syntax used for electronic searches was:

"Pedagog*" or "teaching effectiveness" or "teacher effectiveness" or "classroom practi*" or "classroom strategy* or "teaching strategy*" or "teaching approach*" or "teaching style" or "effective instruction" or "teach* practi*" or "teacher knowledge" or "teach* skill*" or "whole class teaching"
AND
"Primary" or 'elementary" or "middle school" or "Key Stage 1" or "Key Stage 2" or "K-12" or "Grade*" or "infant school" or "junior school" or "mobile children" or "migrant*"
"School outcomes" or "learning outcomes" or "academic performance" or "standardi* tests" or "exam*" or "key stage" or "Grades" or "assessments" or "attainment" or "Grade retention" or "Grade point average"
AND
"Trial" or "experiment" or "intervention" or "randomi* controlled trial" or "RCT" or "regression discontinuity" or "causal evidence"

2.2 Inclusion criteria

In order to be included, a report had to be about:

- Teaching practices
- An empirical study using experimental or quasi-experimental design (e.g. regression discontinuity design, instrumental variables, propensity match scoring)
- Mainstream education (include SEN or learning needs children in mainstream schools)
- Pre-school to 6th Grade (age 4-11/12)

- Behavioural management (if it leads to academic outcomes including learning skills)
- International studies (with population similar in cultural context to UK population)
- School-wide or state-wide interventions delivered by teachers
- Specific interventions implemented by teachers in the classroom
- Classroom behaviour as a learning outcome (e.g. on-task, engagement as outcome)
- CPD (if it leads to evaluation of impact on children's learning outcomes)
- Teacher-pupil relationships (again if it includes analysis of academic outcomes)
- Peer-tutoring (if it is an instructional strategy used by the teacher)
- Interventions to improve thinking skills if they also look at impact on achievement

And it had to be:

- Reported or published between 2000 and 2016 (some older studies are included
- Reported in English (but from any country)

We also included meta-analyses and systematic reviews to summarise the existing evidence on each topic. Using the results of the search, inclusion was judged initially on the basis of title and abstract.

2.3 Hits from the searches

<u>Search 1</u>
Web of Science (n=1,280)
(Science Citation Index; Social Sciences Citation Index; Arts and Humanities Citation Index; Conference Proceedings Science Citation Index; Conference Proceedings Social Science and Humanities Citation Index; Book Citation Index -

science, Book Citation Index - Social Science and Humanities, Emerging Sources Citation Index

After screening for title and abstracts 385 pieces were retained

Ebscohost (n=460)
(American doctoral dissertations, BEI, Child development and adolescent studies, eBook collection, Educational abstracts, Educational admin abstracts, ERIC, Library, information science and technology abstracts, MathSciNet via Ebscohost, Medline, PsyARTICLES, PSYCINFO)

After screening for title and abstracts 195 pieces were retained

Search 2
We included additional parameters in our search, such as migrants, traveller groups, Pacific Rim in the search

Web of Science (n=5,234)
After screening title and abstract 836 pieces were retained

Search 3
Additional searches were also made to look specifically for evaluations of Singapore Maths and whole-class teaching strategies among others.
103 studies were picked up in this round (92 on whole-class teaching and 11 on Singapore Maths)

First round of exclusion
After elimination of duplicates and applying the inclusion and exclusion criteria considering relevance of topic, design and age, the combined number of studies included in the first round was 632.

Second round of exclusion

Further reading of the text excluded another 75, leaving 337 studies. These were data extracted.

We also supplemented these 337 studies with known studies from our previous work and reviews. We searched the EEF teaching and learning toolkit and web pages for relevant and current reports. In each case, this added extra studies that had been missed by the search (in particular, EEF-funded studies were only picked up where they had been published).

2.4 Data extraction

Each included study was then data extracted using a template that included the following sections:

Full reference
Research design
Sampling strategy (sample size, allocation of samples)
Attrition
Brief description of intervention
Outcome measures (how they are measured?)
Reported outcomes
Reviewers' calculation of effect size (if enough details are provided)
Clarity of reporting (evidence of biased reporting, threats to validity)
Level of evidence (quality assessment - see section on quality judgement)

The evidence of impact was judged based on the research design and not the conclusion or reported effects in the study report. Hence, the positive or negative results from these studies should be read in that light.

The identified studies were judged on their quality using pre-set criteria (similar to the padlock security rating developed from our approach by the Education Endowment Foundation) based on study design, sampling strategy, methods of assessing outcomes, appropriate methods of data analysis and clarity of reporting (see below).

2.5 Judging the quality of research studies and reports

We judged the quality of each research report and therefore the trustworthiness of its findings based on its design, scale (sample size), attrition (dropout, missing cases), outcome measurements (standardised, pre-specified), appropriateness, fidelity and validity.

Table 2.1, derived from Gorard (2015), has five main columns representing the kinds of issues that might usefully be taken into account when judging how secure the findings of any piece of research are. Using the descriptors in each column it is possible to decide on a broad classification for each study, ranging from 0 (not research or equivalent to not having done the research) to 4* (the most trustworthy a piece of research can be in real-life). The issues included are study design, scale of the study, bias through loss of data, the quality of data obtained for the study, and other threats such as conflicts of interest. The judgement on these issues assumes that the study has been reported fully, clearly, and without bias. If the study has not been reported properly, so that a fair judgement could not be made on one or more of these factors, it would automatically rate as of lower quality.

Table 2.1 – A 'sieve' to assist in the estimation of trustworthiness of descriptive work

Design	Scale	Dropout	Data quality	Threats	Rating
Strong design for research question (RQ)	Large number of cases (per comparison group)	Minimal attrition, no evidence of impact on findings	Standardised, pre-specified, independent	No evidence of diffusion, demand, or other threat	4«
Good design for RQ	Medium number of cases (per comparison group)	Some attrition (or initial imbalance)	Pre-specified, not standardised or not independent	Little evidence of diffusion, demand or other threat	3«
Weak design for RQ	Small number of cases (per comparison group)	Moderate attrition (or initial imbalance)	Not pre-specified but valid in context	Evidence of diffusion, demand or other threat	2«
Very weak design for RQ	Very small number of cases (per comparison group)	High attrition (or initial imbalance)	Issues of validity or appropriateness	Strong indication of diffusion, demand or other threat	1«
No consideration of design	A trivial scale of study, or N unclear	Attrition huge or not reported	Poor reliability, too many outcomes, weak measures	No consideration of threats to validity	0

The procedure starts with the first column, reading down the design descriptions in Table 2.1 until the study is at least as good as the descriptor in that row. For a causal question, an RCT or Regression Discontinuity Design (RDD), for example, might lead to the first row. A propensity score matched design might lead to the second row. If the design is not reported or there is no comparator this would lead immediately to the final row. Staying in the row achieved for the design, attention moves to the next column and down the scale descriptions until the study is at least as good as the descriptor in that row. An RCT with only 12 cases in each group would end up in row 5 at this stage. This process is repeated for each column, moving down (never up) the rows until the study is at least as good as the descriptor in that row. The final column in the table gives the estimated star rating for that study.

This means that an evaluation will be judged to be as good as the lowest classification it has achieved for each of the six categories. For any column, if it is not possible to discern the quality of the study from the available report(s) then the rating must be placed in the lowest (0) category. In using this aid, the emphasis throughout is intended to be on judgement. The ratings represent how much one might be prepared to stake on an intervention working or not, based on a single evaluation, in the same context or setting again (or for descriptive work how 'accurate' the results are).

The cell descriptions are therefore deliberately non-specific. For example, the phrase 'a large number of cases' might be interpreted rather differently, depending upon the precise context, question or pay-off. There is also an interaction between the simple number of cases, their completeness, representativeness of a wider set of cases, and the integrity of the way they have been allocated to groups. 'A large number of cases' would certainly be in the hundreds, but there is no precise figure such as 400 that can be set, other than as a rough guide. An excellent study might have one case below whatever threshold is suggested (399) and a weak one might have one more (401). Similarly, a true RCT might be considered a 'fair design for comparison' but there will be other designs of equal ability to discriminate between effect and noise. An attrition rate of 2% might be crucial if the missing cases all had extreme scores in the same direction, whereas 10% might still yield reasonably secure results if there was an obvious reason for the dropout that was unbiased across groups and types of cases. As with N, there is no clear threshold between 'minimal' attrition and worse that can be defended. There is a clear difference between trivial attrition and non-trivial attrition. But where precisely that difference lies is a matter of judgement, based on what is known about the context and the nature of the missing cases and where they appeared in the research process.

It is important that the outcome(s) of interest is specified and made clear before the study is conducted, if at all possible. This is to prevent researchers or users subsequently dredging a larger number of variables for those that show 'success' or 'failure'. The outcome also needs to be independent of the intervention itself. A key threat, especially when the outcome measure is tied in any way to the intervention, is that the treatment group might practice the post-test or a close proxy for it, in a way that the control group does not. Other threats to validity include having so many possible outcomes that some must be positive.

There are a large number of further issues that could enhance or reduce the trustworthiness of research results. In practice the overall level of research quality is already set by this point, as the various elements of quality are related in practice to some extent. For example, it is unlikely that a design based on a very weak comparison group would bother with whether the participants were 'blind' as to which group they were in when the outcome data was collected. Perhaps the single greatest threat to any study is a conflict of interest (CoI) for anyone involved. Traditionally this has been interpreted as concern where stakeholders stand to gain financially from the results of the study. However, CoIs are wider than this. Researchers can have prestige or prior claims wrapped up in a study intended to test their own, perhaps well-known, theory. This might make them reluctant to face a robust and independent test of their claims. Practitioners can become enthusiastic about an intervention even though ostensibly they have nothing to gain from an untrustworthy finding. The solution is, of course, that evaluators must be unconcerned about the nature of the results other than their quality, and that all interested parties should be 'blinded' as far as is feasible.

2.6 How did we synthesize the results?

With such a wide-ranging review it was hard to judge how to collate the findings to impose some order. We decided on four parallel approaches. We selected all of the most trustworthy results regardless of topic or outcome (judged secure 2* or better), and built analytical sections around the topics covered by this relatively small number of pieces (listed in the more detailed tables in the next section, with the most trustworthy 3* or better listed in bold). We looked at the EEF Teaching and Learning website, and built analytical sections around the themes that are relevant and deemed successful for classroom teachers in primary schools. These included:

- Phonics
- Peer-tutoring
- Behaviour interventions
- Social and emotional learning
- Collaborative learning
- Digital technology
- Oral language interventions
- Meta-cognition and self-regulation
- Reading comprehension strategies
- One to one tuition
- Early years interventions
- Mastery learning
- Mentoring
- Reducing class size
- Feedback
- Individualised instruction
- Arts participation

We did not include homework or parental involvement as these are not about classroom pedagogy or teaching approaches as such. We have previously conducted a very large systematic review of parental involvement/engagement and its (lack of) impact on pupil attainment (Gorard and See 2013). Nor did we include studies of setting and streaming as such because we already know that these do not work. We did not look at attitudes and aspirations, and have previously conducted a very large systematic review of attitudes and behaviour and their (lack of) impact on pupil attainment (Gorard et al. 2012). We searched for and analysed a few specific topics of current interest as requested by the funder (such as Maths Mastery). And finally, we put together evidence in areas where there were a large number of reports even if none of them was very robust. These four approaches tended to overlap to some extent.

2.7 Presentation of results

Where possible, because a research report either contains or provides sufficient detail for us to compute it, we present the standardised effect size for each relevant outcome. An effect size is here computed as the difference in mean scores between the intervention group and the control, divided by the overall standard deviation of those scores. An 'effect' size of 0 means that there is no difference between the groups (the intervention has caused no benefit or harm). An effect size of +0.02 would mean the same thing in reality. An effect size of -0.12 would mean that there is a discernible difference (but in this example the benefit comes from being in the control group). And an effect size of 0.22 would mean that there is a small but clear benefit from being in the intervention group. However, some studies do not report the 'effect' size (ES) at all and some do not report it clearly. Some have so many effect sizes for so many outcomes that it is hard to summarise. In these cases the column in the summary table is either left blank or the ES shown is a likely estimate.

Of course, an effect size must be viewed in terms of the scale and quality of the study – how trustworthy it is. A simple way to encapsulate many of the characteristics of any study and its findings is to convert the effect size into a number representing how different any missing cases would have to be in order for the effect size to become zero. This number of counterfactual cases needed to disturb the finding (NNTD) is here calculated as the effect size multiplied by the number of cases in the smallest group (intervention or control) minus the number of missing cases or cases missing data (attrition). If this NNTD is above zero then it means that even in the unlikely situation that all missing data were in the opposite direction to the main finding (counterfactual) the effect size would still be non-zero. This would mean a strong finding – all other things being equal (Gorard and Gorard 2015). Some studies do not report attrition, in which case we leave that column blank and reduce the security of the findings, and some do not make their report about attrition clear, in which case the figure given in the summary table is a likely estimate.

We are clearly not claiming that the review found and reported all relevant evidence. Therefore, the question is not whether any studies are missing but whether including further studies would change the substantive findings.

3. General comments on research in this area

Conducting any review, as here, it soon becomes clear that a majority of published and unpublished 'research' is of no consequence or use for any real-life purpose. It can be safely ignored and would not influence the findings of an empirical review. It may, of course, have other uses but its scale and predominance in the field of education suggests that a considerable sum of public and charitable funding is being spent for no gain.

If a causal model is envisaged as formed by evidence of association (correlation), an appropriate sequence of events (cause before or at same time as effect), an explanatory model, and then evidence that altering or introducing the purported cause changes the purported effect, this review can be envisaged as focussing on the fourth strand. There is, apart from the research noted in the last paragraph, quite a lot of work describing the first three components of a causal model. In a sense, some of the studies in this review emerged from work on the first three components. For example, descriptive work may have suggested that a successful teacher tends to use a certain approach. **The key question for policy or practice is whether other teachers can be encouraged to use that approach as well, and if so whether the results improve for their students.** Correlation is not causation and many plausible and well-intentioned interventions just do not work when their developers test them robustly with a wider population.

Aside from a large proportion of work of no consequence, and of a descriptive or explanatory nature, there is much less work that tries to test out an intervention or approach. And of this minority of work, most is still next to useless due to threats to design, minimal scale, or high attrition.

There also appears to be a mismatch specific to improving teaching. Large-scale descriptive, correlational and longitudinal studies have repeatedly identified possible factors describing successful schools, teachers or classes (see above), and risk factors for pupil low attainment. Many of these factors, like good classroom climate, charismatic leadership, or high quality teaching, need clear operationalisation to avoid the charge of being nebulous or tautological. All of these factors could and should be tested by rigorous classroom trials, but most have not been. It was rare in this scoping review to find a trial based on an intervention operationalised from school and teacher improvement studies.

Most actual trials seem to emerge from the ground up – such as testing the product of a company, or the idea of an academic. We know more about some relatively small and sometimes even trivial issues, and much less about some of the key issues emerging from strong descriptive work. There is also a widespread issue that the ground up trials are often conflicted, either because a company wants their product to be successful or an individual does not want their idea to be shown not to work. This lies behind the use of developers' own outcome tests, and may motivate rather partial reporting and the other dangers discussed throughout this report. Evaluations tend to be better when the researchers have nothing to gain or lose from whatever the result is, but gain or lose from whether the result is trustworthy or not.

Another general finding **is how small much of the work is** (even in this last category of evaluation work, which is among the best to be found). We report on studies where there were perhaps 90 students divided in three treatment groups and a control. This is a waste of resources, with 20+ cases per cell not leading to any usefully secure results. Of course, even dividing the 90 cases into only two groups would not lead to secure findings. What is clear is that there is overall sufficient funding for large studies but that it is being frittered away on many small ones. There is a lack of strategic vision and a risk of repeating mistakes of the former ESRC TLRP, in disproportionately funding specific ground-up interventions to the detriment of funding the big unresolved issues for improving teaching.

Looking at the summary tables in Section 4, and the reported outcomes of studies that were excluded as being unable to test a causal model by design it is **notable that the vast majority of poor studies reported a positive impact.** Many tried to find some positive impact on some sub-scales or subtests, or by using a more complex analytical approach than necessary. Many 'interventions' with evaluations were just lessons – as in if we teach pupils about something they tend to know more.

Biased reporting was found to be frequent – even to the extent that the success claimed in the abstract and conclusion of a report did not match the findings actually reported. Positive results are often highlighted in the abstracts or pulled out for more extensive discussion in the conclusion. For example, the paper may be an evaluation of literacy testing different components sometimes using different tests for different outcomes. Almost invariably bigger or positive effects are found for outcomes measured using researcher or developer-constructed assessments. It is often the case, that when standardised tests are used, such positive effects disappeared. For example, Paris and Paris (2007) reported big positive effects from teaching comprehension strategies on children's implicit and explicit comprehension. However, positive effects were found for test items that were related to the intervention, but not on items that were independent of the intervention. In essence, they tested strategies that were taught to experimental children but not the control. This was not explained clearly by the authors in the abstract or the conclusions. Although pre-tests were conducted using standardised tests, they were not used (or at least not reported) in the post-tests.

The issue of different results depending on the independence of the test is widespread and noted in most reviews (e.g. Li and Ma 2010). Yet it continues, for example: An (2015) and Arnold (2010) reported positive impact on teacher report card Grades, but no impact on the state standardised MCAS test for elementary pupils. Arnold (2010) reported impact on teacher-developed tests, but not on the Missouri Assessment Programme. It is also a very common occurrence where standardised tests are used in the pre-test to judge baseline equivalence and then a bespoke test more aligned to the intervention is then used for the post-test (and one wonders whether results have been selectively reported in some cases). Pullen et al. (2010) used the standardised PPVT in the pre-test but a bespoke researcher-developed post-test of target words that were used in the training. Their argument was that the PPVT was not sensitive enough to detect change in short-term intervention. A similar study by Pesco and Devlin (2015) using standardised test showed no effects of explicit instruction on comprehension. Puhalla (2011) tested the effects of booster instruction on vocabulary development. A range of tests was conducted, including the DIBELS. However, only the results for the Storybook Vocabulary Assessment (a researcher-developed test) were reported. This test assessed children on target words taught in the booster sessions, but which were not taught to the non-booster or average performing children.

Another widespread (almost universal) problem was the use and reporting of significance tests from studies in which cases had not been randomised or in which, having been randomised have suffered considerable attrition (missing data). This error shows a general misunderstanding of the use and pre-requisites of portability-based estimation, and the meaning of results. Worse, such studies tend to misuse these approaches instead of and as though they replaced careful consideration of threats to validity such as missing data.

4. The role of the teacher - teacher quality, knowledge and interactions with pupils

In the sections that follow (4 to 8), we have had to make a decision about placing each relevant study. We have not repeated any study, and so a report about research on feedback in maths could appear either under the heading of feedback or general improvement in maths. As far as possible, we have placed each study within the most specific section. This section concerns teacher knowledge.

4.1 Teacher development and pedagogical content knowledge

Many of the studies that reported positive effects included an element of teacher development. In some examples, this involved training by a developer or similar in the use of a specific intervention or approach such as enhanced feedback or Response to Intervention (see below). This may or may not be an essential part of any intervention success but is not the focus here. Rather, this section focuses on the more general subject and pedagogical knowledge that teachers have or develop, including attempts to get teachers to use research evidence more directly to improve their teaching. Slavin et al. (2009) reported teacher development as one of the most useful approaches to helping beginning readers. Teacher development includes professional development training teachers in subject content knowledge, pedagogic skills and teaching strategies for specific interventions. In the US the Reauthorisation of the Elementary and Secondary Act (2010) states that teachers need "effective, ongoing, job-embedded, professional development that is targeted to student and school needs... [and] aligned with evidence of improvements in student learning". As with educational effectiveness more generally, there have been many attempts to correlate measures of teacher quality or experience with pupil attainment (see Kini and Podolsky 2016 for a recent review of teacher experience). However, none of these can directly address causal questions such as does having a more experienced, or more developed, teacher *cause* better pupil outcomes.

As with the following sections, this section is 'driven' by the studies discovered as part of this review and rated as medium or higher quality (as listed in Table 4.2), but for completeness all studies of at least minimal quality are used to construct the summary of 'impact' in Table 4.1.

Table 4.1 - Quality and impact summary: studies of teacher knowledge

	Effective	Ineffective
Higher quality	1	3
Medium quality	4	6
Lower quality	4	3

Tables 4.1 and 4.2 indicate that there is no conclusive evidence whether training teachers to provide them with knowledge (either in content or pedagogic skills) is effective in raising attainment in primary school children. If anything, the weight of higher quality evidence is against and the only higher quality study showing an impact has very small effect sizes.

Table 4.2 - Quality and impact detail: studies of teacher knowledge

Reference	Intervention	Smallest cell	Attrition	ES	NNTD-attrition	Quality
Gersten et al. 2013	**Teacher development (research-based knowledge)**	**88 teachers, 871 pupils**	**Unknown**	**0**	**0**	**3***
Gallagher et al. 2014	**Professional development writing instruction**	**22 schools (472 pupils)**	**5%+**	**0**	**0**	**3***
Blair and Raver 2014	**Tools of the Mind - neurocognition**	**13 schools (340 pupils)**	**5%**	**0 to 0.11**	**20**	**3***
Heller et al. (US)	Teacher content pedagogical knowledge	122 teachers, 1900 pupils	39% of teachers	Teaching Cases 0.37 Looking at student work 0.57 Metacognition 0.60	0 306 366	2*
McCutchen et al. 2009	Teacher summer school	14 teachers (329 pupils)	Unknown	0.54	177 or less	2*
Matsumura et al.	Content focused	14 schools	50%	0.29	0	2*

2013	coaching	(1400 pupils)				
Borman et al.	Teacher content pedagogic knowledge in science	School level, 482 pupils	Unknown	0	0	2*
Diamond et al. 2014	Teacher content pedagogic knowledge in science	32 schools	18%	0	0	2*
Hairrell et al. 2011	Teacher quality in literacy	18 classes, 339 pupils	9%	0.53	115	2*
Coladarci and Gage 1984	Teacher content pedagogical knowledge	16 teachers, 315 pupils	14%+	Reading - 0.2 Maths - 0.08	0	2*
McNally 2014	Evidenced-approaches for lead teachers	462 pupils +562 pupils	33%	0	0	2*
Dorsett et al. 2014	Training in metacognition	20 schools	11 schools missing	0	0	2*
Rienzo et al. 2015	Training in growth	1,505 pupils	39%	Maths 0.01	0 0	2*

	mindsets			English -0.11		
Rimm-Kaufman et al. 2014	Training in Responsive Classroom	1,000 pupils	745 pupils	Maths 0 Literacy 0	0 0	2*

A large-scale and well-conducted study (Gersten et al. 2013) suggests positive impact of teacher development on teacher practices, but no impact on student outcomes. This study involved 182 first Grade teachers (94 treatment and 88 control) and a randomly selected sample of 1811 students (940 in treatment and 871 in control). These were drawn from 61 Title 1 schools (31 treatment and 30 control) from 16 school districts in four states. The aim of the intervention, Teacher Study Group (TSG), was to enhance instruction by helping teachers integrate research-based instructional strategies into their existing curriculum. 11 interactive sessions were held at the school site twice a month. Teachers' knowledge and children's vocabulary knowledge were assessed. Student outcomes were assessed using the Woodcock-Johnson vocabulary test, Group Reading Assessment and Diagnostic Evaluation. Random assignment of schools yielded treatment and control groups that were similar at baseline on all demographics and pre-test measures, except gender of the student sample.

A very large-scale study (Heller et al. 2012) examined the links between professional development, teacher knowledge, practice, and student achievement. In a randomised experiment implemented in six states with over 270 elementary teachers and 7,000 students, this project compared three related but systematically varied teacher interventions - *Teaching Cases, Looking at Student Work, and Metacognitive Analysis* - along with no-treatment controls. The three courses contained identical science content (electrical circuitry). They differed in the ways they incorporated analysis of learner thinking and of teaching, making it possible to measure effects of these features on teacher and student outcomes. The interventions were delivered by staff developers trained to lead the teacher courses in their regions. Results showed the three courses were effective in improving teachers' content knowledge and pupils' test scores compared to controls (ES for Teaching Cases = 0.37; Looking at Student Work 0.57; Metacognition 0.60), and effects were maintained a year later. Teacher attrition was high (39%) so reducing the trustworthiness of the findings. Heller et al. suggested that metacognition alone is not enough. Professional development should incorporate content learning with analysis of student learning.

An evaluation of a teacher summer school suggests that development of teacher knowledge is related to student outcomes with an average effect size of 0.89 for lower-ability learners and 0.54 across other students (McCutchen et al. 2009). The intervention was a 10-day summer course for teachers to develop their understanding of phonology, phonemic awareness, and the role of these factors in balanced reading instruction that emphasizes both word-level and text-level instruction. The course also emphasized the importance of developing students' reading comprehension and composition skills. Teachers developed lessons based on this new learning. Participants were 30 teachers from 17 US schools, 16 in treatment (389 3rd to 5th Grade pupils) and 14 in control (329 pupils), including a subset of 140 children identified (from 29 of the classrooms) as lower-performers (80 intervention, 60 control). However, it was not clear what the attrition was and how children or schools were matched.

The Hampshire Hundreds project (McNally 2014) was a local authority-led intervention. The aim was to provide support for teachers to enable them to understand the needs of the pupils and improve the quality of their teaching particularly in questioning and feedback. It involved 462 disadvantaged children plus another 562 other children. Results showed no evidence of impact on disadvantaged pupils and those eligible for free school meals. Attrition was high at 33% (12 of the 36 schools had dropped out by the end). The study shows that it is difficult to put research evidence into practice.

Another study that looked at professional development for teachers (Gallagher et al. 2014) to support teachers in the 3rd to 5th Grade with their writing instruction also found no impact of teacher training on student writing. This was a school-level randomisation with 44 schools being matched (forming 22 matched pairs). The number of pupils in the treatment schools was 472 and 530 in the control. One pair of schools dropped out and the reporting was rather poor.

Hairrell et al. (2011) conducted a school-level RCT involving 11 US schools, 36 classes and 679 4th Grade children, looking at the impact of teacher quality on student comprehension and curriculum-based measures of vocabulary and content knowledge. Teachers were allocated to either a comprehension or content vocabulary group. Teachers in each condition participated in 15 hours of relevant CPD over 18 weeks. Teacher quality was assessed in terms of their qualifications, instructional practices, treatment fidelity following CPD, structural effectiveness and social studies knowledge. Teacher quality was linked to increased achievement ($r = 0.73$). However, the study was poorly reported, around 64 student scores were missing, and the level of teachers' years of service was clearly different between the groups. Reporting structural equation modelling instead of ES does not address either of the latter issues, and obscures the mean results for each group.

Diamond et al. (2014) conducted a school-level RCT of the impact of improving teacher subject knowledge and teaching practice using Inquiry based learning to promote understanding of science concepts in 32 high poverty elementary schools. Schools were allocated to either treatment or control groups. The intervention included a curricular and professional development intervention consisting of a 5th Grade science curriculum, teacher workshops, and school site support. Of the 227 teachers, 4 did not take part, and 40+ did not provide crucial data such as scores on subject knowledge. As with several other studies, the intervention is reported as being successful in increasing teacher subject knowledge (ES 0.26 on test items from TIMSS). But there was no direct impact on student attainment. Teachers' science knowledge predicted student achievement outcomes regardless of participation in the intervention. There was no link between teacher classroom practice (as observed) and student achievement.

Borman et al. (2009) examined the impact of increasing teachers' content and pedagogical skills in science – via a professional development programme called Teaching SMART. This was a school-level RCT based on 965 3rd Grade children and 129 teachers, with the treatment group having 45 lessons per year. Schools were randomised to treatment or control, but the report does not state how many schools were involved, and the number of teachers involved appears to fluctuate over three years. The intervention was successful in increasing teachers' pedagogical content knowledge, but there was no benefit in terms of student performance in the State standardised test (Florida Comprehensive Achievement Test).

Coladarci and Gage (1984) tested a minimal intervention consisting of providing teachers with instructional methods, strategies for behavioural management and feedback strategies without directly intervening. Six instructional packets were posted to experimental teachers. The instructional packet highlighted large-group teaching, frequent use of question-and-answer sessions, use of visual aids and phonic exercises in reading activities. The manual also taught teachers about seat work assignments, differentiated instructions and exercises, how to rely on textbooks and workbooks (rather than games, technology) and minimising time for organising and giving directions. Another packet was about questioning and feedback strategies. Participants were 32 US teachers from 4th, 5th and 6th grades who were randomly assigned with their classes to treatment conditions. There was no description of what the control teachers did. Four teachers dropped out – so analyses were performed on 28 teachers (631 pupils). Before and after training, classroom observations were conducted for two hours on two occasions. The observations recorded teachers' conformity to recommendations. The ES for reading was -0.2 and for maths -0.08.

Another interesting intervention using an educational approach called Tools of the Mind aimed at closing the achievement gap based on neuroscience research and theory (Blair and Raver 2014). The programme trains teachers to organise and manage instruction so that children can build self-regulation skills through purposeful interactions with classmates. 759 Grade 1 and 2 children from 29 schools across 12 school districts and from 79 classrooms participated in the study. 16 schools were randomised to an experimental condition and 13 to 'business as usual' control. Results demonstrated improvements in reading, vocabulary, and mathematics at the end of kindergarten that increased into the first Grade. However, not all measures were positive. There were small positive effects on reading, vocabulary and maths although the effect on maths was reduced over time. ES range from 0.03 to 0.11. Attrition was 5% at follow-up.

A professional development intervention involving the provision of a specialist content-focused coaching (CFC) coach for schools designed to encourage higher-quality engagement with texts (Matsumura et al. 2013) reported positive effects (ES = 0.29). The CFC programme was implemented in schools for three years, consistent with the literature that suggests it can take several years for multi-level interventions to show effects on desired outcomes. The CFC-trained coaches were introduced to the treatment schools relatively late in the first study year. In the first year the focus was establishing relationships with their schools' principals and gaining teachers' trust. In the second year of the trial, coaches began working with teachers. 32 US schools (three then withdrew after assignment), 15 intervention, 14 control and 2,983 pupils (over 90% were eligible for free lunches and 95% minority ethnic origin) took part in the study. Attrition was high at 8% in the first year and 50% in the second year. This casts doubt on the trustworthiness of the results.

Rimm-Kaufman et al. (2014) examined the impact of Responsive Classroom, a professional development programme for teachers, on student achievement. Responsive Classroom involves teaching teachers practical strategies to support the social, academic development and self-regulatory skills of students, and promote a caring and well-managed classroom environment. 12 elementary schools were randomly assigned to implement Responsive Classroom for three years and another 12 elementary schools were assigned to a comparison group that would not implement Responsive Classroom during that period. The initial number of students was 2,042 (745 left the programme between the end of 2nd and 5th Grades). More students came in than left, leaving a final total of 2,904. Some teachers in two of the comparison schools received training for Responsive Classroom. As a result, the authors randomly selected one of these two schools and re-assigned it to the intervention group, so that the intervention group ultimately consisted of 13 schools and the comparison group consisted of 11 schools. There were about 1,000 students in the intervention group and 1,000 students in the comparison group. The effectiveness of Responsive Classroom was assessed by comparing student performance in math and reading on a state standardised test (Standard of Learning) in fifth grade. There were no benefits for maths (-0.13) and reading (-0.06).

There were several other poorer quality studies that evaluated the effects of training teachers to develop content knowledge and pedagogical skills – not appearing in Table 4.2 and rated as 0 or 1* in quality. These were either small scale or did not have a robust causal design. For example Behrmann and Souvignier (2015) examined the impact of a strategy-based programme on teachers' pedagogical content and improvements in children's reading. The strategy-based programme involves teachers explicitly teaching correct strategy usage and emphasising self-regulation. 65 teachers who volunteered and their classes from Grades 5-7 received training on the reading strategy. Teachers received teaching materials and introduction to the principles of reading strategies. Only 15 of the 65 teachers developed the assumed pedagogical content belief, suggesting that perhaps the training had not been successful in developing teachers' reading instruction. The study reported that the programme was effective, but there was no comparison group. Instead comparisons were made between students of teachers who showed development in pedagogical content beliefs (PCBs) with those who did not. Pupil attrition was 14%.

In a poorly reported longitudinal study of 65 US teachers and 889 students (Kindergarten to 3rd Grade), Waller (2013) found that teachers' pedagogical content knowledge predicted student maths achievement on the Terra Nova Math test. However, there was a larger correlation (0.23) between students' maths achievement gains and their contact hours with Kentucky's main classroom math interventions - Mathematics Recovery, Add+Vantage, Math Recovery, and Number Worlds. This study was rated 0 because it was not a causal study.

One large-scale correlational study (Tchoshanov 2011) examined the relationship between teacher knowledge of concepts, teaching practice and student achievement. Results showed that teachers' content knowledge, knowledge of models and generalisation were not significantly related to students' passing rates on standardised tests, but knowledge of concepts and connections were significantly related to student achievement.

Hasty (2010) looked at the effects of a high quality teaching professional development programme on 4th grade student achievement. It involved 1,186 low attaining Grade 4 students, in schools not making adequate yearly progress. The teachers were on the professional development programme. The author compared the cohort results immediately prior to implementation of CPD programme to those afterwards – and so this is weak evidence. The pupils got higher grades after the programme (ES 0.28).

Overall, the existing evidence on whether primary school teachers' subject and pedagogical knowledge matters is weak. There were about as many higher medium and quality studies showing positive effects and as showing no effects.

Developing or training teachers to use new approaches is also often unsuccessful. Dorsett et al. (2014) looked at training teachers of Year 4 to embed metacognition in their practice (and parental involvement). The study involved 51 schools of which 11 dropped out or are missing data. The result showed no difference for the treatment group. Rienzo et al. (2015) looked at training teachers about growth mindsets and pupils about the malleability of intelligence, in 30 schools, with 1,505 pupils in England. There was 39% attrition. The ES was 0.01 for maths, and -0.11 for English (i.e. there was no benefit).

The situation for teachers' direct use of research evidence to improve pupils' attainment is not promising - partly because the studies in this area are not yet as robust, and partly because the pilot studies that have been done show no benefit.

In one intervention, teachers studied evidence-based instructional practices that cultivate academic engagement and conducted an action research project to implement selected practices in their classrooms (Strambler and McKown 2013). Control teachers participated in a self-study group and read about evidence-based practices to promote student engagement. 18 teachers were assigned to groups (9 in each, with 306 pupils in 16 classes). But only 5 teachers completed the intervention. The authors claim that students with initial low engagement and low reading grades demonstrated greater gains in these outcomes in action research classrooms.

In Kindergarten at least, the use of up-to-date and more reform-oriented instruction (characterised by cooperative learning, student-led discussion and open-ended assessment techniques that require complex cognitive skills and processes) may even be detrimental (Park 2013). In this correlational study, based on 5,238 children in the Early Childhood Longitudinal Study-Kindergarten Cohort data (1998-1999) in the US, it seemed that reform-oriented instruction produced slightly worse results in maths than traditional pedagogy (characterised by textbooks, teacher-directed, chalkboard and routine practice and drill). And highly qualified but less experienced teachers were most likely to use non-traditional methods, and produced the worst results.

Recent pilot evaluations funded by the Education Endowment Foundation found little evidence that getting teachers to use research made any difference (Griggs et al. 2016). The evaluators doubted that such practice was even feasible. Speight et al. (2015) also found no evidence of impact from encouraging teachers to use research evidence on issues such as metacognition. See et al. (2015a) suggests that teachers need clearer guidance, professional development and modelling of effective strategies on the use of research evidence to improve attainment. There needs to be some conduit to translate research evidence into practical guidance for teachers – which could be lesson plans or precise protocols.

4.2 Teacher:pupil interactions

The way teachers behave and interact with their pupils, their teaching styles and their attitudes/expectations of their pupils may affect how pupils respond to teaching and learning. Hastie et al. (2013) suggested that teachers' motivating style that is highly supportive and permits autonomy is facilitating and can help support students' self-determination and achievement goals. This relates to achievement in sports. The study reviewed 27 studies that looked at interventions at all phases of schooling from pre-school up to secondary school level and concluded that giving pupils opportunities to pupils to decide on their own goal can lead to higher skills attainment and perceived competence.

However, none of the studies in this new review could really establish if improving pupil-teacher relationships can improve academic attainment (Table 4.3). Most of the better studies were merely correlational or observational.

Table 4.3 - Quality and impact summary: studies of teacher interactions

	Effective	Ineffective/unknown
Higher quality	0	0
Medium quality	0	0
Lower quality	4	2

Stanford (2014) reported that teachers who adopt delegated and facilitating styles of teaching are more effective in improving maths performance than teachers who are authoritative. Delegated teaching style, also known as group style, uses collaborative teaching and is more suited to inquiry-based learning such as laboratory work (Concordia Online 2016). The facilitating style, or activity style, helps students to develop self-regulation. Facilitating teachers use questions to develop critical thinking skills and this style is most suitably used for teaching science. Stanford also reported that pupils taught by more experienced teachers (defined as those with more than 5 years of service) performed better than pupils whose teachers were less experienced. However, this is a correlational study, so it is not possible to attribute causality to these relationships.

Similarly, Gollwitzer et al. (2011) suggested that children taught to think about how to achieve success did better than those told to think about getting success. This was a small study with 49 2nd and 3rd Grade pupils in Germany. Attrition was at least 10%.

Zhou and Urhahne (2013) tested whether teacher behaviour such as their judgements of pupils' performance can affect pupils' self-concept and self-attribution which, in turn, can affect their academic performance. This study involved 144 German and 272 Chinese fourth-Grade elementary school students. Mathematics teachers were asked to estimate pupils' performances on the applied mathematics test. Discrepancies between teacher judgment and student performance led to groups of underestimated and overestimated students. Underestimated pupils demonstrated maladaptive attributional patterns compared to overestimated pupils. This study was not a trial, so no causal claims can be made.

In another study, Hong (2012) analysed the Early Childhood Longitudinal Study Kindergarten cohort (ECLS-K) dataset using propensity score matching, to establish if the Grade 3 retention policy can be mediated by teacher expectations of pupils' academic achievement. Results suggest positive expectations can result in higher learning gains. However, positive expectations alone are not enough. The policy could be detrimental to pupils' maths and reading skills and nontested subjects if implemented by teachers with high expectations (ES -0.12 in Science, 0 in reading and maths). The results are therefore unclear.

Archambault et al. (2013) looked at how teacher-pupil relationships are associated with student classroom engagement. The study analysed data from the Quebec Longitudinal Study of Child Development (QLSCD) which collected information from a random selection of children born between 1997 and1998. Data were collected from parent interviews, parent questionnaires, individual child assessments and teacher questionnaires at age 5, 17, 29, 41 and 53 months. Children's prior academic measures included school readiness data on maths and vocabulary. These were measured using the Number Knowledge Test (NKT, abridged version) and the Peabody Picture Vocabulary Test (PPVT). 2^{d} Grade academic outcomes were measured using teacher ratings on the child's maths and reading achievements. Teacher-child relations were reported by teachers in Grades 1 to 4 (age 6-10) using the Student–Teacher Relationship Inventory (on a 1-5 rating). Structural Equation Modelling analysis suggests that children who were perceived as being more engaged by their teachers had more positive relationships with their teachers. Cognitive skills in kindergarten were positively correlated with classroom engagement (0.18) and teacher-student relationship at first Grade (0.16), but not at Grade 4. Achievement at 2nd Grade was negatively correlated with classroom engagement and teacher-student relations in Grade 4. The study used a large cohort sample. However, the correlation analysis does not show a causal relationship. Despite the use of SEM (which some believe can establish causality), the design cannot establish whether children with good relations with teachers are perceived by teachers as being more engaged. It could be the case that more engaged pupils are more likely to have a better relationship with teachers. The direction of causation cannot be established. It is also possible that better engagement and academic performance are measuring the same thing.

Principato (2010) examined whether co-teaching, defined as two or more trained teachers delivering substantive instruction to a diverse group of students, had any beneficial effects on children's learning. This was designed especially for teaching children with special needs in an inclusive classroom. It is sometimes also known as cooperative teaching, team teaching or collaborative teaching. The study compared two models of co-teaching. Different schools adopted the relative effectiveness of two co-teaching models (in-class co-teaching and pull-out). In some schools the co-teacher was used to support a small group of pupils in pull-out lessons, sometimes the co-teacher took half a class for repeat lessons. In other schools, teachers shared teaching, e.g. co-teacher may teach English and class teacher teaches maths, resulting in little actual collaboration. Participants were 126 4th grade pupils and nine teachers from five schools; 75 pupils were in co-teaching classes and 51 were in non-co-teaching classes. Outcomes were measured using MAP (Measurement of Academic Progress), a state aligned, computerised and adaptive test; the NJASK and the end-of-year report. Overall, there are no benefits to be had from co-teaching regardless of models on literacy, but the in-class support co-teaching is particularly not helpful for very weak pupils. All groups made similar gains between pre- and post-tests of MAT literacy with the pull-out classes marginally better (ES = +0.01) compared to control. In-class support co-teaching performed worse than control (ES = -0.02) suggesting there is no advantage for having extra support in the classroom. Where there were differences it was in teacher-assessed report card grades and this was due to one particular teacher who scored their pupils very low. There were also no differences in terms of attendance, punctuality and suspension, there were no differences between groups. Comparing progress of children by schools before and after co-teaching was applied, there was also no significant differences. All the schools made similar progress with one school showing marginally lower gains. Comparing by ability levels, it appears that in-class co-teaching can have a negative impact for children with weaker reading skills.

5. Improving science, maths and literacy – one-off evaluations and less promising interventions

5.1 Improving science in general

Other than those covered in other sections (such as on teaching thinking and reasoning), this review found eight studies and one review pertaining to science instruction. Campbell et al. (2015) reviewed 81 research articles on the use of modelling instructions in the teaching of science to aid conceptual understanding. The review suggests that modelling pedagogy was most commonly used to teach conceptual understanding, while expressive modelling was the most often used strategy. Exploratory and experimental modelling were the most frequently observed combination of modelling pedagogies. Half of the research on science pedagogy involved the use of technology. Scientific reasoning, explanation, and peer-to-peer collaborative or cooperative learning were identified as the most important instructional strategies. More importantly, the review did not identify any instructional strategies that can be considered the most effective for science instruction specifically.

Table 5.1 - Quality and impact summary: studies of improving science

	Effective	Ineffective/unknown
Higher quality	1	0
Medium quality	1	1
Lower quality	2	1

In this new review, the most common method tested was the inquiry-based approach to teaching science. Three of the 8 studies were about inquiry approaches and these showed no benefit (Kim 2012, Kukkonen et al. 2014, Lee et al. 2006). There is no evidence that any particular approach used specifically for teaching science or a specific science topic was effective (Table 5.1). Perhaps more successful approaches are those that are common across subjects (such as teaching thinking and reasoning, covered in a later section).

Table 5.2 - Quality and impact detail: studies of improving science

Reference	Intervention	Smallest cell	Attrition	ES	NNTD-attrition	Quality
Wells et al. 2015	**School garden**	**1,530**	**9%**	**0.25**	**244**	**3***
Lorch et al. 2014	Controlling variables	178	6%	0.79	126	2*
Kim et al. 2012	Mastery of concepts	958	34%	0	0	2*

The studies other than inquiry-based learning tend to be very specific. For example, a large-scale RCT testing the effects of a school garden intervention on children's science knowledge was conducted with 49 primary schools. 25 schools were randomly assigned to receive the school garden intervention and 24 to a wait-list control to receive the intervention at the end of the study (Wells et al. 2015). The aim was to use real-life and hands-on experience to encourage learning. The garden intervention consisted of both raised-bed garden kits and a series of 19 lessons. Participants were 3,061 2nd, 4th and 5th grade children (ages 6-12). Science knowledge was measured using a 7-item questionnaire testing knowledge of nutritional and plant science. Attrition was 9%. The results showed that gains were modest (ES around 0.2 to 0.3).

Lorch et al. (2014) examined the effects of using valid and invalid experimental designs to teach variable controls in learning science. They compared three teaching interventions: an intervention that used examples of invalid designs to explain the logic of controlling for variables in science (CVS) (Invalid condition); an intervention that used examples of valid designs to explain CVS (Valid condition); and a control condition, in which no explicit instruction was provided until after an immediate post-test. Participants were 1,069 fourth Grade children (age 9-10) taken from 17 schools. Half of the classrooms were in schools that performed well on a state-mandated test of science achievement, and half were in schools that performed relatively poorly. The sample was originally 1,183, but pupils who already understood CVS were dropped from the analysis. Fifty classes were randomly assigned to the two experimental conditions and 10 classes to the control condition. Steps were taken to balance possible influences of teacher-assignment and school on the instructional conditions. However, within any school that had three 4th grade classrooms, the three classrooms were treated as members of the same "triplet." The authors reported that children taught using valid and invalid conditions performed better than those in the control groups in immediate post-test. However, only the invalid condition did better than control in delayed post-tests. There were only small differences for higher and lower performing schools (regarding 'immediate' and 'far' 'transfer'). Over 6% of observations were missing, and there was some initial imbalance between groups. Because the schools are divided into two groups (halving the cell size) and the reporting is unclear, the quality of this paper has been assessed lower than it otherwise might have been.

Kim et al. (2012) examined the impact of an inquiry-based approach to learning science that emphasized mastery of concepts. Science achievement was measured using the Metropolitan Achievement Test (MAT-8 subtest). In addition a standardised measure of critical thinking was used to assess learning outcomes. Teachers' classroom behaviours were also observed. Participants included 3,300 Kindergarten-3rd grade students from 115 classes across six schools. However, results were reported for only 2,182 pupils (control 958 and intervention 1,224). Teachers were randomly assigned to either the control group or the experimental group. Results showed no beneficial effects on experimental children in the first year of intervention and a small positive effect in the second year (ES = 0.10). The effects disappeared in the third year of intervention. But there were some initial group imbalances in favour of the experimental group so the results are probably biased upwards. Nevertheless, this is a large study that contrasts with the evidence on Maths Mastery (which shows more promise at present).

Ellis (2013) examined the effects on individualised science instruction (ISI) on science achievement using the Reformed Teaching Observation Protocol (RTOP). The RTOP captures five elements in reformed teaching: background knowledge; classroom setting; lesson design and implementation (instructional strategies, student engagement and student exploration); content (teacher's knowledge and understanding of content, making connection between lesson and real life and scientific reasoning) and classroom culture (interactions and teacher/student relationships). Study design was a single-group pre- post comparison. Two science units were developed based on the constructivist and reform-based practices. Using the 5-E Learning Cycle (engage, explore, explain, elaborate and evaluate) reading and science were integrated into each lesson. Outcomes were science achievement measured by the Iowa Science Test; reading comprehension, by the Woodcock Passage Comprehension; and vocabulary, by the Iowa Vocabulary test. Quality of instruction was measured using the Reformed Teaching Observation Protocol (RTOP). Video recordings of 24 lessons were analysed using the RTOP. Participants included six teachers, two graduate assistants and 96 2nd grade children (age 7-8). Attrition was 7%. The findings showed that all pupils made significant progress between pre- and post-tests on reading comprehension, vocabulary and science measures, but no significant relationships were observed between RTOP and any of the achievement variables. The strength of evidence for this study was low because it was correlational and thus could not establish causal relationships. Due to the small number of teachers and pupils involved, and the fact there was no comparison group, there is a possibility of teacher and/or classroom effects. Confounding variables cannot be ruled out and effects might be different on children who did not volunteer.

Another study that looked at the use of an inquiry-based approach to the teaching of science (Kim 2006) used 3-D simulations (modelling) to support learning. Participants were 41 5th grade children (20 control and 21 experimental). This was a non-randomised two-group pre- post-test design. The control group was engaged in the 2-D animation materials covering the same topic (plate tectonics) as those in the intervention group. Regression analysis suggests small positive effects after controlling for differences but this was only for 31 pupils (10 missing). No design-based comparison was possible with unmatched groups. Groups were not close to matched, with big differences in initial test scores between the groups.

Lee et al. (2006) used a semi structured inquiry-based learning approach to teach evaporation to 28 3rd and 4th grade children (age 8-10) from culturally and linguistically diverse backgrounds. Four children were selected by each of the seven teachers in the six schools to take part in this experiment. The impact of the intervention was simply a recording of the number of correct or incorrect responses to questions posed orally to children on a one-to-one basis. There was no comparison group. The focus was instead on the different rates of progress made by different groups of pupils, therefore making it impossible to make any claims about effectiveness.

Tong et al. (2014) evaluated a scheme of ongoing professional development and specific instructional science lessons with inquiry-based learning, direct and explicit vocabulary instruction, and integration of reading and writing, with $^{th}5$ grade disadvantaged English language learners. The treatment group received a Daily Oral and Written Language in Science (DOWLS) activity during their daily English lesson. They were presented with a science-related prompt and asked to think, record written responses, and discuss with a student. Treatment ELLs outperformed their counterparts in English-reading fluency, knowledge of word meaning, and science and reading achievement; in the language/reading intervention treatment ELLs continued to develop faster than their peers in English oracy, reading fluency, and comprehension; ELLs benefited more from the science intervention if they received the prior language/reading intervention.

There is a suggestion that for children with learning disabilities scaffolded simulation-based inquiry learning may be beneficial. Kukkonen et al. (2014) studied the use of this approach with 21 5th graders (age 10-11). Like Lee et al. (2006), this study was based on only one topic (using models of the greenhouse effect) and had no comparators. The findings therefore cannot be generalised to other science topics which may not lend themselves well to such an approach.

5.2 Improving maths in general

A wide range of studies were found that evaluated programmes/interventions aimed at improving maths achievement for primary school children (here focussing on those approaches only trialled once). A review of successful pedagogic strategies for fostering maths skills for very young children identified two programmes: Rightstart and Building Block (Burger 2015). Rightstart involves using games, pictures and objects, while Building Blocks involves the use of a computer software, books and game sheets. Shin and Bryant (2015) reviewed 17 studies on instruction interventions to improve children's learning of fractions. Only two focused on primary age children, and both were doctoral theses with very small numbers. Allsop et al. (2003, p.311) identified the following instructional strategies:

- teaching in authentic and meaning contexts;
- modelling problem-solving strategies and learning strategies using multisensory techniques;
- ensuring that the sequence of instruction moves from the concrete, to the representational, to the abstract;
- giving students opportunities to use their language to describe their mathematical understandings;
- providing multiple practice opportunities to help students use their developing mathematical knowledge and build proficiency; and
- continually monitoring students' performance and offering meaningful feedback in the form of performance charts.

Our review uncovered only two large-scale relevant RCTs (Tables 5.3 and 5.4).

Table 5.3 - Quality and impact summary: studies of improving maths

	Effective	Ineffective/unknown
Higher quality	1	0
Medium quality	1	0
Lower quality	19	4

Table 5.4 - Quality and impact detail: studies of improving maths

Reference	Intervention	Smallest cell	Attrition	ES	NNTD-attrition	Quality
Newman et al. 2012	**AMSTI**	**15,000 pupils**	**8%**	**Maths 0.05** **Science 0** **Reading 0.06**	**0** **0** **0**	**3***
Clements et al. 2012	Building Blocks	592 pupils	Unknown	0.34	-	2*

Newman et al. (2012) involved 30,000 students (from Grade 4 to 8) and 780 teachers across 82 schools in the US. The aim of the study was to evaluate the effectiveness of the Alabama Math, Science and Technology Initiative (AMSTI) on maths and science achievement. AMSTI is a school-wide programme that has 3 main elements:

- Professional development
- access to programme materials, manipulatives, and technology needed to deliver hands-on, inquiry-based instruction;
- and in-school support by AMSTI lead teachers and site specialists who offer mentoring and coaching for instruction.

Pairs of similar schools (maths achievement, minority students and students from low income households) were selected and schools in each pair were randomly assigned either to AMSTI or a control where teachers used the existing maths and science programmes. Student achievement was measured using the end-of-year Stanford Achievement Test (SAT). A small positive effect was found for maths (ES = 0.05). However, the effect for science was not statistically significant. Based on the SAT 10 science test administered by the state to students in Grades 5 and 7, no difference between AMSTI and control schools could be discerned after one year. Positive effects were also found for reading with a difference of 0.06 standard deviation. Effects were maintained after 2 years for both maths and science. The effect is equivalent to a difference of 0.10 standard deviation in favour of AMSTI schools or 50 days of additional student progress. For science ES was 0.13 in favour of AMSTI. Reported as due to changes in classroom instruction (emphasis on active-learning strategies) that are an important aspect of AMSTI theory of change. This was explored, and for both mathematics and science, statistically significant differences were found between AMSTI and control teachers in the average reported time spent using the strategies. The effect of AMSTI on these instructional strategies was 0.47 standard deviation in mathematics and 0.32 standard deviation in science. However, AMSTI did not appear to have an effect on teachers' self-reported content knowledge. AMSTI also did not appear to benefit disadvantaged students, with no statistically significant differential effects on student achievement in mathematics problem solving or science based on racial/ethnic minority status, enrolment in the free or reduced-price lunch program, gender, or pre-test level. It appears that results were not reported for all students as their Figure 1 shows results for only 18,713 students (not 30,000). For science results were available for only Grades 5 and 7 (n = 79 schools and 7,528 students). Student attrition ranged from 5% to 8% and varied with tests.

Four linked studies by some of the same authors evaluated the effects of the Building Blocks (Clements and Sarama 2007, Clements and Sarama 2008, Clements et al. 2011, Sarama et al. 2012). The key elements of the Building Blocks curriculum are technology-enhanced instruction, assessment and CPD. The programme comprised mathematical themes such as sorting and sequencing, communicating, reasoning, representing, and mathematical problem solving. The instructional approach of the programme involved guiding children to extend and mathematise their everyday activities. In practice, children were taught to identify the mathematics in and develop mathematics from their concrete experiences and interests. This occurred in block building, art, songs, and puzzles, through sequenced activities throughout the day.

The earlier study (Clements and Sarama 2007) included two schools and four teachers (4 classes) and 68 pre-school children. One class from each school was selected as treatment and one as the control (30 pupils in treatment and 38 in control). Only those who completed the post-test were included in the analysis. Attrition was 11%. The authors reported that all children made significant progress between pre- and post-tests, but Building Blocks children both schools made bigger improvements on all measures (ES = + 1.2 for number test; ES = +2.7 for geometry test). However, this study was rated 1* because of the small sample (two schools and four classes) which limits generalisability and internal validity. Also the groups were not randomly assigned. The fact that the researchers were also the test developers meant that the assessments could be testing things that were emphasised in the programme but not taught to the comparison children. The programme also provided more opportunities for treatment children to practise (including individualised practice and at home).

Following this study the authors conducted another evaluation the year after but this time using a randomised controlled design (Clements and Sarama 2008). This was a 26-week intervention. Participants included 36 teachers and 276 pre-school children. Analyses included only 253 children (only those who stayed on and who had pre- and post-test data). Teachers were randomly selected for participation, and eight children from each class were selected for the trial. The 36 classrooms/teachers were assigned to one of three conditions (Building Blocks; Pre-school Maths Curriculum/PMC as active control and the business-as-usual control). All three groups covered the same topics but varied in terms of the number of weeks allocated to each topic. The intervention was complex. It included small group, whole group and family activities to support learning at home. PMC was largely whole group teaching, family activities and used Early Childhood Express software for individual practice. Control classes used schools' maths activities. Maths achievement was assessed using researcher-developed Early Maths Achievement test. The researchers claimed that other tests, such as the Woodcock-Johnson's test, were too restricted in range. Overall, the BB and PMC groups outperformed the control group. BB children outperformed control (ES = 1.09), PMC also did better than control (ES = +0.6), but BB outperformed PMC (ES = + 0.54). Although promising, the strength of evidence was downgraded because of the use of intervention-related assessments developed by the researchers.

A scaled up study was reported by the same authors (Clements et al. 2011). This was a longitudinal cluster randomised trial in which schools were randomly assigned to one of three conditions. Participants were 2,076 pre-school (age 4-6) from low income households. Children came from 62 schools. Initial number of children was 2,100. Child outcomes were measured using Research-based Early Maths Assessment (REMA), a researcher-developed test. Children were also assessed on narrative skills using the Renfrew Bus Story. In one state (Nashville), children were also assessed using the standardised test on maths and literacy (Woodcock-Johnson III). Outcome measures for pre-kindergarten, end of kindergarten and end of first grade were compared for the three groups. Building Blocks children outperformed control on REMA (ES = +.35 to 0.69). Positive effects were also found for the Woodcock-Johnson test in Nashville (ES = +0.18 to 0.32). However, no effects were found for literacy (letter/word identification). It is difficult to assess the evidence due to poor presentation.

A follow-up study looking at the long-term effects compared children with and without follow-through interventions up to 1st grade (Sarama et al. 2012). The previous paper (Clements et al. 2011) suggested that there were 62 schools and 2,076 children originally, but this paper reported only 42 schools and 487 children. This suggests extremely high attrition as only 23% of the original children remained in the study. The authors reported that students in both the follow-through condition (g = .33) and non-follow-through condition (g = .22) scored ‘statistically significantly’ higher than children in the control condition. Both groups outperformed the control condition in treatment-on-the-treated analyses (g = 0.38, follow-through; 0.30 non-follow-through). There was a small difference between follow-through and non-follow-through in favour of the follow-through (ES = 0.17, calculated by reviewer).

Baroody et al. (2015) conducted an experiment to evaluate the effects of 9-month training in discovery technique using highly guided discovery learning software to develop children’s reasoning skills. The theory behind this intervention is that when children learn to count, they go through 3 stages. They start with verbal counting, and find a pattern (e.g. add-1 rule) and develop a reasoning strategy (e.g. add 1 gives the next number up) and through practice this strategy becomes automatic (non-conscious). The aim of the study was to find out whether a minimally or highly guided discovery programme was more effective. Participating children (n=100) from kindergarten to second Grade recruited from 3 schools were randomly assigned to one of three conditions: highly guided add-1 rule training, highly guided doubles training or minimally guided add-1 rule and doubles practice. The study reported that there was no difference between guided and unguided/minimally guided training in learning the add-1 rule or the doubles. The level of guidance did not make a difference in learning more salient rules. However, the degree of guidance did matter depending on the reasoning strategies required. This was a lower quality study because of the small sample (about 30 in each intervention group) and the use of researcher-developed tests. Tests items were related to the intervention so it is not surprising that children who did not receive training in add-1 rule or doubles rule did not do as well as those who received training.

Durkin and Rittle-Johnson (2012) tested the use of incorrect examples to teach decimals and place values. The intervention involved getting children to compare correct and incorrect answers. Correct and incorrect examples were presented side-by-side with prompts to compare the examples. In the control condition, students were also presented with two solution procedures to compare, but both procedures were correct. The theory is that the incorrect solution together with the scaffold of comparison would help develop conceptual understanding and procedural knowledge even without prior knowledge. Intervention also included practice sessions and feedback on how children are doing. Participants were 74 Grade 3 and Grade 4 children from 3 schools (age 8-10). Children were randomly assigned to either incorrect condition comparing correct and incorrect examples (n=37) or correct condition comparing correct examples only (n=37). Small positive effects were reported for incorrect examples over correct examples on the test of conceptual knowledge (ES = 0.25); procedural knowledge (ES = 0.5) and misconception errors with whole numbers (ES 0.05). The positive effects were not sustained. In the delayed post-test both groups made negative progress but the treatment group made a bigger loss than the control group. This study was rated zero because of the very small sample and the fact that the same assessments developed by the researchers were used for pre, post and delayed post-tests. Attrition at delayed post-test was 18%.

Scaffolding is often considered as an effective instructional strategy. Bliss et al. (1996) conducted a study to explore the use of scaffolding in maths, science and design and technology. Participants were 13 KS2 teachers (Years 5 and 6). Teachers' instructional practices were observed and analysed to see if the model of scaffolding transferred to school knowledge in the classroom. The description of this study was retained here although not within the inclusion date because it represents many of the studies about effective instructional classroom strategies that are typical of UK research. There was no objective evaluation of teaching practice and no evaluation of the impact of using scaffolding on children's outcomes. The paper started on the assumption that scaffolding has positive effects on children's learning based on prior research (which is itself largely flawed or of low quality).

Another strategy often used in teaching maths is practice. Dennis et al. (2016) tested the effects of teaching number sense with constant practice using a single-subject multi-probe design. Participants were six second Grade children (age 7-8) with mild learning disabilities randomly assigned to number sense lessons with extensive practice (NSF) or practice followed by number sense lessons (EPF). The order of the interventions was varied between the two groups. The results showed that extensive practice helped fact retrieval. On fact retrieval, NSF made improvements from baseline 1.44 points (SD = 0.89) increased from 0.58 points (SD = 0.58); EPF was 3.18 points (SD = 1.99) increased from 0.51 points (SD = 0.69). In the second phase (extensive practice), NSF made bigger improvements 4.02 points (SD = 1.68) increased from 1.47 points (SD = 0.74); EPF was 1.46 points (SD = 0.77) increased from 0.64 points (SD = 0.68). The authors concluded that although teaching number sense helped children to understand concepts, extensive practice improved automaticity and memorisation of basic facts, therefore both interventions should be used in tandem. The evidence for this is weak because of the very small sample. There was no pure control so we cannot be sure how much difference each of the two interventions would make without the treatment. Also the intervention was delivered by trained graduate students and not the regular teacher, therefore similar results may not be seen when delivered by teachers in regular classroom settings.

Hiebert and Wearne (1993) compared the traditional textbook approach (practicing prescribed procedures) to an alternative approach teaching children to construct relationships between place values and computational strategies. In the alternative class pupils were given fewer problems, but more time on each problem. They were frequently asked to suggest and explain alternative strategies. Participants were 2nd Grade children (147) from 6 classes taken from one school. 135 had parental consent. One average-high achieving class (n = 30) and one average-low achieving class (n = 21) were taught the alternative method. A specially trained teacher delivered the lessons during the 12 weeks while the regular class teachers watched. Some classes spent more time on discussion and some an equal amount of time on discussions and seatwork. The alternative class spent most of the time (85%) on class discussions. Outcomes were measured using researcher-developed instruments measuring place values and multi-digit addition and subtraction. Results showed that one alternative class made the most improvement between pre and post-test.

Cook (2008) examined the effectiveness of commonly known effective teaching practices on maths achievement of Grade 6 children in one school. The 8-step strategy incorporates formative assessment, setting goals, developing lessons, small group and peer tutorials, enrichment activities, reviewing and revisiting lesson objectives and monitoring progress. Of the initial 111 children only 46 were retained. These were assigned by the registrar to either treatment (classes that use the 8-step strategy) or business-as-usual. Outcomes were assessed using Criterion-Referenced Competency Test and the Academic Knowledge and Skills Mathematics Test. Scores were analysed using ANCOVA. The study found no 'significant' difference in mathematics achievement between the treatment and non-treatment groups. The data suggested student achievement in mathematics improved following inclusion in a mathematics intervention course, regardless of types of teaching methods. This study was rated zero because of the small sample and the non-random allocation of the treatment groups.

One study conducted in France (Gamo et al. 2010) tested the effectiveness of different strategies used in arithmetic word problems. Participants were 4th and 5th Grade (age 9-11) pupils from 11 classes across six elementary schools (193 were treatment pupils and 68 control from same schools). Treatment classes and their teachers were trained to use these maths strategies. The control classes continued with their regular lessons. Although the abstracts stated that the experimental group improved significantly by choosing alternative strategies, the results table (their Table 2) showed there was no difference in performance between groups.

Wong et al. (2009) used 21 Primary Grade 6 classes (a total of 686 students) in a school, and compared the spiral bianshi curriculum for maths with a reference group using standard textbook materials in Hong Kong. The results indicated an ES of around 0.25 for pre-post comparator difference in computing fractions.

Two papers described how teaching children understanding of text can help improve problem-solving in maths (Glenberg et al. 2012 and Hirashima et al 2007). Glenberg et al. (2012) explored whether improving reading could improve maths performance (worded maths problems). Participants included 97 3 rd and 4 th

Grade (age 8-10) pupils. Attrition was 30%. All children have access to a laptop. Each Grade had a class of EAL readers who were intentionally assigned to intervention groups. The other five classes were randomly assigned to control or intervention. Children manipulate and move things on a computer screen to simulate content. Results showed that the reading group got more correct answers (ES=0.54), more correct solution procedures (0.59) and used less irrelevant information (0.78) than those in the control group. Children in the reading group made improvements equivalent to one z-score on the state test. Analysis was adjusted for maths and reading covariates (no pre-tests). This was consistent across three variables (0.15). This study had attrition of 18%. Results were based on an average over 3 days of use of the strategy. There was no assessment as such but children were given instructions as they went through the texts on the computer screen and answered questions as they went along. This was not a fair test as the reading children were given instructions to work out the answer to a story problem on a piece of paper instead of just answering yes/no to each text. They were also instructed to show their workings. It was not clear if control children were given the same instructions.

Hirashima et al. (2007) tested the use of problem-posing by sentence integration on solving word problems in maths among Japanese children. The intervention was a computer-based interactive programme. Participants were 132 second Grade children (age 7-8) from two schools, divided equally between (66 in each group by class to treatment or control condition. Results showed small effects in favour of the treatment group (0.24). Attrition was not reported and there was initial imbalance. This study was rated low because of the small sample (under 100 in each intervention arm), which was not randomly assigned to conditions. Also the tests were developed by the researchers, which could be intervention-related.

Griffin and Jitendra (2009) evaluated the impact of word problem-solving instruction on the maths performance of 60 third grade children (age 8-9). Children were randomly assigned to either schema-based instruction (SBI) or general strategy instruction (GSI). Children were pre-tested and post-tested repeatedly over 18 weeks. Both groups showed improvements in word-problem and computational skills, but the SBI group made bigger progress (ES = +0.94) initially. However, over time the differences disappeared. There was no 'normal practice' control group, so it is not possible to say if these approaches were better if the children did not have the intervention. This was a fairly small sample (n=60) with some initial imbalance between groups on the word-problem solving test. No attrition was reported.

Another intervention conducted in Israel examined the effects of peer mediation and children's verbal ability on their performance in maths problem solving (Shamir et al. 2006). The intervention, Peer Mediation with Young Children (PMYC) involved children working in pairs. Half of the dyads received the PMYC programme training (intervention); the others received general instruction on working with peers (control). This was a cross age tutoring where the mediators were from Grade 3 (age 8-9) and the learners from Grade 2 (age 7-8). Verbal maths achievement tests were devised for pre/post-tests - one for learners, one for mediators. No 'official' standardised maths test appears to have been used. The MANN abstract reasoning assessment was used though to test verbal reasoning skills. This was a small study with only 108 children (split into 54 dyads). The findings suggest that pupils in the intervention groups (both learners and mediators) made greater improvements in their maths attainment. The ES using control pre-test standard deviation is 0.56.

Carr et al. (2011) tested the effects of combining two instructional strategies (cognitive strategy and computational fluency) on the maths performance of 178 second Grade children (age 7-8) from schools in two states in the US. Six children from each class were randomly selected by their teachers for participation. Selected children were then randomly assigned to one of 4 groups: fluency instruction; cognitive strategic instruction; combined or control (reading). Instruction was delivered using a computer-based instruction. Maths achievement tests were developed by researcher by selecting items from existing maths tests and high stakes competency tests downloaded from the internet. The intervention consisted of 40 half-hour sessions (2 sessions per week for 20 weeks). ANCOVAs indicated that children in the combined fluency and cognitive strategy condition significantly improved their mathematics achievement in comparison to the control group. The combined intervention also appeared to benefit boys more than girls. However, children trained in only cognitive instruction did worse than the control. This study was given a low rating because of the small sample (c. 44 in each treatment arm) and doubt about the validity of the test instrument. The maths achievement tests were specially selected to reflect the items used in the training - questions on fluency in addition, subtraction were selected because children were trained on these items in the Fluency and Combined group.

Some people have argued that teachers' teaching styles may have an impact on children's performance in maths. Stanford (2014) investigated the impact of different dominant teaching styles on maths achievement. The different teaching styles were defined as "facilitator" and "delegator teaching" styles, "expert", "formal authority" and "personal model teaching" styles. The study included 29 upper elementary (Grades 3-5) classroom teachers from 5 schools in the US. Teachers were grouped into the teaching style subgroups based on their predominant teaching style. The Arkansas Augmented Benchmark Examination (AABE) mathematics scores of 855 students in classes of teachers using different teaching styles were compared to see if pupils' academic expected performance was associated with any particular teaching style. Groups were not balanced or clearly matched. The findings of this study revealed the AABE mathematical scores of students in classrooms with teachers using facilitator and delegator teaching styles were higher than students in classrooms of teachers using expert, formal authority, and personal model teaching styles. This was a correlational study, not an RCT although the title suggests that it was a causal study. Overall it was a poor study despite high student numbers. Reporting was poor and overly complex, and there was also the issue of 'defining' teacher style reliably.

Codding et al. (2007) compared the effectiveness of cover-copy-compare technique (CCC) with Explicit Timing (ET). Participants were 98 second and third grade pupils. The intervention was carried out twice weekly over 6 weeks. ET is a process whereby students mark their progress in one-minute intervals constantly providing feedback to the child on how many problems are correctly completed.

565 children from 16 classes were recruited, but only data from 98 were analysed. These were randomly assigned to either control, ET or CCC. Those excluded were those who had no pre-test, or left. Some stopped and some were classified as SEN. HLM analyses suggested that results were mixed for different groups of children. The CCC and control conditions were more effective for children whose fluency levels fell within a certain range. For children whose fluency was in the instructional range, explicit timing was the most effective treatment. This study was rated low because of the high attrition, and analyses were conducted on those who remained and completed the intervention and provided pre and post-test data. See also Codding et al. (2009)

Adams (2012) investigated the effects of the Compass Learning Odyssey Math programme, a computer-assisted programme on children in Grades 3 to 7 (age 8-13). Compass Math incorporates a number of teaching practices such as working with students' ZPD, scaffolding, use of spiralled curriculum, instructional feedback and differentiated instruction. Pupils used the programme 1-2 times a week for 40 minutes in the lab and also 2-3 times a week in the general classroom. Pupils on a 'minimal' or 'basic' rating on the Wisconsin Knowledge and Concepts Examination (WKCE) also received additional sessions on Compass Math. This was a weak quasi-experiment as the treatment school was selected because it was already using Compass Math, while the control school did not. The schools were described as similar in terms of pupil characteristics. The comparison school, however, had multi-age classrooms. It used Connected Maths, supplemental/remediation, student-centred and cooperative learning approaches. The treatment school was also using other programs (e.g. Saxon Math, Accelerated Math) and had a more teacher-directed approach. There were 162 pupils in the treatment school and 119 in the control school. Maths achievement was measured using the state assessment, the Wisconsin Knowledge and Concepts Examination (WKCE) and Measures of Academic Progress (MAP). Apositive effect was reported for MAP. A comparison of gain scores by the reviewers showed negligible effect (ES = +0.05). Although there was a big imbalance between groups at pre-test stage (treatment school M= -.04 and comparison school M= -.35), no comparisons of gain scores were conducted. Instead. The study's author compared post-test scores and estimated a huge effect size of +0.74 and concluded: "*the treatment school made a significant improvement in mean z-scores while the comparison school did not show any improvement.*" Gain score analysis was conducted for the treatment school, but not for the comparison.

Two studies were conducted by Dyson et al. (2013, 2015) to test the effectiveness of number sense; one for low-income kindergarten children (Dyson et al. 2013) and one for low-achieving kindergarten children (Dyson et al. 2015). Number sense addresses basic number concepts, number relations and number operations. The first study involved 121 kindergarten children (age 5-6) who were randomly assigned to either number sense or business-as-usual (treatment n = 56; control n = 65). The intervention was delivered over eight weeks (24 sessions) in small groups. Number sense children made bigger gains than control on the WJ-III subtest (ES for Applied Problems = 0.16; ES for Calculation = 0.34 and ES = 0.3 for overall test). However, the gains were not sustained in the delayed post-test. In fact on the Applied Problems sub-test the control children continued to make improvement whereas the number sense children regressed. The authors claimed that the WJ Applied Problems test involved situations that were not typical of those in the intervention. They also involved larger numbers and children were not prompted to use counting strategies. All these suggest that the intervention was only effective on the intervention-related test and did not help children to perform under normal test conditions. Attrition was low at 4%. There was an obvious attempt to highlight the positive findings. Despite the lack of delayed effects and inconsistent results using a standardised test, the authors concluded thus:

> "Controlling for number sense at pre-test, the intervention group made meaningful gains relative to the control group at immediate as well delayed post-test on a measure of early numeracy. Intervention children also performed better than controls on a standardized test of mathematics calculation at immediate post-test."

In the second study Dyson et al. (2015) included two more elements to number sense instruction: number–fact practice and number-list practice. They compared number sense + number fact, with number sense + number list. Participants were 126 kindergarten children (age 5-6) from 11 classes across 4 schools. Children were individually randomised: number sense followed number-fact practice (NS+NFP); number sense followed by number-list practice (NS+NLP) or business-as-usual control All children received 25 minutes of number sense sessions delivered in small groups over 24 half hours sessions. For the purpose of this review we consider only the results of the intervention-independent standardised test (Woodcock-Johnson III) and the Wechsler Preschool and Primary Scale of Intelligence (test of non-verbal reasoning). For mathematics computation achievement (WJ-III), there was no difference between number-practice and number-list pupils at post-test (number list ES = 0.58, number fact ES = 0.60), but at delayed post-test, the effect of the number-list condition had diminished whereas the ES of the number-fact condition remained well above .25 (number list ES = 0.12, number fact ES = 0.4. This suggests that teaching number sense followed by number-fact is more effective in sustaining the effect of teaching number sense. Compared to control group pupils, number-list children performed better both at post-test and delayed post-test (ES = 0.32; 0.26 respectively) and for number-fact over control (ES =0.82; 0.56). Number-practice was also found to be particularly effective for English learners (EAL) children. The security rating was downgraded because of the small number in each treatment arm (average n = 42). Attrition was low at 5% and the authors only included children who had data for pre-, post- and delayed post-tests (126 out of 133).

One study conducted in China (Zhang and Zhou 2016) reported positive effects of testing using a web-based curriculum learning system on 142 children with mild learning difficulties (72 in treatment and 70 in control). The study claimed that treatment children made bigger gains (ES = +0.64) than control (ES = +0.30). It did not report the level of attrition.

Fuchs et al. (2016) tested the effects of using self-explanation in learning fractions. This was part of a multicomponent intervention and the aim of this study was to isolate the effect of self-explanation. Participants were 4 th graders (although it is not clear where they were taken from and how many schools were involved). It is not clear how many pupils were sampled initially, but the authors reported that after exclusion (on eligibility criteria; children below 9th percentile on Wechsler test of intelligence) and random sampling, 236 from 52 classrooms and 14 schools were included. Children were then randomly assigned to three conditions: intervention with explanation (n = 79); intervention with word-problem component (n = 79) and control (n = 78). Attrition was 8% (18 children dropped out). Both intervention conditions included 36 sessions, each lasting 35 minutes. All but seven minutes of each session were identical. In those seven minutes, students were taught to provide high quality explanations when comparing fraction magnitudes or to solve fraction word problems. The sessions were delivered three times per week for 12 weeks and were conducted in pairs. For this review we consider only the outcomes for fraction knowledge as the other two outcomes were measured using instruments developed by the researchers. Results were mixed. Positive effects were found for both intervention groups on measures assessed using researcher-developed instruments but not on the national assessments (NAEP). Compared to control, the word problem group made the biggest gains between pre- and post-test on the NAEP test (ES = 0.89). The supported explanation group outperformed the control (ES = 0.64) but worse than the WP group. The interventions were delivered by researchers, so the results may not be generalized to real classroom condition where lessons are delivered by regular teachers. There is an obvious attempt to highlight only positive results. Their Tables 2 and 3 presented results for all the tests but the authors only mentioned results for the other tests but not NAEP where WP outperformed the EXP group.

Muthukrishana (2013) evaluated the effects of the Maths Concepts Comprehensive (CMCCE) curriculum. The curriculum claimed to improve maths attainment through "big ideas". It included content knowledge, pedagogy, word problems, algebraic mapping and professional development. There was no pre-test, but teacher evaluation was used. Two cohorts of Grade 3 children were included (188 in cohort 1 and 82 in cohort 2). Children were not randomly allocated to treatment conditions. The lower track children were put in the experimental group while the second track children formed the control. The study reported that the children taught using the CMCCE curriculum did better than those who did not. Effect sizes for cohort 1 ranged from 0.75 to 1.22, while those in cohort 2 ranged from 1.59 to 1.79. The two groups were not equal and thus comparisons cannot be valid. There was no report of attrition.

Another maths intervention involved the use of paraphrasing to teach problem solving to children at risk of maths disabilities (Moran et al. 2014). The intervention was delivered in small groups of three to five children over 20 lessons. In addition to normal maths classes, children also received supplemental intervention in the form of tuition two times a week for 25-30 minutes for approximately 10 weeks (20 lessons). Participants were 99 third grade children from four schools. The authors reported some positive impact (considerable in some cases) for those students involved in the intervention. However, groups were poorly matched, attrition was not clearly reported and interventions and intervention states were not particularly clearly reported.

Mononen and Aunion (2014) evaluated the effects of ThinkMath, an intervention for low performing children. Study participants were 86 Grade 2 children (age 7-8) in Finland (77 treatment and 11 control). Children were taught number words, sequence skills, counting skills and place value. The intervention was delivered twice weekly in small groups. This was in addition to the normal lessons. The study reported improvements for intervention children between pre and post-tests, but in the delayed post-test (3 months later) improvement was seen only in the combined maths scale. However, the findings are meaningless given that the two groups were not matched. The reporting was also unclear. Given these and the small number of cases, no conclusions can be made about the intervention.

One study tested the use of Geometric Motions (GM) in helping children to understand the concept of area measurement (Huang and Witz 2011). 120 fourth grade children were divided into 4 groups: Area Measurement (AM), 2-D Geometric Motion group (GM), 2-D Geometric Motion plus Area Measurement (GMAM) and a control. The study found the curriculum incorporating 2-D geometry motions and area measurement calculations (GMAM) led to an improvement in mathematical judgments and explanations but it did not lead to significant gains in the total post-test score compared to the curriculum involving only area measurement numerical calculations (ES for each treatment group 0.38, 0.59, 0.09 relative to control). The evidence is weak because of the small number of pupils in each intervention group and the class level randomization. Children were also not equal at baseline.

Khodami and Hariri (2013) suggested in a small RCT that metacognitive training improved maths performance for low attaining Iranian Grade 3 children. Reporting was poor and it was no possible to estimate the effect size. No attrition was reported.

Very few studies here were on the same topic, and despite the claims of success in so many papers there is no good evidence. Other than the approaches covered in other sections (such as improving reasoning) the only area with specific promise for maths is maths mastery.

5.3 Maths mastery

"Singapore Math" is a collection of maths curricula originally developed by Singapore's Ministry of Education for use in Singapore schools, using a national framework centred on problem solving that emphasizes computational skills as well as conceptual and strategic thinking processes. "Singapore Math" Maths Mastery textbooks for primary grades tend to provide in-depth coverage of a relatively small number of topics, using the concrete to pictorial to abstract approach to instruction, and covering fewer topics, but addressing them more thoroughly. Darroch (2009) suggests that Singapore Math, by progressing logically, delving into a range of numerical concepts deeply, and carefully connecting one concept to the next, was at least partly responsible for Singapore students coming first in international maths competitions. Key features of Maths Mastery (MM) include a systematic approach to mathematical language, frequent use of objects and pictures to represent mathematical concepts and an emphasis on high expectations. It emphasizes deep understanding rather than procedural knowledge. Every child is expected to understand what they are doing rather than merely repeating routines. MM involves training of teachers, in-school support, CPD and collaboration with peers and teachers in other schools to share best practice.

The What Works Clearinghouse (2009) identified 12 studies of Singapore Math that were published or released between 1983 and 2008. Six studies were rejected by them as having an ineligible design, and the other six for other reasons relating to research quality. In 2009, therefore, there were no studies meeting minimum WWC evidence standards, and so it was not possible to decide if Singapore Math was effective or not. What Works Clearinghouse (2015) updated the picture by examining seven new studies. Again none met minimum quality standards, and therefore no conclusion could be drawn about the effectiveness of Singapore Math. The situation has not changed much.

However, the newer and better studies from our review in Table 5.6 suggest that the approach has some promise, and the weight of evidence in Table 5.5, while weak, is in favour.

Table 5.5 - Quality and impact summary: studies of Singapore Maths

	Effective	Ineffective/unknown
Higher quality	1	0
Medium quality	1	1
Lower quality	3	0

Table 5.6 - Quality and impact detail: studies of Singapore Maths

Reference	Intervention	Smallest cell	Attrition	ES	NNTD-attrition	Quality
Jerrim and Vignoles 2015	**Singapore Maths:Maths Mastery**	**45 schools, 2461 pupils**	**10%**	**0.10**	**14**	**3***
Jaciw et al. 2016	Singapore Maths:Maths in Focus	41 teachers, 985 pupils	27%	Problem solving 0.12 Criterion referenced test 0.05	0	2*
Powell 2014	Singapore Maths v Everyday maths	102 pupils	Unknown	0	0	2*

The poor quality and partial nature of much work is exemplified in Bennett (2015). This study took 40 3rd Grade students, taught them using Singapore Math, and discovered that they had improved their maths knowledge by 5th Grade. There was no comparator group to assess if this gain was more or less than would have occurred using other approaches, and so there is no way of knowing if Singapore Math had been effective. Despite this, and following meaningless ANOVA and other significance tests used with this non-random group from one school, the authors talk of the 'effect of maths in focus' and conclude that "This study suggests the instructional strategies and curricular materials of the Math in Focus: The Singapore Approach may lead to statistically significant mathematics achievement for both average and above average learners".

Many other studies, such as Garelick (2006), Hazelton and Brearley (2008), look at successive cohorts before and after implementing Singapore Math, or merely compare schools that chose to implement it with those schools not doing so.

In a study with a non-randomised comparator (Blalock 2012) compared three US elementary schools implementing the Singapore Math curriculum and approach to teaching in their 1st Grade first term, with other schools in the same district not implementing it. The author reports that "an intact population was utilised", and yet the analysis still used meaningless ANCOVA and other significance tests while not reporting effect sizes. The author concludes that students taught Singapore Math demonstrated more knowledge of mathematics skills than students taught traditional approaches.

Powell (2014) compared the results of 205 5th Grade students using either Math in Focus: Singapore Math or Everyday Mathematics (non-randomised). There were no substantial differences in performance based upon treatment status, whereas student background characteristics (race/ethnicity and SES), and attendance accounted for more of the variation in results.

More promisingly, since the WWC review, Jaciw et al. (2016) randomised 93 teachers in 12 US elementary schools to Singapore Math or usual teaching. Impacts on mathematics achievement were reported as ES of between 0.11 and 0.15. Jerrim and Vignoles (2015) evaluated Singapore Maths (Maths Mastery programme) with Year 1 and Year 7 pupils in 90 schools in England. Half of the schools were assigned to MM, 7 schools dropped out and altogether just over 9% of the original 5,108 pupils were missing post-test scores. The pre-test scores of those who dropped out were lower than average. Maths outcomes were assessed using the Number Knowledge test – an individually and orally administered test which takes 10 minutes to complete. The difference between the groups was small, but favoured MM with ES=0.10.

Overall then, there is some evidence that Maths Mastery works, and could be adopted more widely.

5.4 Improving literacy in general

At least 10% of the children in England used to leave primary school with apparently deficient reading and writing skills (Brooks et al. 2002). Over 30% of children in their first year of secondary school were found not to be able to read at a level suitable for their age in 1997, although this dropped to around 20% by 2009 (National Literacy Trust 2010). Such children are not likely to catch up and are more likely to continue to fall further behind their peers (Sainsbury et al. 1998, Galton et al. 1999). Pupils struggling to achieve their 'expected' reading level at primary school would generally find it difficult to access the full secondary curriculum, since literacy is such a fundamental gateway for further study.

Reading is a fundamental skill for later life and forms a basis for any child's subsequent learning at school (Good et al. 1998). Pupils who read well in early stages of their education are more successful in later years compared to those who fall behind (Hirsch 2007). Differential reading ability is a key determinant of patterns of subsequent learning (Wolf and Katzir-Cohn 2001, Pikulski and Chard 2005). Poor reading ability can have harmful psychological, social and economic consequences, with implications far beyond those directly associated with education (Adams and Bruck 1993). Societal demands for reading ability are increasing in the information age (Cunningham et al. 2004), and a minimal level of literacy is an entitlement for all.

A series of reviews has looked at reading interventions for students with reading difficulties and disabilities (Wanzek and Vaughn 2007, Wanzek et al. 2010, 2013). There were benefits from both comprehension and reading outcomes, and the impact was greatest when the intervention was provided early and to the smallest group sizes.

Marulis and Neuman (2010) reviewed 67 studies of vocabulary interventions on pre-K and kindergarten children's oral language development. The overall effect size was 0.88 for vocabulary measures. Promising approaches included having trained adults in providing the treatment, and combined pedagogical strategies that included explicit and implicit instruction. As usual, researcher-developed measures compared to standardised measures. There were similar results from a later review looking at vocabulary interventions for young children at risk for reading (Marulis and Neuman 2013).

Burns et al. (2016) compared studies based on using data from neuropsychological tests to improve reading and maths with those using more traditional idea such as phonics and fluency. The overall ES for cognitive approaches (0.17) was considerably smaller than for using phonics (0.48) and reading fluency approaches (0.43). The authors suggest that the latter two should be used.

Bowers et al. (2010) reviewed the evidence on the impact of teaching morphology on literacy outcomes. Using 22 relevant studies they found morphological instruction was effective, especially for weaker readers. A review by Carlisle (2010) of 16 studies came to similar conclusions. Goodwin and Ahn (2013) looked at 30 studies, and recorded an overall ES for morphological instruction on language and literacy outcomes of 0.32, with the impact decreasing with school age. There were larger reported effects for quasi-experimental than experimental studies and for researcher-designed measures than for standardised measures

Graham et al. (2012) synthesized evidence on improving writing, and calculated average ES for 13 writing interventions. All but one were deemed effective – including peer assistance when writing (0.89), self-regulated strategy (1.17), and strategy instruction (1.02). A subsequent review confirmed these, and added a few more including frequent writing (0.24) – Graham et al. (2015). In a review of 53 studies, Graham and et al. (2015) found that formal spelling instruction led to better literacy outcomes, regardless of students' Grade level or literacy skills.

Despite these reviews, a lot of the existing and even widely used approaches to improving literacy (and numeracy) for young children have no good evidence that they are effective, or have evidence that they are ineffective (such as the supplemental instruction approach evaluated by Cantrell et al. 2013). The various approaches found in our review (and not covered in later sections) are reasonably well-balanced in terms of reported effectiveness (Table 5.7). No one approach or intervention emerges having evidence of effectiveness with repeated evaluation (Table 5.8). Some of the larger studies show quite convincingly that approaches like READ180, for example, do not work. In terms of the larger synthesis these approaches are therefore ignored. The only approach with any real promise is Grammar for Writing.

Table 5.7 - Quality and impact summary: improving literacy

	Effective	Ineffective/unknown
Higher quality	1	2
Medium quality	5	2
Lower quality	24	7

Table 5.8 - Quality and impact detail: improving literacy

Reference	Intervention	Smallest cell	Attrition	ES	NNTD-attrition	Quality
Horsfall and Santa 1994	Project CRISS	111 pupils	20%	+	-	2*
James-Burdumy et al. 2009	Project CRISS	1,155 pupils	Unknown	0	0	2*
Puma et al. 2007	Writing Wings	1,500 pupils	Unknown	0	0	2*
White et al. 2005	**READ180**	**617 pupils**	Unknown	**0**	**0**	**3***
Kim et al. 2010	READ180	132 pupils	Unknown	+	-	2*
Sprague et al. 2010	**READ180 (Grade 6 to 10)**	**2,775 pupils**	**Large**	**0**	**0**	**3***
Cantrell et al. 2010	Learning Strategies Curriculum	431 pupils	24%	0.22	0	2*
Coe et al. 2011	6+1 Trait Writing	1,931	Unknown	0.13	-	2*

Torgerson et al. 2014	**Grammar teaching**	**408 pupils**	**22%-**	**0.24**	**8**	**3***
Mashburn et al. 2016	Read it Again	168 pupils	Unknown	Alphabet knowledge 0.18 Narrative language 0.17	-	2*

Torgerson et al. (2014) evaluated improving the writing skills of Year 6 pupils by providing contextualised grammar teaching, based on randomising pupils at class level. This was a small group intervention (817 pupils) Attrition approached 22%. The headline ES was 0.24.

Project CRISS (Creating Independence through Student-owned Strategies) is a programme where teachers model learning strategies for students to help develop independent learning. It is aimed at improving reading, writing and learning for 3 rd to 12th Grade students (age 8 to 18). The strategies used by teachers include monitoring learning, and building on prior knowledge with new information. This programme has been the subject of extensive research, but only two studies out of 31 met WWC minimal evidence standards (WWC 2010).

The evaluation by Horsfall and Santa (1994) reported a positive effect on comprehension for students in Grades 4 and 6, but only using a teacher-developed 'free recall' comprehension test. This is not a very appropriate test. There was also dropout of around 20% from each class. This was a randomised controlled trial in three schools, with a sample of 120 students in six intervention classrooms and 111 students in six control classrooms. The duration of the programme was for 18 weeks. James-Burdumy et al. (2009) examined the impact of Project CRISS based on 1,155 students attending 17 Project CRISS schools, and 1,183 students in control schools. The study found no benefit from Project CRISS on a standardised norm-referenced diagnostic test (GRADE), or on the science or social studies reading comprehension assessments. Overall, the evidence of beneficial impact from Project CRISS is weak and suggests no effect.

Writing Wings, a structured writing programme, was evaluated using 3,000 students in the 3rd, 4th and 5th Grades in 39 schools across the US (Puma et al. 2007). No positive effect was found on the writing ability of disadvantaged students.

Read 180 is a small group reading programme designed for both primary and secondary students not achieving the expected level of proficiency. The programme involves a combination of tracking students' progress via the computer, reading practice using a computer program, reading of story books and direct instruction on reading, writing and vocabulary in two 90-minute sessions. It has been evaluated in 111 studies listed by What Works Clearinghouse (WWC 2009). Many of these did not meet WWC standards for evidence and those that did, were not able to provide clear evidence of impact.

A small number of studies portrayed positive effects, but the evidence is not always clear due to compromises made in the research. For example, Interactive Inc. (2002) reported mixed results, but a re-analysis by WWC found no clear differences. Assignment to groups was violated as parents/caregivers and students were allowed to request inclusion or exclusion even though the treatment was meant for those who the school believed would most benefit from it. In a large trial involving 16 schools in the US, READ180 was offered to 617 Grade 4 to 8 students who were not achieving the expected grade level in literacy (White et al. 2005). Results on standardised English Language Arts and Reading tests showed that the treatment group made greater progress in reading compared to a comparator group of 4,619 students from the same schools. However, the average effect across the three Grades was not large enough to be considered important. The use of significance testing was also misplaced as the sample was neither randomly selected nor randomly allocated.

Another evaluation of READ180 involving 384 Grade 6 to 8 students from one middle school found no intervention effect in the first year, although greater gains were reported for the intervention group compared to the control group in the second and third year (Woods 2007). A smaller study by Caggiano (2007) involving 120 Grade 6 to 8 (age 11-14) students found no clear differences between groups in all three Grades on standardised tests in reading. However, differences between groups were reported for Grade 6 only on the Scholastic Inventory Reading Comprehension Assessment, a test designed by the developer of the programme. One study conducted by Scholastic Research (2008), the same organisation who created and marketed the intervention, reported clearly different results in general literacy for 285 students in Grades 6, 7, and 9 after one year of READ180, compared to 285 matched students. All were considered to be struggling readers, and a majority had English as a second language. The outcome measure was the gain score in the English Language Arts subtest of the California Standards Test.

Two fairly large studies using standardised assessments found no positive effects of READ180 on students' literacy. For example, Kim et al. (2010) involved 264 Grade 4 to 6 (age 9 to 12) students identified as struggling readers and found no effects on all outcome measures, including reading fluency, reading comprehension and vocabulary, using norm-referenced and standardised tests. The study involved randomly assigning poor readers from three elementary schools to READ180 or an alternative non-literacy focused after-school programme. Both groups scored below the proficiency level at the end of the intervention period. In the most extensive evaluation of the READ180 programme covering five sites in different states of the US (Sprague et al. 2010), no differences were found in all the sites apart from one, and then only in the middle school (not high school). This site had a very high dropout rate of 55% which was not addressed by the complex analyses used by the authors. This finding is important as it is one of the largest studies of READ180 involving 5,551 students from Grade 6 to Grade 10 (age 11 to 16). In this study, students identified as achieving below their Grade level were randomly assigned to either READ180, Extreme Reading (alternative reading programme) or 'business as usual' where they received regular instruction. The outcome measures in all sites were the standardised, state level assessments.

The overall evidence for READ180 is therefore mostly negative. It is shown to work chiefly with assessments designed by the developers but not on standardised assessments. It did not work in the few randomised controlled trials, the largest studies or for those students most at risk.

Learning Strategies Curriculum (LSC) is a supplementary reading intervention to improve reading comprehension for 6th to 9th Graders (age 11 to 15) where students received 50-60 minutes of LSC per day for the entire school year. Cantrell et al. (2010) evaluated this intervention for 862 students in 12 middle and 11 high schools. The intervention was found to be effective in improving reading comprehension for 6th Graders (effect size of 0.22), but not for 9th Graders on both outcome measures. It has to be noted that there was a high attrition rate of 24%.

6+1 Trait Writing is a supplemental writing programme that complements the schools' existing writing curricula. Coe et al. (2011) examined the impact of this programme on 4,461 (2,230 intervention students and 1,931 control) students in 74 US schools. Students' writing performance rated on the six core characteristics of the 6+1 Trait Writing Model's definition of writing quality was used as outcome measures in the pre- and post-tests. The results showed that experimental students increased their writing scores in a year, by a small overall effect size (0.12 to 0.14). Only three of the six outcome measures were reported as improved.

In the US, Mashburn et al. (2016) evaluated Read It Again – a curriculum which targets children's development of language and literacy - with 506 pre-kindergarten pupils randomly assigned across three study conditions: control, Read It Again, and RIA with expanded professional development. The relative advantage for RIA over control classrooms on each outcome was - print knowledge (0.07); alphabet knowledge (0.18); print concepts (0.25); definitional vocabulary (0.05); phonological awareness (0.02); and narrative language (0.15). Attrition is unknown

The Rainbow Repeated Reading programme was found to have no added effect on reading skills (Wheldall 2000). This was an add-on to an existing programme, MULTILIT (Making Up for Lost Time in Literacy). The programme emphasized repeated reading of short sections of texts, which were graded, to increase accuracy and fluency. This was carried out over nine weeks. Forty students from Years 2 to 7 who were enrolled on the MULTILIT programme in two sites were randomly assigned to receive this additional programme. Two tests were used to assess impact. One showed no difference, while the other showed a positive impact in only one site, indicating a possibility of inconsistency in administration.

Another bespoke programme involved instruction on the learning environment used video-taped lessons with 5th Grade students in Belgium taken from four experimental classes (n=79) and eight control classes (n=149). It showed that although the intervention encouraged students to use reading comprehension strategies, it did not improve comprehension skills (De Corte et al. 2001).

A study of the two-week *Concept-Oriented Reading Instruction* (CORI) programme claimed that it was effective in improving the reading test scores of 156 low achieving Grade 5 students (Guthrie et al. 2009). Participants were from three schools (two intervention and one comparator). CORI students outperformed traditionally taught students on the Gates-MacGinitie Reading post-test, scoring higher on word recognition speed and reading comprehension. However, this study had a number of serious flaws. First, the intervention and comparator students were not drawn from the same school, and no baseline equivalence was established for both groups. CORI students had higher Grades than control students at the outset. There were also more students identified as having special educational needs in the control group (22%) compared to only 7% in the intervention group.

The question-answering programme is an intervention to enhance reading comprehension and vocabulary. Brown (2004) evaluated this programme for 267 Year 5 students (age 9/10) taken from 10 classes across three schools. Students were assigned (in an unspecified manner) to question-answering programme or regular reading classes. Teachers volunteered either to take treatment or control classes. Three outcome measures on reading comprehension, question-answering and vocabulary and reading fluency showed that the treatment group made greater improvements than the comparator group, in this weak design.

Direct instruction means that teachers are primarily responsible for introducing new material, devising student activities, and leading classroom discussion. Mackley (2000) tested the effectiveness of direct instruction on cognitive skills and subject matter. Children whose teachers used direct instruction were compared with children whose teachers did not use this model of instruction. Participants were 124 4th Graders from 3 intact classrooms. Control children were matched using school district's percentage of students receiving Aid to Dependent Children and prior attainment on the Ohio Proficiency Assessment taken in 3rd Grade. Results on the state standardised test (the Ohio Fourth-Grade Proficiency Tests in reading and citizenship) showed no difference between the mean scores of the treatment and control groups for reading.

A randomised experimental design with three levels of intervention was used to compare the effects of beginning reading interventions on early phonemic, decoding, and spelling outcomes of 96 kindergartners identified as at risk for reading difficulty (Simmons et al. 2007). The three instructional interventions varied systematically along two dimensions—time and design of instruction specificity—and consisted of (a) 30 minute with high design specificity (30/H), (b) 15 minute with high design specificity plus 15 minute of non-code-based instruction (15/H+15), and (c) a commercial comparison condition that reflected 30 minute of moderate design specificity instruction (30/M). For students who entered kindergarten with the lowest skills (i.e. naming 3 or fewer letter names per minute or spelling fewer than 13 letters correctly in a list of words), 30 minute of highly specified intervention produced significantly greater effects than 15 minutes of highly specified intervention. For students who entered kindergarten with higher alphabetic skills, 30 minutes of highly specified intervention produced no more reliable differences on word attack or word identification measures than 15 minute of highly specified instruction. In other words, for alphabetic skills, the 30-minute intervention was differentially effective for the lowest performing students only.

Vaughn et al. (2006) examined the effects of systematic and explicit instruction in oral language and reading on first grade English language learners. The intervention was delivered in small groups of three to five children for 50 minutes every day. Although children were randomly allocated to groups, 10 were replaced and seven dropped out. This represented 25% of the total sample of 48. Effect sizes between groups were not calculated, but ES for Letter Identification was 0.15.

Vadasy and Sanders (2008) in an evaluation of repeated reading (Quick Reads) with word-level scaffolding instruction reported an effect size of 0.16. This study involved 2nd and 3rd grade children taught in pairs by para-educators for 30 minutes every day for four days per week over 15 weeks. The level of attrition is above that of NNTD, making the findings unstable.

Zhang and Schumm (2000) compared the effects of the keyword method and the rehearsal method of vocabulary learning. Participants were 60th5grade children with limited proficiency in English. The intervention was delivered in groups of 20. Both interventions were found to have positive effects (ES = 1.0) compared to control. There was no dropout.

Williams et al. (2014) studied the effects of using expository text, emphasizing clue words, generic questions, graphic organizers, and close analysis of well-structured examples of cause/effect text on reading comprehension of 197 second and third grade children (age 7-9). Comparison children used the same social studies text but did not receive training in cause and effect. Outcomes of the two groups were compared to a no-instruction control. Strong positive effects were reported for some aspects of reading comprehension (ES ranged from 1 to 6).

To test whether comprehensive vocabulary instruction (CVD), a multifaceted, metacognitive vocabulary program, could help enhance reading comprehension and vocabulary acquisition of fifth grade children (age 9-10), Lubliner and

Smetana (2005) compared children who received CVD instruction with a comparison group. Experimental children (n=91) came from low-performing and low-income school, while the comparison children (n=30) were from an above-average performing school. The study suggested that there was some evidence of gap closing. Effect sizes were given for the gain compared with the groups own baseline (they range from 0.12 to 1.03), but not with the unmatched comparison group.

Paris and Paris (2007) tested the effects of teaching narrative comprehension strategies on comprehension and metacognition. Participants were 123 first grade children (age 6-7) in 6 classes: 4 were randomly assigned to experimental condition (n = 83 pupils) and 2 to control (= 40 pupils). The intervention was delivered in the classroom in 10 lessons over 5 weeks. Children learned strategies that promoted story structure knowledge, retelling skills, predictions, and inferences about characters' internal responses, dialogue, and theme. The lessons emphasized metacognitive discussion and guided practice. Control children received instruction on language development and poetry and exposure to motivating language arts activities. Similar types of activities and grouping practices were used in both conditions. Although standardised tests (Woodcock-Johnson Expressive Vocab and the state assessment on literacy progress on phonemic awareness) were used for the pre-test, they were not used in the post-tests (or not reported). On the comprehension tasks test of expository and narrative comprehension, experimental children did better than control on test items that were related to the intervention (narrative genres), but not on items not related to the intervention (e.g. expository genres). There was no effect on expository texts comprehension and metacognition. Significant effects were reported for listening comprehension (Cohen's d = +0.67) and retelling narrative elements (Cohen's d = + 0.92). The evidence is weak because assessments were intervention-related, which disadvantaged control children. They test skills that were taught to the experimental children but not the control children.

Aarnoutse and Schellings (2003) tested the impact of using problem formulation to motivate children to read and improve their reading comprehension. Pupils worked in pairs to formulate questions related to the text they read and then use resources (reference books e.g.) to answer the questions. The intervention consisted of 40 lessons across 4 units designed to develop reading strategies and stimulate reading motivation. Experimental children (n= 155) were from six classes in the 10 schools who agreed to take part. Seven classes from the other schools formed the control (n = 172 children). Participants were not randomised to conditions. There is thus a selection bias. No baseline equivalence was established, meaning the two groups of children could be different at the outset. This is even more so given that that experimental children were from volunteer schools. Positive effects were found on reading motivation, use of reading strategy and understanding of reading strategy. Since control children were not taught or required to use these strategies it is not surprising that they did not demonstrate any improvements. On a test of reading comprehension, there was no difference between groups.

Cohen and Johnson (2012) conducted a quasi-experiment to evaluate the effects of using imagery as an instructional tool to help children to learn and retain content knowledge. The idea was to enhance the literacy skills of children so that they can better understand and remember what they have learnt. The theory is that mental images can facilitate making inferences and organising information. Participants were 89 fifth grade children (age 10-11) from 5 classes taken from 2 schools. Children in each class were randomly assigned to 4 intervention groups: picture presentation (word paired with picture): Image Creation-No picture (children draw an image of the word); Image Creation-Picture (children draw an image of a picture shown to them) and Word only method (simply verbal presentation of the word). Students in the imagery intervention groups (Picture Presentation, Image Creation-No Picture, and Image Creation-Picture) outperformed all the other intervention groups for both retention and immediate recall. Students in the Image Creation-Picture intervention scored the highest, followed by the students in the Image Creation-No Picture intervention, those in the Picture Presentation intervention, and finally the Word Only intervention students. The evidence is weak because of the very small sample (average about 22 in each group). Although the pre-test was the standardised PPVT, the post-test was researcher developed test.

The intervention was delivered by researchers, so the results may not be replicated when delivered by regular teachers. Attrition was 10%.

To evaluate the effectiveness of the Reading Acceleration programme, Houtveen and van de Grift (2012) conducted a quasi-experimental study involving 37 schools and 1,021 children (567 treatment and 454 comparison group) in the Netherlands. A significant difference was found in the post-test for reading individual words and comprehension (ES = 0.11). The comparison group had fewer struggling readers in the pre-test so the results could be due to regression to the mean.

Fien et al. (2011) investigated the effects of teacher Read Alouds on the vocabulary and comprehension of young children. The intervention was delivered in small groups and integrated direct and intentional comprehension and explicit vocabulary. Participants were 106 first grade children (age 6-7) from 18 classes across 9 Title 1 schools (Small group n = 54; control n = 52). The groups were not balanced. There were more SEN children in the control (23%) compared to the treatment group (18.5%). Classrooms were first randomised (block randomization) and 10 pupils in the lower 50 percentile on vocabulary and oral test from each classroom were matched. Each matched pair was then randomly assigned to treatment or no-treatment (control) condition. All children received whole-class read aloud but students in the intervention group received small-group instruction for 20 minute, 2 times per week, for 8 weeks in addition to the whole-group instruction. The small-group instruction included additional read aloud activities and opportunities to preview, review, and enhance vocabulary instruction aligned with the whole-class Read Aloud Curriculum. The study showed that students who received small-group instruction reliably outperformed their controls on vocabulary assessments and expository retells (with effect sizes of 0.57 to 0.66), but not on narrative retells. An earlier study by the same authors (Fien et al. 2010) using whole class Read Aloud reported moderate to big moderate to strong effects on first-grade student vocabulary (d= 0.80) and moderate effects on narrative retell outcomes (d= 0.36). It has to be mentioned that the small group intervention was a booster session available only to the treatment group. This means that the children had extra instruction which the control children did not have. There was no pre-test of narrative retells and expository retells- so it is not possible to say which group had made more gains. Again the independent test was used in the pre-test but not in the post-test. Results reported only the Vocabulary Knowledge test – a researcher-developed test (p. 312)

Mathes et al. (2005) compared the relative effectiveness of combining enhanced instruction (where teachers used assessment data to enhance their existing provision) with proactive reading (where instruction is arranged to reduce occurrence of errors and to facilitate ownership and integration of skills and strategies); combining enhanced instruction with responsive reading, providing explicit instruction in phonemic awareness and phonemic decoding, but dedicating less time to the practice of these skills in isolation than did the Proactive approach and enhanced instruction alone. Participants included 399 children (92 in the proactive intervention group, in the responsive intervention group, 114 students in the at-risk enhanced classroom condition, and 101 who were typically achieving). All pupils designated as at risk within a school were randomly assigned were randomly assigned to one of three conditions. Graphs indicate that all groups made progress, with the proactive and responsive groups making more progress than the enhanced regular class. There were differences across outcomes between the two interventions though. The paper had lots of undigested tables, and it was hard to work out effect sizes. Impact was given in terms of slope/intercept coefficients. They reported that the ES was 0.84 for proactive group and 0.78 for responsive. It is not clear what the comparisons were. It could be against the enhanced classroom but it may just be against a baseline - it may not even be a Cohen's d. Attrition was 14%. The intervention was unclear in many places and the poor reporting made it difficult. There were also too many measures used.

McGinty et al. (2011) looked at whether the number of sessions and the intensity of the strategies used mattered in terms of children's development of print knowledge (i.e. awareness of what letters/words look like on the page, alphabet and emergent writing). 367 randomly selected pre-school children and 55 teachers from across 2 states in the US took part in the study. 195 children were in high-dosage frequency and 163 in low-frequency dosage. Teachers were self-selected. 31 were assigned to high frequency and 24 to low frequency doses. The majority of the children came from socioeconomically/educationally disadvantaged families. There was no clear control. Intervention was carried out over 30 weeks. High-frequency dose children received 4 sessions per week and Low dose children received 2 sessions per week. Using structural equation modelling to analyse the data, it appears that there was an interaction between dose frequency and dose. In the ow frequency condition - dose matters greatly, but less so in the high frequency condition. For a high dose condition, both high and low frequency groups were about the same on 2 measures and the low frequency did better on one. This means that if the intervention is given less often, the number of strategies used mattered, whereas if the number of strategies used was high then the frequency did not matter (the results were mixed). Reporting of results was not very transparent given the slightly confusing design with the doses and frequencies.

A study compared the effects of using little books (textbook approach) and literature-based basal anthologies (Menon and Hiebert 2005) on children's word solving skills and decoding. Children who used the little book approach were given scaffolding of different features linked to text content and cognitive load. The control children continued with the existing anthologies with no scaffolding. This was a whole class intervention. The participants were 75 first grade children from 4 classes. Two classes were assigned to little books (n=39) and two classes to control (n=36). Based on increases in mean scores on QRI (Qualitative Reading Inventory) tests the authors argued that even a moderate amount of scaffolding can help improve children's reading and word recognition abilities. No effect sizes were reported. The evidence is weak because of the small number of cases and the lack of similarity between teacher instruction and time spent on literacy in each class. Attrition was not reported.

Morris et al. (200) replicated a one-to-one reading intervention called Early Steps with 86 first grade children (43 experimental and 43 control) from across 11 schools. Children were matched on pre-test. Teachers were provided with 12 Early Steps training sessions over the year and the children received on average of 91 one-to-one tuition sessions with a trained member of staff. Results suggest that students at-risk of under-performing in reading performed better than comparison group following one-to-one intervention. Effect sizes for each test were reported at between 0.67 and 0.91. Attrition was not clearly reported. As it was a matched comparison design, it was not possible to exclude the influence of some unobserved factors. There was some potential bias in the recruitment of schools.

Macedo-Rouet et al. (2013) conducted an experiment with 4th and 5th grade French children to teach them how to evaluate information sources in text comprehension on controversial issues. The training sessions involved practice, feedback, explanations, and discussions. The instructional intervention consisted of five steps of mediated discussion in small groups. The general goal of the instruction was to encourage students to identify the sources presented in the texts, to establish links between sources and content (i.e., who said what), and to assess the knowledge of each source with respect to the topic of the text. Control children were told that they would complete a series of text comprehension practice tasks using the online system they already knew. They then completed the practice task (text and questions) and two experimental tasks. Participants were 96 children who were matched on an initial screening measure and sorted to intervention and control. Results showed that the less abled pupils in the intervention group assessed source knowledge more accurately than those in the control group (ES = 0.77 for lower ability pupils, 0.01 for higher ability). The evidence for this study is weak as children were matched rather than randomly assigned. The number of cases in each group is small given that they were further divided into high and low ability groups. Since high and low ability children were not randomised, there is a potential for bias. Attrition was 12%.

Mason et al. (2013) tested the effects of teaching children reading comprehension with writing instruction. 79 fourth grade children from 4 schools took part in the trial. They were identified by their principals and teachers as having difficulties with reading comprehension and writing. Children were randomly assigned to one of three conditions: reading comprehension only (n=29), reading comprehension plus writing (n=30) or no-treatment control. Results showed that pupils in reading comprehension instruction and reading comprehension plus writing instruction outperformed the control group on oral and written retelling, a standardised reading test, and semantic measures. Syntactic measures, however, did not show statistically significant differences by treatment or control group (ES = 0.59 to 1.129 across the 6 measures for each intervention group compared to the control. The evidence is not strong because of the small number of cases in each intervention arm, the relatively high attrition (15%) and some initial imbalance between groups.

Lee and Moore (2004) analysed the performance of struggling readers who were taught reading strategies that combined information texts. Participants were 58 fourth fifth grade children from two intact classes – one class received the teaching intervention (n=27) and the other class formed the control. The author concluded that the experimental group performed better (ES = 0.77) than control on the Canada Stanford Diagnostic Reading Test. This is a very weak study as only two classes were involved and 9 children dropped out. There might be class differences that were not accounted for. Also the experimental group was taken by a teacher-librarian rather than the regular teacher.

Kamps et al. (2008) examined the effects of a small-group reading intervention for kindergarten children identified as most at risk. The small group intervention included direct instruction, guided reading and phonemic awareness activities. Each session lasted 30-40min for a minimum of three times per week over 2 years. The study reported here was based on a larger longitudinal study. The sample in this study included first and second grade pupils from 11 schools. The curricular used by the children was determined by the scores on the screening test despite it being described as an experimental study. The three types of curricula were 'direct instruction', 'open court' and 'programmed reading'. The study reported effect sizes of 0.4 to 0.66 for the comparison between 3 treatments and the worst performing treatment (guided reading group). Attrition was 22% by the end of the second year. They started with 106 children, but only 86 remained. This study compared the relative effectiveness of three intervention groups. There was no comparison with the 'normal practice' control.

The effects of Fast ForWord are not clear. Fast ForWord is a computerised language programme developed to train processing of auditory information. The programme includes seven different games to train auditory discrimination, perception of speech, phoneme identification, memory, auditory comprehension, and sentence-level comprehension. The students' English skills were examined in pre-test, post-test and follow-up measurements. The TRG students saw an acceleration in decoding-related skills. This smaller study by Bjorn and Leppanen (2013) reported positive effects on 37 fifth grade children identified as having reading fluency problems. 13 were randomly assigned to receive 50 minutes of daily computer programme-based training for 10 weeks, and 11 formed the control continuing with regular classroom instruction. Another 14 average readers formed a second control. The results were mixed. Experimental children made greater gains on some tests but not on others. Follow-up comparisons showed no differences between pure control and experimental children on rapid naming. This was a very small study with samples taken from one school, thus posing a threat to external validity. Classroom and teacher effects therefore cannot be ruled out.

Maridaki_Kassotaki (2002) aimed to find out if training children in phonological memory can help develop reading skills. The study was conducted on 120 Greek-speaking kindergarten children were randomly assigned to a control and an experimental group. Training involved practicing repetition of non words to promote phonological memory. Teachers also received specialist training. Tests of 'Early Reading Comprehension' used. Subjects' reading ability was tested using the Early Reading Comprehension test. The findings showed that the intervention children performed better than control on the comprehension test. This study was rate low partly because of the small groups. Attrition was not reported.

5.6 Use of Arts and music to improve other subjects

A recent literature review commissioned by the Education Endowment Foundation (EEF) assessed the evidence of impact of arts education on cognitive and non-cognitive outcomes of children from pre-school onwards (See and Kokotsaki

2016). It considered arts education to include a broad range of subjects encompassing the traditional fine arts (e.g. visual arts, music, dance, performing arts, theatre and dance) as well as modern dance and movement, hip hop, poetry and creative writing. A total of 199 relevant studies were identified from a search of eleven educational, psychological and social sciences databases. The vast majority of studies were about music education and a combination of arts forms. Most of these studies were conducted with primary school aged children. Very few involved pre-school age children. No higher quality single studies were found. It is therefore difficult to state conclusively what the evidence of impact of arts activities in education might be. However, given that a large number of weak or medium quality studies do suggest positive effects it seems that more work in this area, taking into account some of the most promising avenues, would be justified.

Music (instrumental, music education and music integration) shows some promise across all age groups. There is little evidence that visual art (painting, drawing, sculpture) had any positive effect on academic outcomes. Few empirical studies were found about the use of poetry for school-aged children, especially for pre-school and primary school children. Although rhymes and rhythms are routinely taught in pre-school, its impact on children's literacy has not been evaluated. The gap means that this could be an area worth exploring. Few studies have been conducted on creative writing as an activity to support general literacy at school. Most research in this area was either on creative writing as an outcome or for older students in higher education. It could be valuable to explore if creative writing has any impact in developing literacy for primary and secondary school pupils.

This new scoping review does not add much to the clear result of that prior review conducted in the same style (and there was very little work about causal models for improving arts performance *sui generis*). It is not at all clear that teaching arts has any value for improving attainment more generally (Tables 5.9 and 5.10).

Table 5.9 - Quality and impact summary: use of Arts to improve attainment

	Effective	Ineffective/unknown
Higher quality	0	1
Medium quality	1	0
Lower quality	5	2

Table 5.10 - Quality and impact detail: use of Arts to improve attainment

Reference	Intervention	Smallest cell	Attrition	ES	NNTD-attrition	Quality
Haywood et al. 2014	**Music v Drama**	**454 pupils**	**10%**	**Maths 0 Literacy 0.03**	**0 0**	**3***
Greenfader et al. 2015	Performing arts	902 pupils	50%	0.06	0	2*

Haywood et al. (2014) used an intervention called Act, Sing, Play (ASP) which offered music and drama tuition to 909 Year 2 pupils. There was 10% attrition. The aim of the programme was to evaluate whether music workshops had a bigger impact than drama workshops in terms of pupils' maths and literacy attainment. The relative ES for maths was 0.003, and literacy 0.03. This does not help decide if either is useful, but it does slightly confirm that music is the more promising approach.

Greenfader et al. (2015) evaluated a 2 year programme using movement, gesture and expression to stimulate English engagements, dialogue and vocabulary. It involved 5,240 K-Grade pupils (902 treatment. 4,338 control). Eight teaching 'artists' implemented the programme. Teachers participated within activities. Nearly half of the children had missing data. Effect size is 0.06.

A small trial conducted for EEF by Styles et al. (2014) found no impact from Rhythm for Reading used with 175 Year 7 pupils.

Runfola et al. (2012) examined the impact of 'musically trained' early childhood specialists on the music achievement and emergent literacy achievement of preschool children. The sample consisted of 11 teachers (control 4, experimental 7 – the primary reason for the imbalance was lack of motivation by some teachers to be in the control group) who met the criteria for the project and their respective students (N=165). Following a year of intensive staff development training in musicianship skill and pedagogical strategies for guiding young children's musical development, the teachers implemented the curriculum in the second year and several measures were used to collect data relative to student music and literacy outcomes. Results were mixed for music achievement. Median scores were similar for the experimental and control groups on use of singing voice. Students' tonal pattern achievement in the experimental group was significantly higher but no significant differences were found in children's rhythm-pattern achievement. When controlling for age and prior knowledge, children's oral vocabulary and understanding of grammar was greater in the music intervention, especially so for children who began with lower literacy skills. Literacy development was measured using the Test of Language Development which is a standardised measure comprised of different components of spoken language and key emergent literacy development skills such as phonemic analysis and word discrimination. Each child's oral-language abilities were tested prior to the music intervention to provide a baseline measure.

Hardiman et al. (2014) looked at an arts-integrated (AI) intervention that incorporated a variety of forms of artistic activity (music, visual arts, and performance arts) into instruction, and was compared to conventional instruction of same topic. Participants were 97 fifth Grade African American pupils from a US school. Control groups did better on post-test for both lower ability and other pupils. Lower ability pupils in the intervention group did better in terms of retention on the delayed post-test (thereby having a higher score at the end point).

Elisana et al. (2011) evaluated the effects of music and movement on maths performance using a randomised controlled, pre-post-test design. Participants were 110 first Grade children (age 6-7), randomly assigned to music and movement (n=55) and control (n=55). Both groups followed the maths curriculum of the Greek Ministry of Education. The music and movement group were taught all the topics of the first 12 weeks of the curriculum (i.e. orientation in space, recognising geometry shapes, comparing and evaluating quantities, numbering, reading and writing to 5, inverse counting, comparing size, time, comparing numbers, symbols, numbers 1 to 20, double sums, the half, designing lines). These topics were taught using music and movement in the 4/4 rhythm. The experimental group performed better but attrition is not known.

Keehn (2003) considered Readers Theatre Intervention and the effect of instruction and practice on young readers' oral reading fluency in the US. A wide range of tests was used to measure different aspects of reading competence/level - Qualitative Reading Inventory, Gray Oral Reading Test, Oral Reading Fluency Test. The study used 66 2nd Grade pupils in 4 classrooms. But both groups got something like the intervention, and the report is very unclear.

Courey et al. (2012) examined the effects of using music notation to teach 67 3rd graders about fractions. Children were assigned by class to general maths instruction or academic music. The intervention was delivered twice a week for 45 minutes / session over 6 weeks by music teacher and researcher together. The researcher guided students to connect music to more formal maths representations and symbols. Both control and experimental children were taught the standard state curriculum, the only difference being that for the experimental children two lessons per week were for academic music. Both groups had the same amount of maths instructional time. Results showed that Music children made bigger gains than comparison children on fraction concept test (ES = +0.35, and the weakest children made the most gains. This could be regression to the means (ES = 1.15). On fraction computation the weakest children in the experimental group also outperformed the comparison group. The evidence is weak because of the small sample and the fact that children were allocated by classes. There is therefore a possibility of class or peer effect, and teacher expectation effects. It is also not clear if the tests were standardised or not intervention-related.

Baumer et al. (2005) evaluated the use of dramatization and play on the narrative competence of 38 kindergarten and first grade children. Children were all from the same school. For 14 weeks both the intervention and control classes used the text from C.S. Lewis's novel, *The Lion, the Witch and the Wardrobe*. In both classes the teacher used the traditional practice of reading the text to the class, followed by writing and discussions (whole class, in pairs or individually) as well as adult participation. The difference is that the intervention class had dramatization and play. These sessions took place once a week for 2 hours. Children's narrative competence was assessed by getting them to arrange pictures in sequence and narrate the story. Children's narrations were videotaped and transcribed. The length, number of words used, linguistic complexity and narrative coherence were coded and counted. The study reported that intervention children made bigger gains between pre- and post-test on length of story, number of words used and coherence. However, the effect on linguistic complexity is unclear because of the high standard deviations among the experimental children. This study was rated weak in evidence because of the very small sample (n=38) meaning that there were fewer than 19 in each intervention arm. Attrition was high at 23%. Participants were not randomly selected nor assigned, and no baseline equivalence was established. Groups could be different at the outset. As children were from different classes there could be a teacher effect. This was not tested. Moreover, the assessment was very subjective. There could be a potential bias if coders were not blinded to condition.

One study (Carmon 2011) used musical notations (Toy-Musical Notes) to teach reading to 150 pre-school children. The results were not clear cut. The musical conventional group did better on correct reading than both musical notation and control groups, while the musical notation group did better on another measure. The small sample (n = 50 in each group) means that the results can be volatile. Also the groups were not randomised to conditions.

In summary, a few specific approaches show promise, but the evidence for most ideas is weak (other than those covered in more focused sections below).

5.7 Use of technology to support learning

Computer-assisted instruction (CAI) or technology is increasingly used in the classrooms to augment or assist classroom instruction. Broadly, technology or IT refers to programmes that use technology either as supplementary instruction (Computer Assisted Learning or CAL) where pupils gain additional practice or remediation or as part of instructional strategy in the classroom. It is now routine for most schools to use technology-based products such as software packages and websites in teaching and learning – for literacy and other core subject skills. Part of the reason for this growth has been enhanced government funding for technology-based purchases and for staff development in the use of ICT.

A review by Slavin et al. (2009) of effective instructional strategies reported no convincing positive effects of the use of IT programmes (including Compass Learning and Read 180). Of the 31 studies (including 8 with random assignment) and covering over 10,000 students, the mean effect size was +0.06 or +0.05. Only one programme (My Reading Coach) which involved more intensive use of computerised instruction of 45 minutes every day showed large effects of +0.24 in a large randomised evaluation. Large RCTs (e.g. Dynarski et al. 2007 and Campuzano et al. 2009) found no significant effects of the use of a variety of modern software on the reading achievement of fourth Graders (ES = +0.02). Most IT studies used computers as supplements to regular classroom instruction. Overall there was no convincing evidence that using IT worked.

Meta-analyses by Li and Ma (2010) and Slavin and Lake (2008) suggested that in general the use of IT in mathematics education positively affects learning outcomes, but in these analyses games were not taken as a separate category. One common computer game used in maths education is the mini-game. Previous studies have shown positive effects of mini-games on mental computation skills of 10-11 year olds (Miller and Robertson 2011). Research suggests that to develop multiplicative reasoning, it is necessary to develop knowledge of number facts and calculation of multiplication and division operations and number relations (e.g. Anghileri 2006, Nunes et al. 2012). Or perhaps the advantage of these computer games is that they have a motivational effect.

Cheung and Slavin (2013) looked at the effectiveness of educational technology applications in improving the reading achievement of poor readers in elementary schools, by synthesising 20 studies. Overall, there was a small benefit noted: ES=0.14, compared to usual practice. Most interventions were represented by only one or two studies and so the overall picture is probably more valid than the results for any one product. Small-group integrated applications such as Read, Write and Type and the Lindamood Phoneme Sequence Program appeared to be the most effective. Technology use as supplemental instructions produced moderate effects (ES=0.18), while comprehensive models, such as READ 180 and ReadAbout and Fast ForWord, did not produce meaningful positive effect sizes. It is not reported to what extent, if any, the quality of the research was used to weight the results by taking into account sampling, attrition and threats to validity in their review.

Archer et al. (2014) reviewed 38 studies from 3 previous meta-analyses and also showed a small overall effect of IT on literacy (ES=0.18). They suggested that implementation fidelity was crucial to the success or otherwise of computer-assisted instruction. However, the review did not examine the effects of computer based IT for different age groups of children. Although 2 of the 3 meta-analyses included RCTs and one of them also included quasi-experiments, it is not clear whether the quality of the included studies were taken into account (e.g. sample size and attrition).

Many of the studies directly addressing the efficacy of ICT in literacy education have been descriptive in nature, relying on the impressions of participants. These studies often find an apparently positive impact on the acquisition of pupil literacy skills (Blok et al. 2002, Silverstein et al. 2000, Cox et al. 2003, Pittard et al. 2003, OFSTED 2004, Rose and Dalton 2002, Pelgrum 2001, Sivin-Kachala and Bialo 2000). But others have argued that the small sample sizes, the lack of comparators, indeed the lack of research design, and the passive retrospective nature of some of this work combine to offer a potentially misleading picture (Waxman et al. 2003).

In this light, it is interesting that experimental studies of the effectiveness of software packages in improving literacy skills tend to show rather different results. Rigorous intervention studies with suitable controls often find little or no positive impact from the use of technology-based instruction compared to standard or traditional practice. A number of studies and systematic reviews have found that software packages had no effect on reading achievement (Borman et al. 2009, Rouse and Krueger 2004, Andrews et al. 2005, Torgerson and Zhu 2003, Angrist and Lavy 2002, Goolsbee and Guryan 2005, Dynarski et al. 2007, Lei and Zhao 2005). An overview of reading instruction interventions by Slavin et al. (2008) suggested that mixed methods and co-operative approaches are more effective than technology alone, although this conclusion is itself the subject of some dispute (e.g. Greenleaf and Petrosino 2008).

The current review uncovered a wide range of studies examining the effects of CAI or IT on pupil achievement. Of these only 3 were of higher quality and all showed no benefit (Table 5.11). These are discussed in more detail below.

Table 5.11 - Quality and impact summary: studies of ICT/CAL

	Effective	Ineffective/unknown
Higher quality	0	3
Medium quality	1	3
Lower quality	19	9

Bai et al. (2016) used 6,304 5th Grade pupils from 127 primary schools in China to test the impact of computer-assisted learning to complement regular English lessons. The 40 minute sessions were conducted twice weekly, involving two pieces of software - animated reviews and game-based remedial exercises, and a collection of additional exercise questions. A lesson implementation protocol was developed to assist teachers to deliver the programme. 44 schools were randomised to receive either the CAL integrated into their lessons, or as a stand-alone intervention. 4,000 students in 83 schools forming the control did not receive any intervention and were blinded to the treatment condition of the other schools. Outcomes were measured using the standardised Endline English test. Attrition was just over 6% of cases, and there was baseline equivalence between the groups. The two CAL interventions provided no overall benefit compared to traditional teaching (although the integrated version was the better of the two).

Khan and Gorard (2012) evaluated a piece of commercial software claimed by the publisher to be effective in improving children's reading in six weeks. In a cluster randomised controlled pre-post comparison trial involving 672 pupils in 23 schools, Khan and Gorard compared the outcomes of children using computer-assisted instruction with those that followed the standard literacy provision. Results showed that the experimental group did improve their literacy scores (ES = +0.56). However, the control group made even bigger gains (ES = +0.99). Overall effect is -0.37. This shows that results of 'evaluations' where there is no appropriate comparator can be completely misleading.

Table 5.12 - Quality and impact detail: studies of ICT/CAL

Reference	Intervention	Smallest cell	Attrition	ES	NNTD-attrition	Quality
Bai et al. 2016	**Integrated CAL in English**	**44 schools (2000+ pupils)**	**6%**	**0**	**0**	**4***
Khan and Gorard 2012	**Literacy software**	**336 pupils**	**2%**	**-0.37**	**0**	**3***
Alvarez-Marinelli et al. 2016	CAL in English	25 schools (270 pupils)	Unknown	Unknown	-	
Chambers et al. 2011	Tier 2 CAL in reading	274 pupils	Unknown	0 or worse	0	2*
Bebell and Pedulla 2015	iPad apps in literacy	8 classes, 130 pupils	0 (confused reporting)	Unknown	0	
Bakker et al. 2015	Computer games in maths	16 schools	47%	0.22 (but not ICT alone)	0	2*
Rosas et al. 2003	**Video games**	**347 pupils**	**Unknown**	**0**	**0**	**3***

Bakker et al. (2015) looked at the impact of playing mathematics computer games on students' multiplicative reasoning ability as used in regular US 2 nd Grade 2 and 3rd Grade 3 maths lessons. The intervention consisted of 4 game units, each lasting 10 weeks and in each unit 8 different mini-games were played. The mini games focused on 'automatising multiplicative number facts and multiplicative operation skills (through practicing), and on developing insight in multiplicative number relations and properties of multiplicative operations (through exploration and experimentation)' (p. 59). The study recruited 66 schools but 19 dropped out at different stages. Schools were also excluded in if classes in both grades did not complete more than half of the mini games. Results are reported for 719 children from 35 schools, representing attrition of over 50%. Multiplicative reasoning ability was measured using the knowledge, skills and insight test. There were 4 groups. It seemed that mini-games played at home and debriefed at school had a positive effect in enhancing overall multiplicative reasoning compared to the control (ES=0.22). However, it seems to be the school debriefing that works (if it does) and not the use of the technology itself. Use of the mini-games at home, school or both had no clear benefit.

Rosas et al. (2003) tested the effects of the use of video games in the classroom on maths and reading. Video games instruction was used daily for 20-40 minutes over 12 weeks alternating between maths and Language content. Participants were 1,274 1 st and 2 nd Grade children and 30 teachers and directors from 6 schools in Chile. Schools were paired by academic achievement, SES and level of vulnerability. Students were divided within schools to internal experimental or internal control group matched by educational level. An external control group was made up of schools where the tool was not used and pupils have a similar education level as the experimental group. There were 758 experimental children from 19 classes, 347 internal control from 9 classes (teacher used regular instruction), and 169 external control from 4 schools (with no contact with experiment). Attrition is not known. There was no clear difference between treatment and control children in maths, reading and spelling.

Alvarez-Marinelli et al. (2016) report on the first year of a two year RCT in Costa Rica, involving 816 3rd Grade students from 76 schools over 25 weeks. There were three groups – a control, and two groups using computer assisted English language learning with different time on task. All instruction took place during regular English lessons. Oral English proficiency measured on four subtests from the Woodcock Munoz Language Survey-Revised (WMLS-R), a norm-referenced, standardised instrument, were selected to monitor participants' oral English development. Attainment was linked to treatment and time on task.

Chambers et al. (2011) evaluated the relative effects of Tier II computer-assisted tutoring in small groups (Team Alphie) and one-to-one tutoring provided to struggling readers in 33 high-poverty Success for All (SFA) schools. Team Alphie is a small group literacy intervention, providing daily 45-minute lessons in phonemic awareness, phonics, fluency, vocabulary, and comprehension, with the focus on decoding and fluency skills. Team Alphie also used Peer Assisted Learning Strategies. In this year-long study, struggling readers in the Team Alphie schools were tutored in groups of 6. In the control schools, students were tutored using the standard one-to-one tutoring process used in SFA. Participants were the lowest 50% of 1st and 2nd Grade children. Students were replaced by the next lowest scorer if they left (and therefore attrition is not clearly reported). The CAL group had 372 pupils and the control 274. Pre-post data was only available for Letter Word Identification (Woodcock LWID), although the authors reported positive effects on all three reading measures (Letter Word Identification; Word Attack and Comprehension). They concluded that 'computer-assisted, small-group tutoring programme may be at least as effective as one-to-one tutoring and serve more struggling readers'. However, calculation of gain scores for this review shows that the CAL group performed worse.

The report by Bebell and Pedulla (2015) is an example of authors appearing to have a conflict of interest, or at least wanting the use of technology to be shown as successful. The study involved 266 kindergarten children from 16 classes in one school district, with 8 classes allocated to receive iPads with access to 22 types of apps for learning listening, phonemic awareness, phonics/writing mechanics, reading and writing. The most frequently used apps were Word Wisard, Spelling Magic and Montessori Crossword. The intervention lasted 9 weeks. Outcomes were measured using the Rigby, Children's Progress Academy Assessment (CPA) and the Observation of Early Literacy Achievement (OSELA) tests. The authors reported in abstract and conclusion that iPads had a positive impact on literacy using the CPA and OSELA tests, but their Figures 2 and 4 (pp.200-201) show that the differences are very small, sometimes negative, and might be disregarded in a study with only 8 clusters. A follow-up after three years no longer had a clean control group, and so the results were compared with different cohorts (i.e. no longer even a quasi-experiment). This aspect of the study reported large gains for literacy, but equally large negative 'impacts' on maths.

There were several other poorer quality studies (poorer quality in terms of either size, attrition, reporting or design or a combination). Results from these studies are mixed, but because of the poor quality we cannot conclude anything much from them. Among these were a number of studies reporting positive effects on a range of children's learning outcomes, and an equal number showing no real benefits. There was also an interesting variety of technology used, from power-point use, interactive whiteboards to toy-musical notes technology and humanoid robots.

The most common use of technology in the classroom is the interactive whiteboard. There is no evidence so far that such technology on its own enhances learning. An evaluation of the interactive whiteboard called ACTIVboard which uses software to create instructional activities claimed that schools using ACTIVboard significantly outperformed schools using differentiated instruction (Sterling 2010). However, there were only 3 schools and these were not matched. Pupils were also selected as a convenience sample. Schools and pupils were not well matched at all in terms of prior attainment. It would have been better to compare gain scores than just post-test scores. Reporting was also poor. Using a pre-post comparison design, Morales (2013) compared four classes of first Grade children from 2 schools – two classes used the interactive whiteboard (SmartBoard) and the other two without. Results showed no impact on maths attainment. The use of Webcam in the classroom also showed no particular advantage compared to children taught face-to-face although the article suggests that children might benefit with teacher fidelity and efficacy (Vernon-Feagans et al. 2015). Both groups made equivalent gains across literacy measures. Digital presentation tools like power-point are widely used in the classroom, but its impact on learning is unclear. Chou et al (2015) concluded that Prezi was more effective than traditional chalk and talk, while power-point presentation was more effective for long term retention. This was a very poor study with small sample (n=78), no random assignment to treatment, no report of missing data or attrition. Only the means for each test were compared, but no pre-tests to gauge gain scores (especially if the groups were different). All 3 classes were taught by the same teacher to control for teacher effects, but possibility of unconscious diffusion. The tests were developed by the teacher.

Although technology is widely used for teaching literacy and language, its effects are not clear. An evaluation of Fast ForWord by Soboleski (2011) suggests that the intervention was not particularly beneficial for primary school children. In fact, children receiving traditional teacher-led small group reading instruction demonstrated significantly more growth. A Canadian study of 512 Grades 1 and 2 children also found no beneficial effects for children taught using interactive multi-media software (Lysenko and Abrami 2014). Troia (2004) warned against the claims of Fast ForWord, having found no clear impact on any aspect of language skills except word recognition (0.31). The study involved 191 pupils in US elementary schools.

Fehr et al. (2012) evaluated an online computer assisted vocabulary learning programme and reported positive effects on Grade 2 to 4 (age 7-10) children on picture vocabulary test (not clear if this was a standardised test or a made-up test). There were only 43 children across the 3 Grades. There is thus a question of validity here since we do not know how many children in each Grade were in the treatment or control (full text of the paper is not available). It is possible that comparisons were made between older and younger children. Although positive effects were found for Living Letters (an adaptive computer game to teach proper name sounds), the effect was very variable ranging from 0.01 for letter knowledge to 0.53 for reading comprehension. However the attrition was so high that the groups were no longer equal (Van der Kooy-Hofland et al. 2012). White and Robertson (2015) reported gains in reading fluency and comprehension for children with special needs using a text-to-speech computer assisted software. The study was based on only 5 children and had no comparison groups. Children were withdrawn from their classroom for special individual lessons. The findings are therefore not reliable and cannot be generalised to regular classroom situation.

Dina et al. (2014) reported positive results for a silent reading smart game programme. Groups were not matched and comparison was between high and low ability children (age 8-9), so we cannot be sure if children would make the same progress otherwise.. Results could be regression to the mean. Boden and Boden (2007) also suggested that the use of adaptive computer software can help improve the spelling of children (ages 8-10). Children showed progress over the 5 weeks. There was comparison group, so cannot be sure if this approach is more effective than the regular classroom practice. Assessments seemed to be intervention related, that is, testing children what they have been taught. An interesting study in Taiwan tested the use of humanoid robots in the classroom to present instructional materials (Zeng et al. 2016). Comparison was between two intact classes. The experimental class performed better than the control class in the school's formal exam, but the effect size for writing was very small. The classes may be different to begin with and with no pre-test to estimate gains, it is difficult to say which class has actually made more progress.

The use of technology is widespread in maths and science instruction. Five studies suggested that the use of technology could improve maths/science performance of primary school aged children. All of these had one or more methodological flaws. Fößl et al. (2016) was based on three teachers in one school. Two teachers formed the control while another teacher taught both the control and experimental classes (introducing diffusion). Classes were not randomly assigned. The programme included a number of other components, such as small-group cooperative learning, self-regulated strategy and feedback strategy. So it is not clear which of these elements or a combination of these good practices or indeed the creation of video podcasts enhances learning. More importantly, the test items were selected by researchers, and the very low pre-test marks across groups (averaging about 1.00 and high post-test averaging about 14 suggests that the pre-test tested children on a topic that had not been taught to the children). Serin (2011) conducted a proper RCT with pre- and post-tests on 54 fifth Grade children (age 10-11). Experimental children outperformed control children on the 3 topics taught and on problem-solving. What is wrong with this study is that the test was intervention-related, and it was rather small (26 and 27 in each intervention arm).

Technology has also been used to develop self-regulation in maths learning (Choi 2013). The author reported significant differences in achievement in favour of the group using the revised digital textbook. However, the data in the article showed that control group did better on post-test for lesson 1, while the experimental group did better on lesson 2. There was no pre-test, so unable to estimate gain scores. The small sample (n = 70) taken from one school poses a threat to external validity. Results cannot be generalised. The results could be due to the volatility of small sample. Test items were based on content in the textbook and developed by instructional designer and content expert – not sure if they were standardised. Chiang et al. (2014) investigated the use of mobile phone to teach inquiry-based learning in science. The authors reported that experimental group performed significantly better than control on learning achievement, but the data showed that there was no difference between groups (ES=0.015). The small sample (n =57) from two classes, with no random allocation to conditions (classes were selected for treatment condition) means that the two were not equal. Also the same teacher taught both classes. There is thus a possibility of teacher expectation, which could affect outcomes. Lai et al. (2015) claimed that the use of remedial CAL programmes improve standardised maths scores by 0.15 standard deviation using additional after school classes. The authors claimed this was a randomised experiment, and it was certainly large, but it was not clear from the abstract how the groups were randomised, and there was no comparison of test scores reported in the abstract. This was a remedial programme held outside regular school hours, suggesting that experimental children had additional lessons.

One study of flipped learning showed no effects on maths (Ripley 2015). The pupils (n=55) where the teacher used a flipped instructional method was compared with other pupils not taught using this approach (n=2,315).

Several studies relating to the use of computer software designed to improve literacy for students have failed to show any positive impact. In fact, a number found the use of technology actually slowed down students' progress. Brooks et al. (2006) found the use of computer had a negative impact on students' reading.

Potocki et al. (2015) involved 39 second Grade children identified as having difficulties with processing literal information, from 7 primary schools in France. They were classified (not randomised) into four groups, and given computerised comprehension training. Most groups made about the same progress. See also Potocki et al. (2013).

Altiparmak and Ozdogan (2010) divided 150 pupils aged 11 to 12 into two groups. One received teaching using a computer assisted teaching strategy, and the other continued with the traditional teaching approach commonly used in Turkey. Although a positive impact is reported, it is not clear how the groups were allocated, nor whether they were balanced at the outset. The outcome was a test developed by the researchers.

One paper examined the effects of the educational software Frisbi Mathematics 4 on 4th Grade student's mathematics achievement, retention, and attitudes toward mathematics (Pilli and Aksu 2013). Participants included 55 Grade 4 children (treatment 29; control 26). The experimental group scored higher in the post-test.

A small RCT involving 24 4 th Grade pupils in US suggests mobile phones can be useful for taking notes during science field trips (Zacharia et al. 2016).

Sterling (2010) looked at the impact of using ACTIVboard - an interactive wall-mounted, computer connected white board with software that is used to create instructional activities in the US. Two schools were compared. They were not well matched. The gain for the white board school was minimal, although emphasized by the author on the basis of totally irrelevant significance tests No randomisation was involved). For example, 27% of third Grade students from School A exceeded expectations while only 20% of third Grade students from School B did. Only 24% of students from School A did not meet expectations, as opposed to 29% from School B.

Ecalle et al. (2009) looked at syllabic and phonological training using computer software on literacy skills - teaching children segmented words rather than whole word recognition using software that highlights syllabic words inside words. Participants were 28 first Grade French-speaking children. Children were split into 2 groups: treatment children received training in segmented words while the other group was trained in whole word recognition. There is no report of attrition. The ES for word recognition was around 0.8, for reading aloud and spelling it was 0, but for both of the latter the experimental group later performed better at follow up. A second paper had even smaller cell sizes (Ecalle et al. 2013).

Wijekumar et al. (2014) trialled an intelligent web-based tutoring system to promote the structure strategy for US 5th Grade reading in 128 classrooms. The intervention group used the intelligent web-based tutoring system for the structure strategy (ITSS) for 30 to 45 minutes each week as a partial substitute for the language arts curriculum for the entire school year – meaning that they had more teaching relevant to the test outcomes. Results show that the ITSS delivered structure strategy training improved reading comprehension measured by a standardised test and researcher designed measures.

Ercan (2014) describe a quasi-experimental non-equivalent control group design to examine the effects of using multimedia materials in teaching science. 65 fifth Graders in one Turkish school were randomised to two groups (balanced at pre-test). One topic (Food and Healthy Nutrition) from the science curriculum was used for this experiment, and the intervention was delivered over 8 weeks (32 class hours). 4 pupil scores were missing. The treatment group made greater gains in science tests (0.96).

On balance, this review found little evidence that the use of commercial software or new technology in itself helps improve the academic performance of children. Although many studies reported positive effects, these were often of questionable quality with no controls or comparators, or very small samples in one school. Positive studies tend to be small, do not use standardised tests, have no comparison groups or do not establish baseline equivalence. Where more robust evaluations involving large randomised samples were used, these often found small or no effects. The best studies here find IT use in the classroom to be ineffective or worse. In fact, this is the only widespread approach discussed in this review which may be harming children's learning.

6. Enhanced feedback

6.1 Feedback and self-regulation

There are claims that enhanced feedback or formative assessment may be beneficial in raising the academic performance of kindergarten and primary school children. In 1988, the National Curriculum Task Group on Assessment and Testing (TGAT) for England and Wales recommended that assessment should be an "integral part of the education process, continually providing both 'feedback' and 'feedforward' and ought therefore to be 'systematically incorporated into teaching strategies and practices at all levels" (DES 1988, paragraphs 3 and 4). The proposed system advocated a combination of both formative and summative approaches. Many reports on effective pedagogy identify feedback as a characteristic of effective teaching and learning (Harris and Ratcliffe 2005, Creemers 1994, Scheerens 1992, 1999, Siraj-Blatchford and Taggart 2014, Coe et al. 2014, DfE 2000). However, this work does not, in itself, establish clearly that enhanced 'feedback' is generally effective. It is widely agreed that good teachers tend to use more and stronger feedback naturally. But what is not so clear from these passive correlational and longitudinal designs is how easy it is to enhance the use of such feedback by other, perhaps more reluctant, teachers, and whether this would make any difference to pupils' attainment

Assessment for learning (AfL), a kind of formative assessment (defined as an activity that provides feedback to inform teaching and learning) is one of the strategies advocated for use in the classroom. An early experimental study called "Inside the Blackbox" indicated a substantial impact for AfL on learning for all age groups (from pre-school to undergraduate level), and claimed that formative assessment was especially effective for low achievers (Black and Wiliam 1998). Black (2000) cited research where the use of formative assessment techniques produced learning gains with effect sizes of between 0.4 and 0.7, larger than those produced by some other significant educational interventions. Fuchs and Fuchs (1986) reported benefits for children with special needs. White and Frederiksen

(1998) also reported that feedback was more effective for low achieving students (effect size of 1.0) than for high achieving students (effect size of 0.27).

The Education Endowment Foundation Teaching and Learning Toolkit recorded Feedback strategy as having an impact equivalent of +9months progress and Assessment for Learning with an impact of +3 months progress (Education Endowment Foundation 2015).

A meta-review by Hattie and Timperley (2007) was based on an impressive number of meta-analyses (n=74) of studies relating to feedback, involving a large number of studies (n=4,157) and 5,755 effect sizes. Such meta-meta-analyses often synthesize results from several small and flawed studies. Large effect sizes were cited – these often involved assessments of outcomes using researcher-developed tests. Hattie and Timperley reported wide variations in effect sizes depending on the types of feedback used, but there was no comment on the quality of these studies nor the reliability of the evidence. A synthesis that heavily informed their model was by Kluger and DeNisi (1996) because it was 'the most systematic' and 'included studies that had at least a control group, measured performance, and included at least 10 participants'. This suggests that most of the other studies in the 73 other meta-analyses were not particularly systematic, had no control group, had fewer than 10 participants or did not even measure performance. How many of such studies were in these meta-analyses was not known. Therefore, the number of studies whose evidence we can rely on is unknown. Hattie and Timperley added that many of these studies were not classroom based. Presumably these studies were undertaken in a laboratory condition, which may be less relevant. They then went on to say that their evidence based on 131 studies (conducted largely in controlled conditions) included 470 effect sizes and involving 12,652 participants showed an average effect size of 0.38 (SE=0.09). Of these 32% showed negative effects or decreased performance. This cannot be explained by scale (sampling error) or even by theories of feedback use. But an explanation might involve the kinds of feedback such as praise, reward and punishment, the nature of the pupils or students involved, or the quality of implementation which is often not very helpful. Hattie and Timperley reported that the 'average sample size per effect was 39 participants'. This is a very small sample per study.

Of the studies that Hattie and Timperley cited, we could not locate all of the effect sizes listed in the summary table (Table 1, p.83). For example, the review states that the effect size of 54 studies in Lysakowski and Walberg (1982) was +1.13 whereas the original paper reports it at 0.97 (study-weighted). The figure 1.13 appears nowhere in their paper. In Hattie (1992) and repeated subsequently, it is said that "Skiba, Casey and Center (1986) used 315 effect-sizes (35 studies) to investigate the effects of some form of reinforcement or feedback and found an effect-size of 1.88", but the later 2007 paper reports this review as having 35 effect sizes not studies, and an effect size of +1.24. While none of this undoes the work that has been done or eliminates the evidence for the impact of enhanced feedback it ought to lead to caution. Overall, the evidence is not as clear as some commentators have suggested. We are also not sure what the outcome measures were for these studies. Anyway this one was only about special education rather than mainstream students.

Most of the studies cited did not use random allocation of subjects and yet quote p-values, which must therefore be meaningless. If Hattie used meta-analyses based on p-values but did not eliminate the majority where it was used incorrectly then the results will be incorrect. For example, one study synthesized had used MANOVA based on those students who agreed to participate compared to those who refused, presented as evidence of the impact of the intervention.

What these meta-meta-analyses appear to do is aggregate scores from a wide variety of research designs, practical approaches and educational settings taking no account of the bias introduced by attrition, treating a study with full response as equivalent to one with high dropout or missing data. Some include both passive designs along with randomised control trials (RCTs), some only the former, and no distinction seems to be made between them.

Some research reports cited in the meta-analyses went back as far as 1960. These meta-analyses used different calculations of effect sizes, for different measures of the same parameters (e.g. different types of reinforcement and a range of feedbacks) for different groups of children at different phases of schooling (even university and postgraduate study). Some studies were specifically for SEN children, children with behavioural, emotional and disruptive behaviour. Some were based on very young children, and some used undergraduates at university. How Hattie and Timperley arrived at the effect sizes in the paper was not explained.

There are two other problems with this array of evidence. Some of it is not particularly robust, and little of it sheds light on what happens when feedback practices are implemented across a wide variety of schools and teachers. Other studies are not directly about the impact of enhanced feedback on attainment. For example, some are about how possible it is to implement an intervention such as AfL (Jonsson et al. 2015), while others are about the nature and perception of the feedback generated by teachers (Carvalho et al. 2014).

The second problem is that few of the studies come with a practical guide on how to apply the research evidence in real classroom situations. For example, Kluger and DeNisi's meta-analysis was based on studies where the research was undertaken largely in controlled or laboratory conditions. Results may be different in real classroom conditions. Others have suggested that feedback may not always be effective if introduced without proper training for implementing it (Black and Wiliam 1998). Black and Wiliam stressed that for the successful implementation of formative assessment, pupils needed to be trained to set goal oriented criteria ('Success Criteria' in Hattie and Timperley 2007, p. 88), assess their own progress, identify areas that need improvement, and understand strategies needed to achieve this. White and Frederiksen (1998), on the other hand, suggested that pupils should be told explicitly by teachers what the criteria of success should be.

Many of the studies conducted so far have been small-scale. For example, most of the 1,387 studies in a recent review by Hopfenbeck and Stobart (2015) on AfL were small case studies (with one or two schools), while very few were large-scale or well-designed evaluations. The White and Frederiksen (1998) study was based on only three teachers in two schools. Truckenmiller et al. (2014) had only 39 cases in the smallest group, and Lipko-Speed (2014) involved only 65 5 th Grade students (10-11 year-olds) altogether. The original Black Box experiment involved six volunteer schools, and it is evident that the approach does not always lead to equivalent success in less propitious circumstances (e.g. Smith and Gorard 2005). These small studies generally reported positive effects. For example, Truckenmiller et al. (2014) reported an effect size of 0.66 effect size, while Lipko-Speed (2014) confirmed that use of enhanced feedback was better than using additional study or summative testing only.

Ennis and Jolivette (2014) reviewed 14 studies of Self-Regulated Strategy Development – an explicit instruction approach that includes goal setting, self-monitoring, self-instruction and self-reinforcement for students with and at risk of emotional and behavioural disorders. Many used non-standard outcomes, and were delivered by researchers rather than teachers. Most presented positive outcomes. The three RCTs suggested large, zero to large, and negative to large effects. See also Losinski et al. (2014).

Table 6.1 - Quality and impact summary: studies of Feedback

	Effective	Ineffective/unknown
Higher quality	1	1
Medium quality	1	2
Lower quality	11	3

Joseph and Eveleigh (2011) conducted a review to synthesize the effects of self-monitoring methods on reading achievement for students with disabilities. Findings suggested that reading performance improved when self-monitoring methods were used. Among the many findings derived from this review, more studies explored the use of self-monitoring on comprehension skills than on other reading skills, and more studies included participants with learning disabilities (followed by students with emotional and behavioural disorders) than students with other types of disabilities.

Table 6.2 - Quality and impact detail: studies of Feedback

Reference	Intervention	Smallest cell	Attrition	ES	NNTD-attrition	Quality
Lang et al. 2014	**Formative Assessment**	**15 schools, 2000+ pupils**	**1 school, unknown pupils**	**0.20**	**500+**	**3***
Phelan et al. 2011	**Feedback (Year 7)**	**2045 pupils**		**0.03**	**0**	**3***
Decristan et al. 2015	Formative assessment in science	11 teachers (232 pupils)	10%	Unknown	0	2*
See et al. 2015	Enhanced feedback	5 schools		0.04	0	2*
Torgerson and Torgerson 2014b	Self-regulation and writing	130 pupils	11%+	0.74	Unclear	2*

Donker et al. (2014) reviewed 58 studies of learning strategy instruction to improve self-regulation and so enhance academic performance. Results indicated big positive effects on writing (1.25), science (.073), mathematics (0.66) and reading (0.36). Metacognition strategy was deemed to be the most useful across all the 4 domains. As usual studies using self-developed tests showed bigger effects than intervention-independent tests. And it is not clear if or how studies were quality appraised.

In this new review we found five large-scale studies of at least moderate quality (Tables 6.1 and 6.2). The most promising was Lang et al. (2014) which suggests that feedback may be beneficial in raising the academic attainment of very young children. It was the best in terms of quality with a large sample size (over 4000 pupils) and low attrition. Three others were of lower quality. One of these reported positive effects, but the tests were developed by the researchers, and teachers were trained to teach the topics tested (Decristan et al. 2015). This poses a threat to validity and reliability. Torgerson and Torgerson (2014b) evaluated self-regulation and writing in England using 261 pupils in Years 6 and 7 allocate by school. The ES was +0.74, with at least 11% attrition but the reporting is unclear on this.

See et al. (2015) used a matched comparison design comparing intervention children (n =1,677) with 1,177 pupils in matched comparator schools. The study showed that Year 6 (age 10-11) pupils in intervention schools made bigger gains than comparator schools in reading, maths and writing (ES = +0.04) in national exams (from KS1 and KS2) and also when compared to all the other state schools in the area (ES = +0.6). However, when value-added scores were used intervention schools did not show much progress compared to comparator schools. For all other year groups where national exam scores were not available, comparisons were made using teacher assessments. The results showed small but mixed effects - positive for maths (ES = +0.06) and negative for reading (ES = -0.04) and writing (ES = -0.05). However, the results were more promising for free school meals eligible pupils. The gain score 'effect' sizes were positive for FSM-eligible pupils in all three subjects – reading (+0.17), writing (+0.12) and maths (+0.41), but because of the small number of cases (n = 360), there may be some volatility. This study was rated lower because of the design.

Lang et al. (2014) evaluated the Formative Assessment System (MFAS) in 31 US elementary schools involving 2,317 kindergarten and 2,515 first Grade children and 301 teachers. One school dropped out. This was a block cluster-randomised study with randomisation at school-level. MFAS is aligned with the Common Core State Standards (CCSS) and was intended for both teachers and students. The formative assessment process provides feedback to teachers to adjust ongoing teaching and learning to address gaps in children's knowledge related to the instructional objectives. In lessons teachers ask students to perform tasks, explain their reasoning, and prove their solutions. The evidence collected enables teachers to differentiate instruction based on students' mathematical thinking and reasoning rather than solely on incorrect answers. The MFAS-CCSS programme was designed to provide teachers with tasks and rubrics to employ the following five key strategies: (1) assess the student's level of understanding during instruction, (2) identify the student's specific misconceptions and errors, (3) examine samples of student work for further evidence of student understanding, (4) pose additional questions to elicit student thinking, and (5) obtain guidance on next steps for instruction.. The result showed a positive effect on children's maths outcomes (ES = 0.2 for kindergarten and ES = 0.24 first Grade.

Another large-scale but slightly weaker study evaluated the impact of embedding formative assessment as teaching practice on children's academic outcome (Decristan et al. (2015). 551 third Grade German children (age 8-9) and 28 teachers and their classes were randomly assigned to receive professional development training on embedded formative assessment (treatment teachers = 17; control teachers = 11; treatment pupils = 319; control = 232) or to control. Treatment teachers were also taught how to teach the target topics. Control teachers received training in parental counselling. Treatment students showed higher levels of science understanding than control. However, the test instruments were developed by researchers – so there is possibility of bias e.g. teaching to the test, teacher and researcher expectations since teachers were not blind to the intervention. Researchers claimed that the test items had been judged as valid by experts in science education (i.e. relevant to the topics). Teachers were trained to teach the topics that were tested. The question is whether the same results can be produced if teachers taught other topics without CPD but just using embedded formative assessment.

One large-scale study involving 4,091 pupils from 25 schools tested the use of a toolkit made up of a list of formative assessment items for teachers to use to check their pupils' understanding of mathematical concepts so that they can tailor their instruction and feedback to their pupils (Phelan et al. 2011). Experimental teachers received CPD and instructional resources. Control teachers had no access to the resources. Small effects were detected between randomised schools (ES=0.03). The authors reported that higher ability pupils benefitted more from the intervention than lower ability pupils. The participants were Grade 6 children (age 11-12).

Another study for older children (Meyer et al. 2010) reported that children receiving elaborated feedback made substantial progress in reading comprehension (d=0.55) compared to those receiving simple feedback (d=0.15). Weaker students also made greater progress between pre- and post-tests (d=0.73) compared to more competent readers (d =0.27), although this could be result of regression to the mean. The participants were 111 5th and 7th Grade students. However, the results of this study have to be taken with caution because of the small sample size in proportion to the large number of groups, meaning that there were on average only four students per grade and treatment condition. There was also no pure control group.

There were several other lower quality studies. One did not actually evaluate outcomes but indicated that there was little evidence that children benefitted from the intervention (Skipp and Tanner 2016). Two suggested positive effects, but were not actually evaluations of feedback as such. Rather they were comparisons of the relative effectiveness of different ways in which feedback was implemented. For example, with or without goal-setting (Codding et al. 2009) or whether feedback was given via personal computer, interpersonal computer or pen and paper (Alcoholado et al. 2016). Hier and Eckert (2014) reported positive impact immediately after the intervention (ES = 0.6) but the effects faded progressively from 2 weeks after the intervention (ES = -0.01) and ES = -0.08 after 4 weeks. The reporting was poor and there was a lot of volatility in the test scores. The groups were also unbalanced at pre-test.

Sontag and Stoeger (2015) examined if highly intelligent and high-achieving students benefit from training in self-regulated learning conducted in regular classrooms as much as their peers of average intelligence and with average scholastic achievement. Fourth-Graders participating in a training programme of self-regulated learning (SRL, n = 123) were compared with 4 th Graders receiving regular classroom instruction (REG, n = 199) in a pre-test, post-test, follow-up design. Students in the SRL group practiced self-regulated learning while working on identifying main ideas in expository texts. The training was effective for highly intelligent and high-achieving students as well as for their peers of average intelligence and with average scholastic achievement.

In a classroom intervention study, reciprocal teaching (RT) of reading strategies was combined with explicit instruction in self-regulated learning (SRL) to promote the reading comprehension of fifth-Grade students (N = 306). Twelve intact classes were randomly assigned either to an RT+SRL condition or to an RT condition without explicit instruction in self-regulation (Schünemann et al. 2013). Three additional classes served as a no-treatment comparison group. Strategies instruction was delivered by trained assistants in conventional German language lessons. Students practiced the application of these strategies in small groups. Both at post-test and at maintenance (8 weeks after the intervention), students in the two intervention conditions (RT and RT+SRL) outperformed comparison students in measures of reading comprehension, strategy-related task performance, and self-efficacy for reading. Relative to RT students, students in the RT+SRL condition were better able to maintain training-induced performance gains over the follow-up interval.

Brunstein and Glaser (2011) conducted an RCT involving 117 4 th Grade children from 4 schools in Germany to test the effectiveness of self-regulation strategies on composition skills. Randomisation was at the class level where half of the class was trained in self-regulatory writing strategies (experimental) and the other half were taught writing strategies (control) only without self-regulation training. Pupils' writing quality was assessed using pre-post comparisons. Results showed that experimental children outperformed control children on all the writing components measures, but the test was intervention-related. ES ranged from 1.2 for story quality to 3.6 for story plans. See also Glaser and Brunstein (2007).

McEldoon et al. (2013) compared three groups of 2nd to 4th Grade pupils from three US schools – control (17), additional practice in maths (31) or self-explanation (21). Attrition was 14%. All students were taught a procedure for solving two mathematical equivalence problems and then worked through six or twelve practice problems. Answer feedback was given on all problems. Students in the self-explain condition were prompted to explain examples of correct and incorrect answers. Both self-explanation and additional practice groups scored higher than control and by about the same amount (ES range from 0.04 to 0.62 depending upon the outcome).

A similar result emerged from Fuchs et al. (2016), using self-explanation to help learning fractions. 4th Grade US children in 14 schools were randomly assigned to three conditions - intervention with explanation (n=79); intervention with word-problem component (79) and control (78). Attrition was 8%. Both intervention conditions included 36 sessions, each lasting 35 minutes. All but 7 minutes of each session were identical. In the varied component, students were taught to provide high quality explanations when comparing fraction magnitudes or to solve fraction word problems. Outcomes included fraction knowledge (using the National Assessment of Educational Progress test items); Fraction magnitude comparisons/explanations (using Fraction Battery-revised); Multiplicative Word Problems. For this review we consider only the outcomes for fraction knowledge as the other two outcomes were measured using instruments developed by the researchers. Compared to the control, the word problem group made the biggest gains between pre- and post-test on the NAEP test (0.89). The supported explanation group outperformed the control (0.64) but made lower gains than the WP group.

Does talking to oneself when learning multiplication work? Arnold et al. (2014) looked at the use of inner speech as a pedagogical tool to develop strategies in learning multiplication. The study was a 50-week intervention conducted with children in the 3 rd and 4 th Grade to train them to develop inner private speech to silent inner speech. Training involved teaching children to move from audible to inaudible private speech (starting from singing and reciting rhymes with a loud voice to whispering and finally in silence). Then the teacher introduced a new multiplication table for 2 weeks and an additional week to repeat what they had learnt. Students wrote down their answers, repeated the task and answered in a loud voice, then in a whisper and finally in silence. The study reported a significant difference between a comparator and intervention group at Grade 4 but not at Grade 7. The study is so badly reported that it is not clear how many groups there were, and who was compared with whom. The sample was described as 77 intervention children in the 7th Grade (5 children had moved away – suggesting that there were 82 initially). Control children were 83 children from 3 schools. It is not clear how many schools intervention children were drawn from and how many (if any) control children were lost.

Lipowski et al. (2014) used 41 1st Graders, 44 3rd Graders to learn one list of words in a test-restudy condition and another in a restudy condition. Those tested earlier had higher scores (could be a test practice effect).

Baker et al. (2012) compared the effects of a paired bilingual programme and an English-only reading programme on the English reading outcomes of 214 Spanish-speaking English learners from 1st to 3rd Grade. The children were from high-poverty, low-achieving schools. There was no difference in reading comprehension by the 3rd Grade (and some gain for the bilingual group in oral fluency). There was no report of attrition.

Enhanced feedback, therefore, may hold promise and is a relatively cheap intervention, but the evidence is not as strong as sometimes envisaged. Only one strong study of the right age group was found, which reported positive effects on maths outcomes for kindergarten and first Grade pupils.

Retrieval practice involves having learners set aside the material they are learning and practice actively reconstructing it on their own. When students are capable of successfully retrieving knowledge, and when they practice doing it repeatedly, retrieval practice is intended to promote learning (Agarwal et al. 2012). Karpicke et al. (2014) report on three experiments with elementary school children. In the first, 94 children were divided into 4 conditions (free recall, concept mapping, cued recall and study only control). There was little difference in recall outcomes. In the second, 103 children were divided into three treatments using a concept map with different levels of intensity, and a control. Children with less support actually performed better (-0.12). In the third, 89 children were allocated to either guided retrieval or reread. The guided retrieval group performed better (0.82). The results are therefore very mixed. It would have been far preferable to have had only one study with nearly 300 pupils in only two groups, and come to a more trustworthy answer.

6.2 Peer tutoring

Peer tutoring is an intervention where students work in pairs and one of the pair acts as the tutor and the other the learner. Peer tutoring can involve same age partners or cross age partners (where an older student tutors the young ones). Another form of peer tutoring is reciprocal peer tutoring where pupils alternate between the roles of tutor and tutee. It could also involve mixed ability pairs where a higher performing pupil is paired with a lower performing pupil to provide the model and the support. Peer tutoring can also be used as a whole class intervention where teachers divide the class into pairs. Typically class wide peer tutoring is highly structured and may involve competitive teams.

There is extensive research on peer tutoring with the majority of studies reporting moderate to large effects in maths and reading. According to the EEF teaching and learning toolkit peer tutoring can have an impact of as much as 5 months progress. Eight meta-analyses cited in the EEF toolkit reported effects ranging from 0.33 for tutors and 0.40 for tutees (Cohen et al. 1982) to 1.05 for cross age peer tutoring (Jun et al. 2010).

WWC (2012) identified 45 studies on Peers Assisted Learning Strategy (PALS) for beginner readers. Only 3 were RCTs that met WWC standards of evidence (McMaster et al. 2005; Stein et al. 2008; Mathes and Babyak 2001). McMaster et al. found that compared to adult one-to-one tutoring children who had PALS performed equally well on seven alphabetic outcomes, but negative effects on comprehension. It has to be mentioned that this study was based on only 66 children with 38% attrition, since results were reported for only 41 children. Mathes and Babyak (2001), on the other hand, found positive effects on the Woodcock Reading test of comprehension. Although not statistically significant it was large enough to be considered substantive by WWC. WWC considers effects of over 0.25 as important. Attrition was 14%, and the sample size was small (60 in PALS, 20 in PALS plus additional skills lessons and 49 in comparison group). For analyses, the two PALS groups were combined and compared with the no PALS group. It is therefore not clear whether it is the additional mini lessons given to one of the PALS group that produced the effects. Stein et al. (2008) involved 2,959 kindergarten children across 67 schools in the US looked at whether the effects of PALS on children differed with the amount of training and support given to teachers. Teachers were randomly assigned to 3 groups of PALS with varying degree of support or to business-as-usual group. Compared to no intervention control, positive effects were found among all the children in the 3 PALS group on alphabetics. Attrition was low (under 10%). Thus for early readers, PALS shows promise on alphabetics given the positive effects of the fairly large study by Stein et al., but no effects on fluency and mixed effects on reading comprehension. WWC (2013) found no discernible effects of PALS on maths achievement for elementary school pupils.

In a review of 17 studies on instructional process progress Slavin et al. (2009) reported an effect size of 0.46 for PALS and class peer tutoring for beginning readers. For upper primary children positive effects were also found for peer tutoring (ES = +0.21 for cooperative learning and ES = +0.26 for cross age and same age tutoring and +0.32 for reciprocal teaching).

A recent meta-review of peer tutoring by the Washington State Institute for Public Policy (Pennucci and Lemon 2014) concluded that both cross age and same age peer tutoring were effective in improving test scores. In a review of modelling pedagogies in science, Campbell et al. (2015) identified peer-to-peer collaborative/cooperative learning as the most important instructional strategies in science teaching. However, the review stopped short of saying which instructional strategies were the most effective for science instruction.

In a meta-analysis of effective writing instructions for elementary grade pupils, Graham et al. (2012) identified a long list of effective instructional practices including explicit teaching of process, skills and knowledge of writing, self-regulation, scaffolding, text instructions and word processing. And all the writing interventions apart from one showed statistically significant effects. Peer assistance when was one of the strategies identified as being effective (ES = 0.89).

A meta-analysis of 15 studies on maths teaching practices (Baker et al. 2002) concluded that "Providing teachers and students with specific information on how each student is performing consistently enhances achievement [and in addition] the use of peers to provide feedback and support seems to be consistently supported by research as a solid means to improve computational abilities and a promising means to enhance problem-solving abilities" (pp. 63-67).

A review of effective pedagogical strategies for teaching literacy to young immigrant students by Adesope et al. (2011) looked at 26 studies, and concluded that collaborative reading interventions, in which peers engage in oral interaction and cooperatively negotiate meaning and a shared understanding of texts, produced larger effects than systematic phonics instruction and multimedia-assisted reading interventions.

Puzio and Colby (2013) conducted a meta-analysis of the effectiveness of cooperative and collaborative learning on literacy in regular classroom settings (not pull-out instruction), for pupils from 2nd to 12th Grade. They found 18 causal evaluations and 29 cohort studies. As usual, it is not clear how the quality of individual studies was assessed, and cooperative learning is often used in combination with other interventions, meaning it is not possible to estimate the exact effects that can be attributed. The authors report that most studies are positive with ES around 0.16 to 0.20.

In a later review for pupils with learning difficulties (Gersten et al. 2009), providing feedback with goals to students did not produce consistent effects across studies. Cross age peer tutoring produced impressive effects in the two studies reviewed (1.15 and 0.75). Peer assisted learning within the class, on the other hand, did not produced beneficial impacts for children with learning difficulties, and this was consistent across the studies.

It has to be remembered that all the meta-analyses included studies for participants across a wide age range. In this current review the focus is on primary school age children in mainstream education.

Our new review identified 4 studies of reasonable quality. Two of these were of higher quality, one reporting positive effects on comprehension (Dion et al. 2011) and one showed no effects on maths (Lloyd et al. 2015). One medium quality study (Fuchs et al. 2002) reported positive effects on maths, but only on items that were aligned with PALS. No effects were found for items not used in PALS training. In summary there is stronger evidence of positive effects of PALS for literacy, than for maths. The evidence for cross age tutoring and collaborative is also weak. The strongest study of collaborative work (Baines et al. 2007) found little or no evidence of impact.

Table 6.3 - Quality and impact summary: studies of Peer tutoring

	Effective	Ineffective/unknown
Higher quality	1	1
Medium quality	1	1
Lower quality	4	3

Table 6.4 - Quality and impact detail: studies of Peer tutoring

Reference	Intervention	Smallest cell	Attrition	ES	NNTD-attrition	Quality
Fuchs et al. 2002	Peer Assisted Learning Strategies	161 pupils	49	0.31	0	2*
Dion et al. 2011	**Peer tutoring and Good Behaviour Game v Peer tutoring v control**	**19 teachers (136 pupils)**	**2.4%**	**Combined comprehension 0.38**	**48**	**3/4***
Lloyd et al. 2015	**Cross-age tutoring**	**1,583 pupils**	**15%**	**Maths Year 3 0.01 Year 5 0.02**	** 0 0**	**3***
Baines et al. 2007	Group work	560 pupils	Unknown	0.04	-	2*

Baines et al. (2007) looked at an intervention known as the *SPRinG programme* - a collaborative group work strategy for science to be used in natural classroom condition. The programme was developed collaboratively with teachers and researchers. It was designed to provide teachers with the strategies to engage pupils in group work. Teachers received training and a handbook containing key principles and practical advice. The intervention was delivered over 14 weeks. It involved 560 intervention Year 4 and 5 pupils in England, compared to 1,027 children from 19 schools in another part of London. The comparator group had proportionately more disadvantaged children, and considerably more EAL pupils (61% against 27% in the control). The control children were taught strategies on peer relations, classroom engagement and learning. Science attainment was measured using a modified version of the Standard Assessment Tasks for Year 6 (modified for lower year groups). There were small positive gains on the overall SAT test (+0.04) compared to control. FSM-eligible pupils did worse in the treatment group.

Lloyd et al. (2014) evaluated a cluster RCT of the shared maths programme (a cross age peer tutoring programme). This study included 6,472 pupils (3,305 in Year 3 and 3,167 in Year 5) in 82 primary schools. Older Year 5 children (tutors) mentor the younger Year 3 pupils (tutees). Children work together to discuss maths problems through a structured stepped approach. Elements of what are considered good pedagogical practice, such as formative assessment and differentiation were also incorporated. Matching of tutor/tutee pairs were performed by teachers. The intervention was delivered in the classroom during regular maths lessons. Outcomes measured using the gains from pre- and post-test scores on the InCAS assessment showed no beneficial effects for Y3 tutees (ES = 0.01) Y5 tutors (ES = 0.02). Attrition was moderate at 15%.

Dion et al. (2011) compared the relative effectiveness of peer-tutoring (reading intervention) and Good Behaviour Game (to increase attention) on reading. The study included 409 Canadian first Grade pupils identified as at-risk for reading and 58 first Grade teachers assigned to 3 conditions: peer tutoring and GBG, peer tutoring only or control. Compared to control both peer tutoring and peer tutoring combined with GBG had small positive effects on comprehension (ES = +0.38); word recognition (ES = + 0.28; 0.34 for PALS and PALS + GBH respectively) and non-word recognition (ES = + 0.28; 0.32). Peer tutoring had moderate effects on attentive pupils (ES = +0.6) and comprehension (ES = +0.76), but no effects on inattentive pupils (ES = +0.1 for non-word recognition and 0.25 for comprehension). Attrition was low (under 3%)

Fuch et al. (2002) is a study on Peer-Assisted Learning Strategies conducted with 328 first Grade pupils (age 6-7) in the US randomly assigned 20 teachers/classes to either PALS or control where they used the teacher-directed instruction with student work. Lessons were conducted in whole class, but PALS were used to replace parts of the teacher-directed and student group activities. Teachers received 2-hour after school workshop. Children were paired by performance. Highest performing pupil from one half paired with highest in the next half and so on. Every 3 weeks the pairs were reassigned so that children were exposed to different students. The stronger pupil would be the coach and mid-way through they switched roles. Children were to encourage partners to use correction procedures they were trained during PALS' activities. PALS strategy included high levels of engagement and frequent correct feedbacks. Fuchs et al. reported positive effects on the Stanford Achievement Test (SAT), but only for items which were aligned with PALS (ES = +0.31). No effects were found for items unaligned with PALS. PALS appear to be more effective for children with learning disability. ES increased to .55 standard deviations for these children. Attrition was difficult to work out.

Some success has been reported for collaborative approaches with older students. Boardman et al. (2015) investigated the efficacy of a multi-component reading comprehension instructional approach, Collaborative Strategic Reading (CSR), compared to business-as-usual instructional methods with 19 teachers and 1,074 students in middle school social studies and science classrooms in a large urban district. Researchers collaborated with school personnel to provide teachers with ongoing professional development and classroom support. Using an experimental design, teachers' classrooms were assigned either to CSR or to a business-as-usual comparison condition. Students receiving CSR instruction scored higher on a standardised reading comprehension assessment compared to their peers in comparison classrooms (0.18). While implementation varied across classrooms, students in the CSR condition were observed using CSR strategies and working together in small groups. Teachers attended to the quality of student work and provided more feedback when teaching CSR. CSR is an effective method to improve the reading comprehension of adolescents and to increase their access to complex informational text.

There were other weaker studies (mostly because of scale or inappropriate designs for causal questions).

Mathes, et al. (2001) evaluated a complex intervention comparing PALS with and without computer-assisted instruction and with business-as-usual control. 6 teachers were randomly assigned to PALS or PAL + CAI and 3 teachers within the school were identified to form the control. Another 27 teachers were recruited and randomly assigned to one of 3 conditions. CAI was introduced to enhance phonological awareness. Results showed that low ability pupils in both PALS and PALS + CAI made bigger gains than control pupils on some subtests of reading and phonological awareness. No differences were found for high and average ability pupils for all the measures. The groups were not balanced at pre-test. Lower ability children in PALS + CAI had significantly lower scores than PALS and control in the Woodcock reading master pre-test. So the bigger gains made could be regression to the mean. Analyses were quite convoluted.

Van Keer (2004) compared explicit reading strategies in a whole class teacher led instruction with direct teaching plus same age peer tutoring and direct teaching with cross age tutoring. The study conducted in Belgium included 22 teachers and 454 pupils. The study reported positive effects of peer tutoring at post-test only rather than gain scores. The author also assumed that using MLM takes care of missing data. Substantial missing data was reported but did not say how much. Both the whole-class and the cross-age peer tutoring groups made significantly larger pre-test to post-test gains than the control group. No significant differences were detected in the same-age peer tutoring group compared with the control group. Although the pupils were reportedly from 9-12 years old, the results were only reported for one age group without specifying which age group that was. Also with three age groups, three conditions and a control, it is not clear that 22 teacher clusters is sufficient. Therefore, while there are suggestions that peer mentoring could assist, the evidence is not strong, not based in the UK, and not specific to disadvantaged and struggling Years 6 and 7 Pupils.

Schünemann et al. (2013), on the other hand, reported positive effects for cross age but not same age tutoring. This was a Dutch study on combining whole class explicit teaching with peer tutoring. They concluded that explicit training in self-regulated learning in a whole class instruction had positive effects on reading comprehension for 2nd Grade children when combined with cross age peer tutoring but not for same age tutoring. The older 5 th Grade children who received explicit reading strategy instructions made bigger gains than the control group. Long-term effects were not maintained for 2nd Graders, but for 5th Graders, direct explicit reading strategy instruction and cross-age tutoring maintained effects after 6 months. Low achievers in the experimental group seemed to make bigger gains. This was a fairly large study involving 444 second Grade children and 454th5 Graders from 25 schools. However, the evidence was considered weak because groups were not strictly randomised to conditions. Teachers were allowed to choose either to be in cross-age or same-age tutoring groups. These teachers may differ in characteristics as they have to find a colleague willing to collaborate with them. Control classes were chosen to match the experimental teachers and classes. Results of the comprehension tests were not presented so effect sizes could not be calculated.

Fuchs et al. (1997) is an earlier study used mixed ability peer tutoring. This was a small study involving only 120 pupils (60 in PALS and 60 in comparison). The study reported significant gains for the PALS group on reading comprehension. However, WWC (2012) reanalysed the data taking account of clustering and found no significant difference, despite a reasonable effect size. Given the small sample size, the high and uneven (between groups) dropout rate of 45% is sufficient to render the results unreliable. It is also worth noting that the evaluation was conducted by the developer of PALS.

Fuchs et al. (2001) conducted a similar study but looking at the effects on kindergarten children's maths readiness. 20 teachers from 3 Title 1 schools and 2 non-Title schools were assigned randomly within school to experimental or control groups (n = 168 pupils). Experimental teachers implemented the peer-mediated treatment twice weekly for 15 weeks. Results were mixed. On the Stanford Test, there were no differences between groups. Positive effects were found on the SESAT (a test which is closely aligned with PALS), but on the more neutral test (Stanford Achievement Test), no significant effects were detected. It is not clear what the pupil attrition was, but one teacher dropped out. It is also not clear how many children there were but on p. 499 it seems to suggest there were 248 children, but it also suggests that SESAT pre-test was administered to 228 children (wondered whether these could be PALS).

Another study by the same developers (Fuchs et al. 2002) suggested that children assigned to phonological awareness with PALS (Peer Assisted Learning) outperformed children assigned to phonological awareness and business-as-usual control. However, no causal inferences can be made because of wide variations in individual children's responses to the intervention. There was no comparison of gain scores.

Klinger et al. (1998) investigated the effects of daily collaborative strategic reading with 114 4 th Graders, in 5 classes randomised by class. Pupils received additional interventions from the researcher on reading strategies (e.g. preview, prediction, monitoring and getting the gist and wrap up). Whether the same findings can be observed when implemented by classroom teacher was not tested. ES on reading comprehension using the Gates MacGinitie Test was 0.44. A similar study conducted by Klinger et al. (2004) with 211 4 th Graders in 10 classes, also showed that collaborative strategic reading children made bigger gains than control children (0.19).

7. Teaching content and how to process it

7.1 Teaching content knowledge in the whole class

There are attempts in the US and now the UK to teach wider and greater content knowledge to primary age children. A theory behind this movement is that children, especially those from disadvantaged backgrounds, do not read well because they do not possess the necessary background knowledge to make sense of what they read. One programme addressing this is the Core Knowledge Language Arts curriculum, whose aim is to expose children to new words and concepts so that the new words stay in their long-term memory and thus facilitate future learning. And if children understand the words they read they can understand the text. In cases where children have less exposure to a wide range of vocabulary, they do not have the background knowledge to build on or a context in which to place what they are trying to read. Their learning is therefore hindered, leading to a so-called Matthew-effect where the gap between the good readers and the poor readers widen.

Core Knowledge Language Arts (CKLA) is a US imported programme that has received much attention in England. It first gained popularity in the US after the publication of the book Cultural Literacy (Hirsch 1987). Core Knowledge is now being used in classrooms in thousands of schools across the US. The philosophy behind Hirsch's idea is that young people need to learn basic facts and ideas in order to make sense of what they read. Literacy depends on understanding of context and textual references and so on the possession of relevant facts. The CK curriculum aims to provide a content-specific core curriculum.

Several influential commentators in England including a Minister of State for Education (Nick Gibb) and an Education Secretary (Michael Gove) have spoken openly of their admiration of Hirsch's philosophy (The Guardian 2012). In 2013 Michael Gove set out to reform the curriculum to emphasize knowledge (Coughlan 2013). Two primary schools were set up in London specifically using a curriculum that is built on the philosophy of CKLA. The journalist Toby Young also opened a secondary free school in West London basing its curriculum on the Core Knowledge Sequence.

Although the Core Knowledge curriculum has been widely implemented in the US, the programme has not been as widely (or rigorously) evaluated. Where it has been evaluated, the evaluations have often been conducted by or directly for the CKLA foundation, and even so the results so far have been mixed and unimpressive (Table 7.1).

Table 7.1 - Quality and impact summary: studies of Core Knowledge

	Effective	Ineffective/unknown
Higher quality	0	0
Medium quality	0	1
Lower quality	4	1

A large-scale pilot RCT of the Word and World Reading programme (WWR), which borrowed the curriculum sequence from CKLA, was recently conducted in the UK (See et al. 2015b). WWR is a whole-class intervention where classroom instruction was highly scripted. Children were taught historical and geographical facts using set textbooks, teaching resources and workbooks. This programme is interesting in that it encompasses several elements of classroom teaching. First, it involves whole-class teaching but controls teachers' pedagogical skills since the lessons were highly scripted. Teachers were given prompts in the text as to when and what questions to ask. Even the classroom small-group activities were prepared for the teachers. Although children worked in small group for the workbook activity, there was no interaction among the pupils. Children worked quietly and individually.

It has to be noted that the WWR programme differed from the original CKLA sequence. The original idea of the Core Knowledge Sequence was to give children a foundation in basic knowledge so that they can apply the knowledge and to question the facts. The programme as used in some US schools encouraged pupils to explore and question. 50% of the curriculum was to be devoted to the teaching of content and the other 50% for wider discussions of the topics covered. The WWR programme, on the other hand, was highly prescriptive and the lessons were scripted. There was little interaction and opportunities for in-depth discussions as teachers were given set questions and set answers. Pupils were not encouraged to question or explore the content, or to think critically.

The study involved 1,628 Year 3 and Year 4 pupils (age 7-9) from 17 schools. Schools were randomly assigned to either WWR or business-as-usual control. The results based on a standardised test of reading comprehension showed no obvious benefit of the curriculum (ES = -0.03).

Table 7.2 - Quality and impact detail: studies of Core Knowledge

Reference	Intervention	Smallest cell	Attrition	ES	NNTD-attrition	Quality
See et al. 2015	Core Knowledge	814 pupils	10%	-0.03	0	2*

Whitehurst-Hall (1999) reported mixed results of a longitudinal study following 301 7th and 8th Grade children over three years using a matched comparison design. Impact was measured using the Iowa Test of Basic Skills (ITBS) subtests on reading, language and maths. Positive 'impacts' were noted for some measures but not others. There were no clear differences between CK and control pupils in terms of Grade retention and Grade failure.

An evaluation of CKLA conducted by Johns Hopkins University (Stringfield et al. 2000) using four matched pairs of CK and comparator schools across the US with norm-referenced tests also showed mixed effects. The overall impact of CK on reading was negative for children who had CK for three years starting when they were aged six (effect size of -0.06) as well as for older children who received the programme from aged 8 to 11 (effect size of -0.08). The programme appeared to be more beneficial for low achieving younger pupils (effect size of +0.25), but not older pupils (effect size = -0.53). Schools in each state (Washington, Maryland and Texas) apart from Florida registered a negative impact on reading. The authors explained that the exceptionally poor performance of CK pupils in one low implementing school in Maryland had skewed the overall results. The overall impact is therefore unclear despite the authors' claims of success.

Dartnow et al. (2000) reported that schools that implemented the programme successfully showed greater improvements in standardised test scores (Comprehensive Test of Basic Skills). The abstract stated that "Core Knowledge students' basic skills standardised test scores were about the same as, or slightly better than, demographically matched control students' scores". But on p.179 the paper said "There was considerable variability in the overall mean effect sizes across sites, ranging from -0.56 to +0.51. Mean effect sizes across all schools were close to zero, averaging -0.05 for math and -0.06 for reading". The CK results are actually slightly worse overall. The paper went on to say that when the children were assessed on Core Knowledge content, CK pupils performed significantly better than their non-CK counterparts, but this is to be expected.

The study did not take account the fact that not all the pupils were retained in the final analysis. Only 59% of the first Grade children and 70% of the third Grade children took the basic skills test three years later, representing attrition of 41% and 30% respectively. For the Core Knowledge content test, the dropout rate was even higher. Only 44% of first Grade and 52% of third Grade pupils took the test three years later, representing dropout of 56% and 48%. The results are therefore largely meaningless. There is a sense across the prior evidence we have read that authors want to report success.

An independent evaluation of the Core Knowledge curriculum across schools in Oklahama city reported on the Core Knowledge website (Core Knowledge Foundation 2000) suggested promising results. On both the ITBS Norm-Referenced test (ITBS) and the Oklahoma Criterion-Referenced Tests, CK pupils

performed, on average, better than those in the comparison group on reading comprehension, vocabulary and social studies. However, pupils were not randomly assigned to the intervention, and although the author claimed that pupils were precisely matched, matching is never perfect especially when there is attrition.
The Core Knowledge curriculum may be more promising for younger children. A study of an early literacy pilot in New York City in 2012- The NYC Core Knowledge Early Literacy Pilot (NYC Department for Education 2012) reported gains in reading tests (Woodcock-Johnson III) especially in kindergarten, although the differences decreased by the third year. Using the standardised TerraNova test, however, no differences were detected in oral reading comprehension and vocabulary. Although the summary report suggested that children who were on the programme for the longest had the highest post-test scores compared to those with only one and two years of exposure, these children had higher pre-test scores too. In other words, they started from a higher base score. The only reference to this study is on the Core Knowledge website.

There are some concerns that the prescriptive Core Knowledge sequence might stifle creativity. To address such concerns Baer (2011) compared the creative writing (poems and short stories) of seventh and eighth Grade pupils (n=540) in Core Knowledge schools with those in non-Core Knowledge schools. The writing exercises were graded independently by experienced writers and teachers using the Amabile (1982) Consensual Assessment Technique. The results showed that 7th Grade CK pupils outperformed non-CK pupils while 8th Grade CK pupils did worse.

In summary the evidence base for the impact of CK on literacy is not yet clear. Results from the non-randomised studies have been mixed – positive effects were found for only some year groups, in some states and for only some sub-tests. The largest study found no benefit from CK.

7.2 Explicit teaching

Explicit teaching is an instructional strategy used by teachers to meet the needs of their students and engage them in unambiguous, clearly articulated teaching. Teachers plan for explicit teaching to make clear connections to curriculum content, through a concise focus on the gradual and progressive steps that lead to a student's development and independent application of knowledge, understanding and skills. Features of explicit teaching include:

- focusing instruction on identified curriculum content
- connecting to prior knowledge and skills when beginning a learning sequence
- establishing and maintaining clear learning goals and expectations for each lesson
- teaching and expecting students to use metalanguage in ways that support learning
- deconstructing and sequencing teaching to focus on the steps that lead to new knowledge, deeper understandings and/or more sophisticated skill
- describing and modelling concepts and processes clearly, using 'think aloud' and examining models and inferior examples
- varying instruction in response to immediate and reflective feedback
- asking questions to continually monitor understanding and progress and inform immediate feedback
- providing scaffolded learning experiences for students to practise, synthesize and consolidate learning
- developing the capability of students to self-regulate and learn independently.

Siraj-Blatchford et al.'s (2011) longitudinal study explored the associations between value added measures of school effectiveness and variations in classroom pedagogy in Year 5 classrooms in England. The study collected data from 125 schools (out of 850) which had full contextual value-added scores (a volatile measure). These were correlated with 11 observed pedagogic strategies – one of which was making links explicit. Others included the use of plenary, shared goals, collaborative and personalised learning, teacher knowledge, and use of homework. The remainder tends to be vague or tautological such as effective behaviour management, well-organised teaching and positive classroom climate.

Gersten et al. (2009) analysed 41 studies targeting students with MD (mild disabilities).. Interventions were coded on seven dimensions including (a) explicit instructional techniques, (b) the use of visual representations of quantitative relations, (c) student verbalisation of mathematics concepts and strategies for solving problems, (d) attention to the range and sequence of examples used during instruction, (e) frequent assessment feedback to teachers and students, (f) peer-assisted instruction, and (g) use of heuristics. In the explicit instruction studies teachers demonstrated step-by-step routines for solving problems and then students applied these routines to solve similar problems. Of the seven dimensions, explicit instruction had the second largest impact (1.22).

Explicit instruction is widespread and apparently successful in dealing with children with learning disabilities (Swanson and Sachse-Lee 2000, Van Luit 2009), or poorer English language learners (Cena et al. 2013). Our new review found only one further large evaluation (Tables 7.3, 7.4).

Table 7.3 - Quality and impact summary: Explicit teaching

	Effective	Ineffective
Higher quality	1	0
Medium quality	0	0
Lower quality	2	1

Table 7.4 - Quality and impact detail: Explicit teaching

Reference	Intervention	Smallest cell	Attrition	ES	NNTD-attrition	Quality
Doabler et al. 2015	**Explicit maths instruction**	**61 classes, 1267 pupils**	**9%**	**0.08**	**0**	**3***

Doabler et al. (2015) made 379 observations in 129 US Kindergarten classrooms (46 schools), involving approximately 2,200 students across a 2-year span. This was a randomised controlled trial involving 129 classes from 46 schools (68 randomly assigned to Early Learning in Maths (explicit teaching) and 61 to control (standard maths instruction), ELM is a one-year kindergarten maths curriculum designed for whole class teaching, Children were kindergarten age (n = 2,681), attrition was 8.8%. Teachers demonstrated step-by-step routines for solving problems and then students applied these routines to solve similar problems. Characterising high-quality, explicit instructional interactions are three key components: (a) clear and concise teacher demonstrations, (b) frequent opportunities for students to practice what teachers demonstrate, and (c) timely academic feedback from teachers to students related to students' attempts to solve academic problems. See also Doabler et al. (2013). After adjusting for pre-test and other factors, there is a 0.08 link between rate and quality of instructional interactions and maths test outcomes.

Puhalla (2011) looked at the impact of explicit booster instruction in vocabulary for 1st Grade struggling pupils (44 at-risk and 22 average) and two teachers. At-risk children were randomly assigned to either a booster group (receiving explicit instruction) or no booster (receiving vocabulary instruction through the Read Aloud Curriculum). All children participated in Read Alouds but experimental children received five extra 20-minute sessions per unit for the first 2 units. Booster children made bigger gains between pre and post-test in Story Book

Vocabulary Assessment (0.46). However, the booster group had extra teaching and the test assessed words that were taught in the intervention only.

Moore et al. (2014) used explicit instruction to improve word learning from story read alouds in 6 schools in Australia. The Year 1 pupils in 3 schools assigned to treatment (127 pupils). The authors claim success for the intervention but give no figures for the control schools making the claim impossible to assess.

Pesco and Devlin (2015) reported on a small study looking at the impact of explicit instruction on French-speaking kindergarteners' understanding of stories. Half of the 30 kindergarten children were randomly assigned and taught explicit instruction. Outcomes were measured using a standardised test that measures expression, reception and recall of narrative. The control group actually did slightly better on understanding stories (-0.04).

7.3 Social, emotional and behavioural interventions

Most studies of behavioural interventions, including the best, look at chiefly or solely behavioural or psychological outcomes (e.g. Jones et al. 2010, Brackett et al. 2012, Capella et al. 2015). The balance of evidence in the subset that portrays attainment outcomes is that behavioural interventions are not clearly effective in this respect (Table 7.5, 7.6). See also Gorard et al. (2012).

Table 7.5 - Quality and impact summary: Behavioural interventions

	Effective	Ineffective
Higher quality	0	0
Medium quality	2	2
Lower quality	1	0

Manchester Institute of Education (2016) conducted a trial for the EEF of the impact of social and emotional learning for Years 5 and 6 in 45 schools in England.

It made no difference to attainment. 588 of 2,336 cases were missing scores (over 25% attrition).

Table 7.6 - Quality and impact detail: Behavioural interventions

Reference	Intervention	Smallest cell	Attrition	ES	NNTD-attrition	Quality
Manchester Institute of Education 2016	Social and emotional learning	1,168 pupils	588 pupils	0	0	2*
Diperna et al. 2016	Behavioral	19 classes (192 pupils)	20%	Maths -0.04 Reading -0.09	0 0	2*
O'Connor et al. 2014	Behavioral	217 pupils	20%	Maths 0.16) Reading 0.14)	0	2*
Bradshaw et al. 2009	Behavioral	219 pupils	56% 10 years later	Unknown	-	2*

Diperna et al. (2016) looked at a 12 week behavioural intervention to improve classroom behaviour (Social Skills Improvement System Classwide Intervention Programme) with 402 US 2 nd Grade children in 39 classes from 6 schools. Pupils were randomly assigned to treatment (210) or business as usual (192). Attrition was 20%. Although there were mall positive effects on motivation (0.02) and engagement (0.3), the impact on attainment was negative for mall (-0.04) and reading (E-0.09).

O'Connor et al. (2014) looked at the impact of INSIGHT (a schoolwide social and emotional learning intervention) on children's academic achievement, attention and behaviour. It involved 435 US kindergarten and 1st Grade children from 122 classrooms and their parents and teachers. 11 schools implemented INSIGHT and the other 11 participated in a supplemental reading programme. Children received the intervention in the 2nd half of kindergarten and the 1st half of 1st Grade. Attainment outcomes were measured using the Letter Word Identification and Applied Problems subtests of the Woodcock-Johnson III test. Attrition ranged from 0% to 20% across the study variables. The effects were partially mediated through a reduction in behaviour problems, and partially through an improvement in sustained attention.

Bradshaw et al. (2009) conducted longitudinal analyses of RCT results of a classroom centred behavioural management intervention which combines the Good Behaviour Game with an enhanced academic curriculum. The target children were 658 first Graders whose parents gave consent took part in the trial. Follow-up data was collected when children were in high school and at age 19 (n=574). Three classrooms from each of the 9 schools were randomly assigned to one of three conditions (control, school centred intervention or family-school partnership). For the purpose of this review we analysed the results for the school centred intervention only. The aim of the intervention was to address risky behaviours, aggressive and shy behaviours by enhancing teacher instructional and behaviour management practices. The Teacher Observation of Classroom Adaptation—Revised was used to measure externalising behaviour. Children's performance at in class from Grades 6-13 was assessed using teacher-rated academic performance. Academic outcomes at high school were assessed using the Kaufman Test of Educational Achievement for maths and Reading. The classroom-centred intervention was associated with higher scores on standardised achievement tests (for boys), greater odds of high school graduation and college attendance, and reduced odds of special education service use. However, no baseline equivalence was established in terms of academic performance. Only children's contextual background were compared. There was a high level of attrition. Data at age 19 was available for only 56% of the initial Grade 1 children.

The Unique Minds School Program is a teacher-led programme designed to promote cognitive-social-emotional skills, including student self-efficacy, problem solving, social-emotional competence, and a positive classroom climate, with the dual goal of preventing youth behavioural problems and promoting academic learning (Linares et al. 2005). It was tested with 119 US pupils, 13 classes, 2 schools (57 intervention, 62 comparison pupils. The schools were matched. About 35% of cases are missing scores. The intervention school had better maths scores (unspecified).

7.4 Teaching thinking, reasoning and argumentation

Turning instead to learning about how to use information and ideas effectively, the focus here is on learning critique, reasoning and argumentation. As with other areas such as behaviour there is some research on how to improve reasoning that does not test improved attainment or progression (e.g. Bottino et al. 2009, Shayer and Adhami 2010). This can be valuable because any successful intervention must address something malleable, but does not in itself show that it works.

There have been some small trials evaluating attempts to teach reasoning skills. Mercer et al. (1999) evaluated the impact of the TRAC programme (Talk, Reasoning and Computers) which trained pupils to follow certain ground rules for collaborative talking of the kind necessary to implement P4C in a primary classroom. It consisted of nine structured teacher-led lessons of collaborative activities, each an hour long, including some that were computer-based carried out over ten weeks. The study involved 60 Year 4 and 5 pupils (age 9 to 10) from three middle schools in England. Pupils' reasoning abilities were assessed using the Raven's Progressive Matrices test of non-verbal reasoning. Observational data and pupils' interactions were also recorded. Experimental pupils made significantly bigger gains between pre- and post-test compared to control pupils. Bentham et al. (2015) evaluated an attempt to improve reasoning via the use of connectives (such as 'if', 'because') for 14 to 15 years olds studying business studies. The use of connectives was correlated with attainment outcomes, and the intervention group made bigger increase in outcomes (ES of +0.2). The group sizes were only 86 intervention and 71 control students.

Philosophy for Children (P4C) is an educational approach centred on philosophical enquiry and dialogic teaching, the aim of which is to stimulate pupils' abilities of reasoning, disposition to question, construct argumentation and ability to communicate collaboratively with others. Through the training and development of teachers, the initiative is intended to foster cognitive improvement and greater self-confidence, leading to eventual higher academic attainment in children.

Philosophy for Children (P4C) itself was developed in 1970 with the establishment of the Institute for the Advancement of Philosophy for Children (IAPC). P4C has since become a worldwide educational approach, and something like it has been adopted by schools in 60 countries across the world, although the nature of the practice varies (Mercer et al. 1999). In the UK, the Society for the Advancement of Philosophical Enquiry and Reflection in Education (SAPERE) was established in 1992 to promote the use of P4C in schools.

The evidence base so far has been weak or mixed. An initial evaluation of the original scheme was conducted using a matched comparison design involving only 40 pupils from two schools (Lipman et al. 1980). The study reported significant gains in logical reasoning and reading, measured using the California Test of Mental Maturity (CTMM).

One of the earliest studies in the UK was conducted by Williams (1993). The study examined the effects of 27 one-hour P4C lessons (using Lipman's materials) on reading comprehension, reasoning skills and intellectual confidence. Participants were 42 pupils from two Year 7 classes in one school in Derbyshire, UK. Results were obtained for 32 children. Children were randomised to receive P4C lessons (n=15) or extra English (n=17). Pre- and post-test comparison of reading comprehension using the London Reading Test showed that the P4C group made significantly bigger gains than control pupils. Significant gains were also reported for reasoning skills and intellectual confidence. These were measured using bespoke evaluation tools and video recordings of pupils' interactions during lessons which the evaluators had to make subjective judgements about. Nevertheless, the study showed that the philosophy group registered improvements in reasoning behaviour, while the control group showed no such improvements.

A systematic review of evidence for P4C was conducted by Trickey and Topping (2004) suggesting consistent moderate effects on a range of outcome measures. The mean 'effect' size for the studies included was 0.43. However, these studies were not always fully comparable because of the different outcomes measured and the different instruments used for measuring them. For example, Campbell (2002) and IAPC (2002) used the New Jersey Test of Reasoning Skills (NJTRS), while Doherr (2000) assessed emotional intelligence using a Cognitive Behavioural Therapy Assessment. Campbell (2002) evaluated listening and talking skills using questionnaires, focus groups, interviews and observations. It has to be noted that the NJTRS was specially developed for Lipman and the IAPC to measure reasoning skills taught in the P4C curriculum. This is likely to bias the results against the control group of pupils not exposed to the P4C curriculum. Moriyon and Tudela (2004) noted that studies using NJTRS showed larger effect sizes than more generic tests of literacy and numeracy.

The longer-term impact of P4C was assessed by Topping and Trickey (2007). They followed pupils over two years. A total of 177 pupils (105 experimental and 72 comparator) from eight schools were matched and tracked from the penultimate year of primary school to the first year of secondary school. Pupils' cognitive abilities were measured using the Cognitive Attainment Test (CAT). Complete data were available for only 115 pupils. After 16 months of intervention (with 1 hour of P4C per week) the treatment pupils made substantial improvements in test scores whereas control pupils performed worse than when they started (ES = 0.7). Results two years later indicated that treatment pupils maintained their advantage in follow-up test scores compared to the control pupils.

A more recent longitudinal study of the long-term impact of P4C was conducted in Madrid (Colom et al. 2014). This was intended to track children from two private schools over 20 years. 455 children aged 6 (first year of primary school) to 18 (final year of high school) from one school were trained in the P4C programme. Another 321 pupils from another school matched on demographic characteristics formed the control group. Data on children's cognitive, non-cognitive and academic achievements were collected at three time points when children were aged 8, 11/12 and 16. Preliminary analyses of 281 treatment children and 146 control children showed that the programme had positive impacts on general cognitive ability (ES = 0.44), but results on academic achievement were not yet available. The authors implied that the programme was particularly beneficial to lower ability pupils, but this was not clear from their presentation of the analysis. Moreover, although large scale and long term, the students were not randomised in terms of receiving P4C instruction, and the study may not be generalisable as pupils came from relatively prosperous families in private schools. In short, the results from this preliminary analysis should be treated with a high degree of caution.

A recent randomised controlled trial was conducted with 540 pupils in years 7 and 8 (Fair et al. 2015). The study found positive relative gains in the CAT scores for year 7 pupils who received the treatment, compared to control pupils who were taking language arts classes. The equivalent gains for year 8 pupils were much lower. This could be because pupils in year 7 were exposed for 26 weeks and pupils in year 8 were given P4C session for only 10 weeks. The difference in gains between the two groups was attributed to the difference in dosage. The study does not establish baseline equivalence of pupils who were allocated to the two groups and there is an indication that pupils were not equally balanced as pupils in the treatment group were ahead of their counterparts in CAT pre-test scores.

Several of the studies so far have used a matched comparison design (e.g. Tok and Mazi 2015), and most have measured cognitive abilities, reasoning skills or other affective outcomes rather than school attainment directly. Moreover, while there have been several studies in the UK, they have tended to be small scale. There are some unsystematic observations of beneficial impact from OFSTED reports. It is therefore difficult to say if philosophical enquiry can lead to enhanced performance in academic domains and whether it would have the same impact in UK schools with British children. Also few P4C interventions were tested on primary school children. No proper large-scale randomised controlled trial has been conducted on this as far as we know.

Table 7.7 - Quality and impact summary: studies of teaching thinking

	Effective	Ineffective/unknown
Higher quality	3	0
Medium quality	0	1
Lower quality	10	3

Table 7.8 - Quality and impact detail: studies of Philosophy for Children

Reference	Intervention	Smallest cell	Attrition	ES	NNTD-attrition	Quality
Gorard et al. 2015	**P4C**	**757**	**10%**	**0.12**	**15+**	**4***
Reznitskaya 2012	P4C	125	31%	0	0	2*
Worth et al. 2015	**Maths and reasoning**	**517 pupils**	**13%**	**0.2**	**36**	**3***
Hanley et al. 2015	**Higher order thinking in science**	**1513 pupils**	**16%**	**0.22**	**60**	**3***

The largest true randomised control trial conducted in the UK with primary school children was Gorard et al. (2015a). The study involved 48 primary schools in England with no prior experience of using P4C, and all had at least 25% of their pupils known to be eligible for free school meals. Of these 22 were randomised to the treatment group (772 pupils in year 5 at the outset and Year 6 by the end), and 26 to the control (757 pupils). The two groups were well-balanced in terms of sex, FSM-eligibility and SEN status. The intervention lasted just over a full academic year. The study found promising results for reading (ES = 0.12) and maths (0.10), but slightly weaker effects for writing (ES = 0.03). These were measured as progress from KS1 to KS2. Bigger gains were reported for children eligible for FSM (ES = + 0.29 for reading; ES = +0.17 for writing and ES = +0.20 for maths). However, because of the smaller number of FSM pupils (n = 497) and the fact that they were not randomised, the results do not have the power of a trial but it does suggest that P4C is as effective for disadvantaged children. Very few pupils were missing a post-test score. At the outset the treatment and control groups were slightly unbalanced, with the control group having better KS1 scores in reading, but the lowest attaining half of the pupils did not improve their scores more than the higher attaining half, across both groups combined. Therefore, the result cannot be due to regression to the mean.

Reznitskaya (2012) examined the impact of dialogic discussion in a P4C tradition on writing and reading comprehension, with random assignment of 12th5 Grade classes in five schools to P4C (138 pupils) or normal classes (125). It appears that there are no follow up scores for 63 pupils (31%). There were no benefits in terms of post-intervention assessments including essay, recall and interview. The small number of cases (n = 6 classes in each group), the high attrition (31%) and the subjective measures of outcomes all weaken the security of the findings.

Worth et al. (2015) compared the use of mathematics and reasoning, with literacy and morphemes and a control, with Year 2 in 55 schools in England. There were 517 pupils in the smallest group, with 13% attrition. The authors reported ‘significant’ success for maths 0.2 but not literacy.

Hanley et al. (2015) considered a programme to make science lessons in primary schools more practical, creative and challenging. Teachers were trained in a repertoire of strategies to encourage pupils to use higher order thinking skills. For example, pupils are posed 'Big Questions', such as 'How do you know that the earth is a sphere?' that are used to stimulate discussion about scientific topics and the principles of scientific enquiry. There were 41 schools, of which 21 (with 655 Year 5 pupils) were randomised to treatment. Attrition was 16%, and the advantage for the treatment schools on average was 0.22.

Other less robust studies uncovered in our review provided some insight into the pedagogical aspect of teaching critical thinking that could support learning. For example, Larrain et al. (2014) demonstrated that whole class teaching of critical thinking did not yield any benefits (ES = 0.09), and that it was learning to provide justifications and contradictions among peers that prompted learning. This was a weak study because of the high attrition for both pupil (83%) and teachers (36%). Also assessments of learning were based on researcher-developed instruments. Tseng (2014) confirmed the findings of Larrain et al. in that teaching children to question, argue and reason could be beneficial in science learning (but presumably not only in science). Children taught an inquiry-based approach made bigger progress than children taught using the traditional didactic approach.

Fung (2014) provided some evidence that teaching critical thinking was more effective using group work than whole class, and group work with effective strategies was even better than just group work alone. However, results were reported only for children's rating of their own critical thinking disposition. No results for the test of critical thinking skills were presented. Again this was a weak study with only 200 children from 2 schools. Attrition was not reported.

Foster (2001) looked at the impact of teaching higher order skills on reading for African -American elementary school students. Participants were 30 fifth Grade students from one school. 15 who were enrolled in a regular education programme formed the control and the other 15 enrolled in a HOTS programme formed the experimental group. Reading outcomes were measured using the Degrees of Reading Powers (DRP) pre and post. No difference was found.

Cattle and Howie (2008) used a quasi-experiment to test the effects of a cognitive intervention programme, Cognitive Acceleration in Science at KS1. Participants were 10 Y1 children taught in a mixed age class. Another group of 10 Y1 pupils from another rural village formed the control. Intervention was delivered by classroom teacher, alternating with small groups and whole class teaching over a period of 8 months. Thinking skills were assessed using the Raven's Coloured Progressive Matrices, Drawing (developed by the programme developer) and the Boehm-R Test of Basic Concepts Form D (more-less, first-last). There was no support from this tiny study using standardised tests (although the authors reported support for the thesis, as is all too frequent).

Cornoldi et al. (2015) found gains of around 0.34 for working memory and 0.04 for problem solving after an intervention that involve training in metacognition and memory. Participants included 156 children from Grade 3 to Grade 5, with 21 missing cases. Children were from 8 intact classes – four received 8 hours of training in metacognition during maths lessons and the other 4 had 8 hours of usual maths lessons over 3 months.

Khodami and Hariri (2013) ran a small RCT (20 cases) which suggests metacognitive training improved maths performance for low attaining Iranian Grade 3. There was poor reporting, with no mention of attrition, and not possible to estimate ES.

Overall, the evidence here is reasonable. It suggests that critical thinking can be improved and is generally associated with improved outcomes, perhaps especially in science, maths and reading. The largest study suggests that P4C might have a positive impact on pupil attainment at KS2.

7.5 Mindfulness

Studies of mindfulness promotion in schools often involve only psychological outcomes and so are excluded from this review. In a review of 24 evaluations mindfulness interventions, Zenner et al. (2014) looked at range of such outcomes. The closest to an attainment-related outcome was the G score for cognitive performance, which has a synthesized ES=0.08.

Table 7.9 - Quality and impact summary: Mindfulness

	Effective	Ineffective/unknown
Higher quality	0	0
Medium quality	0	0
Lower quality	2	0

Bakosh (2013) conducted a quasi-randomised controlled study to examine the effects of a daily audio-guided mindfulness training regime on the academic outcomes of 337 students from two US schools. Four schools were recruited and 2 dropped out. This was a whole-school programme (Inner Explorer Program) which involved 90 audio-guided tracks of 10 minutes each delivered via an MP3 player and docking station. Students and teachers were given the opportunity to practice mindfulness each day over 10 weeks. Participating teachers were those who volunteered. These were then randomised and all the teachers received 30 minutes of training which was basically an informational introductory session. Treatment teachers received another 30 minutes of mindfulness training prior to implementation. Treatment classrooms received a classroom kit consisting of preloaded iPod MP3 player with 90 Inner Explorer MBSEL tracks, a docking station with speakers, Teachers' Manual, parent letter student journaling notebooks, as well as a few classroom tools including a rain stick and glitter ball, as well as a teacher gazing stone. There were only 8 teachers in School A and 10 in school B. In School A there was no difference between treatment and control groups in terms of changes in GPA for Grade 1 children. For 2nd to 5th Grades there was a strong positive effect. In School B a small positive effect was detected for all Grades combined. Attrition was not reported. Subject Grades were teacher-assessed. As the teachers were not blinded to the intervention there is a possibility of bias.

Bakosh et al. (2016) conducted a quasi-experimental study to examine the effects of a mindfulness training intervention called the Inner Explorer Programme on the academic outcomes of 191 3rd Grade children from 2 US schools. Two classes from each school were assigned to treatment and another 2 to control. Small effects were reported. The results showed that the intervention group outperformed control children in all the subjects (reading, writing, science, maths and social studies). It is not clear whether the classes were randomly selected, and the outcomes were based on teacher assessments.

8. Tiered approaches

8.1 Teaching phonics

Other than the approaches to improving literacy and other core skills described above, the next section consider a range of specific and more promising approaches trialled more than once. This section describes interventions involving phonics in helping children to learn to read. The teaching of phonics is defined here as the teaching of letter-sound correspondences in an organised, regular, explicit and sequenced manner.

Schools under pressure to show improvement in their literacy goals have various approaches available, but it is not always clear to them which approaches to teaching literacy will be the most effective, with national policies liable to change over time (House of Commons 2005). From 1998, England had a National Literacy Strategy for primary schools, based at least partly on an 'analytic approach'. Children first learnt the alphabet, and words were then introduced to illustrate the sounds associated with each letter. Subsequently, children used the whole word as the context to work out the sound of each letter (Johnston and Watson 2004). The Rose Report (2006) changed all that. The report, based on a large-scale review, suggested that there was no evidence that the analytic approach had been effective, and so proposed changes. This led to a greater use of phonics and teaching reading through phonics.

The evidence on generic phonics training is not entirely clear (Table 8.1). It may be effective for some groups and for some measures (fluency, decoding and comprehension) but less effective for other measures, such as spelling. Most of the positive studies in two reviews also suggest that phonics training alone is not enough (Slavin et al. 2009, Slavin et al. 2011). Many programmes included other elements such as cooperative learning or phonological awareness as well. For English language learners, programmes involving phonetic small group or one-to-one tutoring have shown positive effects (Cheung and Slavin 2012). Wise et al.

(2007) suggest that knowledge of grapheme-phoneme correspondences is necessary for the development of phonological awareness, when dealing with children with learning disabilities.

Table 8.1 - Quality and impact summary: studies of Phonics

	Effective	Ineffective/unknown
Higher quality	1	0
Medium quality	1	1
Lower quality	12	3

Two 'experiments' seem have had a considerable influence on the move to phonics after the Rose report. One involved 304 first year primary school children, allocated to three groups to receive different literacy interventions (Johnston and Watson 2004). But the groups were not randomly allocated – indeed they were not even matched and the most disadvantaged pupils received the synthetic phonics intervention (p.12). This makes the finding insecure as the phonics group started from a lower base so more improvement was possible in a short time. The second experiment by the same authors allocated the groups via matching, but involved only 92 first year pupils and these were divided into three groups – synthetic phonics, analytic phonics, and analytic phonics with phonological awareness training. This is a small study with only about 30 pupils per group, and it was ended early for ethical reasons. Other commentators have suggested the implementation of the three conditions may have led to bias (Wyse and Goswami 2008).

A subsequent review of 20 RCTs on phonics interventions concluded that systematic phonics teaching (teaching letter and sound links in a clear sequence) was more effective than not using phonics or using phonics non-systematically (Torgerson et al. 2006). But importantly, it excluded the first Johnston and Watson 'experiment' (above) on the basis of their lack of a valid control (but included the second because the authors personally communicated that the cases had been randomised even though this contradicts what they said in the original paper). The overall effect size for systematic phonics compared to other approaches was estimated as +0.27, and the results largely confirmed a previous review by Ehri et al. (2001). This review of effective reading programmes summarised the results of 68 experimental studies (22,000 children) for beginning readers. They identified the key features of successful programmes as those that included teacher development and cooperative learning where children work with other children on structured activities and where there was a strong focus on phonics and phonics awareness, although focus on phonics alone could not guarantee positive results. Effects were stronger for decoding (ES = +0.27) than for comprehension (ES = +0.2). 13 studies for kindergarten children all reported strong positive outcomes. Most focus on phonics and /cooperative learning and phonological awareness training. However, a combination of relatively few trials, and poor evidence or poorly-reported methods in some existing trials meant that the result cannot be seen as definitive, especially in relation to exactly how phonics should be taught.

Johnston et al. (2012) conducted two follow-up analyses using some of their cases from their assessment of the impact of synthetic phonics teaching in Scotland (see above) by comparing them with cases from England, unmatched on prior attainment. The cases being compared have therefore been neither randomly selected nor randomly allocated. They can have no standard error by definition. Despite this, the authors analysed their results using techniques such as analysis of variance that are based on standard errors (and they similarly cited p-values erroneously in their 2004 study).

There have been four RCTs of the phonics-based 'Sound Partners' intended for below average readers in K-3. Overall, these suggest a benefit for beginning readers in terms of letter recognition, fluency and comprehension. But there is no discernible benefit for reading 'achievement' (What Works Clearinghouse 2010).

Two generic meta-analyses of reading interventions for struggling readers, like the previous reviews described above, reported that phonics was the most promising approach. Galuschka et al. (2014) found 22 randomised controlled trials of phonics interventions. McArthur et al. (2012) found 12 studies using a variety of evaluation designs. Their conclusion was that teaching phonics was more effective than other methods for reading accuracy, but not for spelling or reading fluency.

More recently, two studies in England have come to opposing conclusions (Table 8.2). An evaluation of 'Rapid Phonics'- a popular synthetic phonics programme used as a catch-up literacy intervention for pupils moving to secondary school – found no benefit. In fact the pupils in the treatment group did worse than those in the control (King and Kasim 2015). However, 'Butterfly Phonics' was found to be effective for pupils who were not achieving expected reading levels in the transition stage from primary to secondary school (Merrell and Kasim 2015). The evidence is thus mixed. The generic phonics approach may be effective for some measures and in some contexts but not others.

Table 8.2 - Quality and impact detail: studies of Phonics

Reference	Intervention	Smallest cell	Attrition	ES	NNTD-attrition	Quality
King and Kasim 2015	Rapid Phonics	87 pupils	13%	-0.05	0	2*
Merrell and Kasim 2015	Butterfly Phonics	155 pupils	17%	0.43	40	2*
Gorard et al. 2015	**Fresh Start (Year 7)**	**216 pupils**	**3%**	**+0.24**	**45**	**3***

There have been several poorer quality studies on phonics training each introducing a different element, and most suggest some positive results. One was about additional phonics instruction in small groups on top of their regular classroom instruction (Kerins et al. 2010), one was about phonics instruction as a supplemental lesson on a one-to-one basis (Vadasy and Sanders 2011). Another was about integrating phonological awareness and phonics training into whole class mixed-ability classroom (Shapiro and Solity 2008). Kerins et al. reported mixed effects with effect sizes ranging from -0.74, -0.38 to 0.69 and 1.00 for different measures. This study was rated low because it was small-scale (n=23), based on one classroom teacher and her pupils plus an SEN teacher. This was also not a fair comparison as treatment children had additional instruction. Vadasy and Sanders reported positive effects on most measures and for some sub-groups.

A correlational study of 13,609 kindergarten children from 788 schools (Xue and Meisels 2004) using data from the Early Childhood Longitudinal Study compared systematic and direct instruction of phonics and whole language teaching. Integrating language teaching with phonics instruction was found to be the most effective. Children performed better when teachers used integrated instruction more often than just phonics alone. Phonics instruction seemed to benefit lower ability children more than integrated language instruction. This study was rated low because the correlational design cannot rule out confounding factors and also there was a high percentage of missing data. Data from non-English speaking children, those from low SES background and of low cognitive ability were excluded.

Castiglioni-Spalten and Ehri (2003) randomly assigned 45 K1 children (age 6-7) to one of 3 groups - Mouth condition (children taught to associate mouth movements with pictures and sounds), Ear condition (children learn to associate blocks with sounds, and learn to use blocks to represent sounds in words) and control (no special instruction). No attrition reported. This experiment aimed to find out teaching kindergartners to segment words into phonemes or teaching them to manipulate blocks is more effective on their ability to read and spell. There were no differences for reading or decoding. The ear and mouth groups were both better at segmenting words and spelling.

Phonological awareness is one of several key precursor skills to conventional literacy that develop during the preschool period. Significant amounts of research support the causal and predictive relation between phonological awareness and children's ease of learning to decode and spell (Phillips et al. 2008).

Ritter et al. (2013) undertook a quasi-experimental study to test the effects of teaching phonological awareness on children's reading. Participants were Grades 1, 2 and 3 children with learning difficulties, assigned to either treatment (n =34) or control (n =30). Outcomes were measured using Woodcock-Johnson subtests, e.g. Letter Word Identification, Passage Comprehension and subtests from Comprehensive Test of Phonological Processing (CTPP). The treatment group made bigger gains than control children on selected subtests of PA skills (blending words and non words) and the effect sizes were medium (ES=0.57 to 0.72).
Ryder et al. (2008) looked at explicit instruction in whole class teaching on phonemic awareness and phonemically based decoding skills, in New Zealand. Participants were 24 children from 1st and 2nd Grades, matched in pairs and one pair randomly assigned to treatment or control group. Both groups made gains between pre- and post-tests but the treatment group made bigger gains on all measures of phonemic awareness, pseudo-word decoding, context free word recognition, and reading comprehension. Experimental children also outperformed control children in the follow-up test. The effect sizes were 0.72 for the Burt raw score and 0.81 for the Neale Accuracy raw score. However, the treatment group received more teaching, which was more relevant to the topic of the tests.

In a small study using 57 pre-schoolers in England, O'Connor et al. (2009) concluded that while whole class phonological awareness may appear effective in the short term, it does not lead to any benefit by 2nd Grade.

One popular approach to phonics is Fresh Start (FS). FS is a 'systematic synthetic approach' produced by Read Write Inc., whose literacy programmes are cited by OFSTED (2010) as used by the 'best' performing schools. A study by Brooks et al. (2003) evaluating FS for use with low attaining pupils at Key Stage 3 (KS3) claimed success but with only 30% of its initial 500 pupils retained, such claims cannot be taken seriously. One report of the FS programme adopted by all the secondary schools in one local for pupils not meeting or not likely to meet expected levels of literacy (Lanes et al. 2005) only evaluated the outcomes of pupils in one school using the before and after results with no comparators. Despite no proper evaluation the authors claimed that the approach was popular and considered effective by teaching staff. Oddly, a later summary of reading interventions for KS3 included these studies of FS, reporting effect sizes of +0.25 to +0.34 for reading comprehension (Brooks 2007). The study reported no benefit for spelling, perhaps precisely because of the phonic nature of FS. All of the samples were small, with one study having only 29 cases, and there was high dropout, with studies not clearly reporting comparator groups, the allocation of cases or whether the groups were equivalent at the outset.

A recent RCT of FS suggested some promising results (Gorard et al. 2016). This was a school-led trial where 10 schools came together to trial this approach – however, it involved Year 7 pupils not of primary age. This was a fairly large study involving 433 pupils in Year 7, individually randomised to treatment and control conditions. The intervention showed a small positive impact on reading comprehension (ES=0.24). The results have to be taken with slight caution because of initial imbalance (control group had higher pre-test scores than the treatment group).

As with phonics more generally, the evidence related to FS is far from strong, again because studies have too often been small, non-randomised, with high dropout or poorly reported. Overall, the evidence of the effectiveness of phonics approaches is that it works, at least for struggling readers, but the picture is not entirely secure.

8.2 Reading Recovery/Switch-On reading

Reading Recovery (RR) is an intensive one-to-one intervention for the lowest performing 20% of first Graders, and has been widely used in the US, Australia,

New Zealand and the UK (Kelly et al. 2008). It appears to have been less widely evaluated at scale (Table 8.3).

Table 8.3 - Quality and impact summary: studies of Reading Recovery/Switch-On

	Effective	Ineffective/unknown
Higher quality	1	0
Lower quality	1	0
Minimal quality	4	1

The What Works Clearinghouse (2013) found only four out of 78 evaluations of RR that met minimal evidence standards, and even these RCTs were rather small in scale. They involved 168, 91, 79 and 74 students respectively (Baenen et al. 1997, Pinnell et al. 1988, 1994 and Schwartz 2005). One other study (64 students) met WWC criteria with reservations because it was not a randomised controlled trial (Iverson and Tunmer 1993). Of these five studies, four reported positive effects for RR on first-Grade general reading achievement, using the Observation Survey subtests for Dictation and Writing Vocabulary. Baenen et al. (1997) did not find positive effects using Grade retention as an outcome measure. In addition, Tanner et al. (2011) compared 57 RR schools with 54 other schools, and reported that pupils at the RR schools had performed better. However, the schools were not randomised to treatment and baseline equivalence was not established. The comparator schools had more boys, more FSM and more SEN students.

Subsequently, May et al. (2013) reported an effect size of +0.68 for RR with 866 randomly assigned low achieving first Graders, based on measurements using the Iowa Tests of Basic Skills. May et al. (2015) looked at one-to-one RR and found an effect size of +0.47. And Holliman and Hurry (2013) looked at the impact of Reading Recovery in Year 1 on literacy progress and subsequent prevalence of SEN in Year 4 in Schools in England - 73 children who had received RR three years earlier and 48 pupils who had been in RR schools but had no intervention.

RR children were more likely to be on track for Level 4 at end of KS2 and less likely to have been diagnosed with SEN. Effect sizes 0.53 (reading) and 0.43 (writing). Attrition was 17%.

Overall, it appears that this intensive one to one approach is effective (Table 8.4).

Table 8.4 - Quality and impact detail: studies of Reading Recovery/Switch-On

Reference	Intervention	Smallest cell	Attrition	ES	NNTD-attrition	Quality
May et al. 2013	**Reading Recovery**	**433**	**17%**	**0.68**	**220**	**3***
Gorard et al. 2015	**Switch-On (but Year 7)**	**157**	**1%**	**0.24**	**37**	**4***

Switch-on Reading is derived from RR and is shorter in duration than the traditional Reading Recovery and, if found to have positive impacts, could represent a cost-effective way of rolling out an intervention like this. There has been less research on Switch-on Reading itself than of RR. It has previously been evaluated with Key Stage 2 primary age children (Coles 2012). Of 100 pupils randomised to treatment or control, 8 are unaccounted for (7 from the control). For the remaining 92, the 'effect' size for Switch-On Reading was reported as +0.8. Switch-on was evaluated in England at a larger scale by Gorard et al. (2015b), with 157 pupils in each group, and an ES of 0.24 for reading. However, this study involved Year 7 at risk pupils.

8.3 Accelerated Reader

This section looks at the evidence for Accelerated Reader (AR), a computerised reading programme which includes elements of explicit and systematic teaching and differentiated instruction (all believed to be effective instructional practice) to address phonemic awareness (PA), phonics, fluency, vocabulary, and reading comprehension, in addition to writing and spelling. AR incorporates a number of strategies known to be best practice – direct instruction (DI), understanding by design (UBD) which is teaching and testing for understanding (a form of feedback from pupils to teachers).

The evidence from our review is not fully convincing that Accelerated Reader is effective in raising the academic outcomes of primary school children (Table 8.5). Even where there is evidence that AR as a packaged worked, it is not possible to identify which aspect of the programme is the driver because AR is a multi-component intervention including explicit and systematic teaching, use of technology and differentiated instruction and self-regulated reading. So it is not clear which of these components are the key ingredients, or is it a combination of all of them. Therefore, there is a considerable research base on AR, making it one of the most researched interventions in which reading is practised through online resources. Prior research has mainly been carried out in the context of US schools. Also, the quality of the evidence on the effectiveness of AR on attainment is mixed, with much of the research small, with high attrition, using AR-led measurements, or based on weak research designs. Some of it also shows no benefit from using AR anyway, especially when standardised tests that are not intervention-related are used.

Table 8.5 - Quality and impact summary: studies of Accelerated Reader

	Effective	Ineffective
Higher quality	2	0
Medium quality	0	0
Lower quality	12	6

Produced by Renaissance Learning Company, AR monitors and manages pupils' reading practices and encourages them in independent reading. In the UK, over

2,000 schools are using AR on a regular basis, which means that well over 400,000 students are reading what is recommended in AR or what AR supports through quizzes (Topping 2014). However, it is not clear that the implementation of AR at such a large scale can be justified solely on the basis of the pre-existing evidence of effectiveness. Evidence gathered from research so far has been inconclusive.

In addition to simple snapshot surveys suggesting that AR participants read more than other pupils (Clark 2013), there have been several weak evaluations reporting success for AR such as with no comparator group (Johnson and Howard 2003). For example, Scott (1999) involved only 28 pupils, had unbalanced groups at the outset, and the report is unclear how the cases were allocated. There are also studies showing no effects or even negative impact. Mathis (1996) compared the progress of 37 AR pupils over one year with the whole year cohort, using the Stanford Achievement Test. There was a large negative effect size for AR pupils on reading comprehension.

AR is one of 24 reading interventions considered by the What Works Clearinghouse (WWC 2008) in their review of evidence. According to the findings of their systematic review, AR has no visible effect on reading fluency, a mixed effect on comprehension and a possible positive effect on reading achievement. These results are based on only two studies that met WWC minimum standards.

Table 8.6 - Quality and impact detail: Accelerated Reader

Reference	Intervention	Smallest cell	Attrition	ES	NNTD-attrition	Quality
Ross et al. 2004	**AR**	**286**		**0.25**		**3***
Siddiqui et al. 2015	**AR (but Year 7)**	**357**	**2%**	**0.24**	**78**	**4***

In one study, 45 teachers (with 572 K-3 Grade students, aged 11-14, in 11 schools) were randomised to teach using AR or another commercially available reading programme (Ross et al. 2004). The results were calculated after one year. The authors reported what they termed a 'significant' impact on reading comprehension using the STAR reading test, but WWC recalculated and reported that they found it was not statistically significant, although the effect size was over 0.25. Similarly, there was no significant effect on general reading achievement based on the STAR Early Literacy test for each year group, but the overall effect size was over 0.25. Also, the STAR tests are produced and marketed by Renaissance Learning as part of the AR programme itself (http://www.renlearn.co.uk/accelerated-reader/reports-and-data/). They should, therefore, not be regarded as independent assessments in any way (Krashen 2007). The second study involved only 32 Grade 3 students attending one school in the Pacific Northwest (Bullock 2005). They were individually randomised to receive 90 minutes of AR reading or not per week for 10 weeks. At the end there was no difference in terms of oral reading fluency. As above, the author reports no 'significant' effect on reading comprehension using the STAR reading test, but the effect size is greater than 0.25.

Siddiqui et al. (2016) conducted an evaluation of AR in England involving 349 pupils in Year 7 (and therefore strictly the age range for this review) who had not achieved secure National Curriculum Level 4 in their Key Stage 2 results for English, randomised to two groups. AR is a whole-group reading management and monitoring programme that aims to stimulate the habit of independent reading among primary and secondary age pupils. The intervention group of 166 pupils was exposed to AR for 20 weeks, after which they recorded higher literacy scores in the New Group Reading Test (NGRT) post-test than the control group of 183 pupils (ES 0.24).

Brooks (2007) conducted a meta-synthesis of UK studies involving reading interventions for pupils with reading difficulties. The meta-synthesis for AR found 47 studies conducted mostly in the US, but only two were selected for inclusion (Vollands et al. 1996, 1999). According to the reports, AR produced positive effects. However, the cell sizes in comparison were only 11 in one study and 12 in the other. This is too small to draw conclusions on the effectiveness of the intervention. It is not clear how the groups had been created, nor whether baseline equivalence was established between the treatment and control groups. And anyway in tests three months later, the control group had made more progress.

Another study conducted with 108 primary age pupils from two schools in the US (Nichols 2013) found no difference after one year (or rather a small negative effect of -0.02) between the two groups in terms of the Standards of Learning (SOL) test. Pupils were randomly allocated to AR in one (treatment) school, and to a literacy plan in the other (control) school. In contrast, a more recent study in the US based on 19 teachers randomly allocated to AR or not (Shannon et al. 2015) reported a positive impact for the AR group. However, the groups were not balanced at the outset with the treatment group having markedly lower prior test scores. Their subsequent improvement might indeed be a sign of regression to the mean. The outcome measure used in the study was again the STAR reading test, which is an integral part of the AR intervention itself – meaning that those in the treatment group had more practice at this kind of test.

There have been some larger studies, all with weaker designs and non-random allocation of cases (and that are incorrect in using the concept of 'significance' in determining differences between groups). For example, Paul et al. (1996) had a large sample of 6,000 schools in which 58 percent were non-AR comparison schools in similar geographic locations. According to official records, the schools having access to AR had better pupil attendance records and reading performance scores compared to the schools not using AR. A similar study, based on schools that had already adopted AR or not was conducted by Peak and Dewalt (1993), who reported greater success for the AR group at both primary and secondary levels. Pavonetti et al. (2000) developed a test to measure the quantity of books read, called the Title Recognition Test (TRT). Pupils were asked to mark the book titles they had read and in order to check if they were guessing rather than giving true responses, some foils for book names were added in the list (25 titles were actual books and 16 were foils for book names). AR claims that pupils' quantity of book reading increases if they use AR in schools. This claim was assessed using a school -level matched comparison design, with 10 secondary schools. There was no difference in the quantity of reading between the pupils using AR and those not using AR (reported mean difference was -.008). See also Pavonetti et al. (2003). Goodman (1999) involved 282 pupils in one US secondary school with no comparator, and claimed a positive gain based on pre- and post-test only. Using a small sample, Facemire (2000) reported gains of five months for AR pupils compared to gains of only three months for comparison group on the STAR reading comprehension test. Again positive effects were based on the intervention-related test.

Rudd and Wade (2006) used matched comparison schools, and found that the average gains in reading from not using AR were greater than for the intervention schools, but this finding appears neither in their summary nor their conclusion. Instead, the authors reported that it needs "to be emphasized that there were improvements in average standardised test scores in the treatment schools for mathematics (both secondary and primary) and in the primary schools for reading. These were not spectacular improvements, but they can be seen as an important step in the right direction" (p.51). The authors also did not report attrition clearly either at school or pupil level, but it is clear that the reading attainment results are based on only 11 schools of the 21 originally allocated. It looks like a case of data dredging or highlighting only the positive results.

Duke (2011) reported that AR pupils made significant progress in the Standardised Test of Assessment of Reading (STAR), but not in the Missouri Assessment Programme (MAP), the state standardised test. Participants were 99 children in the 3rd and 4th Grade taken from 3 districts. Pre-post- comparisons were made with no control group. So it is not possible to say if the children would have made similar gains if they had not had the intervention. Ysseldyke et al. (2003) studied 157 4th and 5th Grade children comparing them with 61 in the same schools and 6,385 in the district. They reported that AR children made bigger gains in maths than control in one year. Participants were not randomly assigned to treatment condition, so the groups could be different at the outset, and other confounding variables that could explain the different results were not controlled for.

Overall, the weight of evidence is that AR is probably effective, and the two largest robust evaluations concur.

8.4 Response to Intervention and tiered approaches

Response-to-Intervention is a multi-tiered approach that involves initial screening to identify students' learning needs using research-based instructions with on-going monitoring of progress and with different levels of intensity (or tiers) to meet pupils' learning needs. The evidence on RTI so far is predominantly from the US, and has mostly involved small samples or focused on those with learning disabilities. Much of it is very weak (Table 8.7).

Table 8.7 - Quality and impact summary: studies of RTI

	Effective	Ineffective/unknown
Higher quality	3	0
Medium quality	3	0
Low quality	15	4

On balance, the evidence suggests that the small group and individualised approaches of RTI are effective both for literacy and maths. The three largest studies have a substantial positive effect size, and the medium quality studies similarly offer promise at least for some forms of test outcomes (Table 8.8).

Piper and Korda (2011) looked at a combination of intensive teacher training, teacher support plus regular information of student achievement to parents and communities. There were three groups of schools serving 2nd and 3rd Grade in Liberia were randomly selected into full treatment (59 schools, 934 pupils), light treatment (60, 1,065), and control group (57, 989). These groups were clustered within districts, such that several nearby schools were organised together. Attrition was at least 3%. In the “full” treatment group, reading levels were assessed, teachers were trained on how to continually assess student performance focusing on reading instructional strategies, teachers were provided with frequent school-based pedagogic support, resource materials, and books, and, in addition, parents and communities were informed of student performance. In the “light” treatment group, the community was informed about reading achievement using school report cards based on EGRA assessment results or findings and student reading report cards prepared by teachers. Outcomes included early reading tasks (letter naming, reading fluency, phonemic awareness, reading comprehension and listening comprehension. These were assessed using the EGRA Plus: Liberia tool. The light intervention made no difference, but the full intervention pupils made bigger gains between baseline and final assessments on all 7 tests of reading, with effect sizes ranging from E S= 0.39 (for reading comprehension) to ES = 1.23 (for unfamiliar word fluency). Overall impact was 0.79.

Fuchs et al. (2014) looked at teaching arithmetic calculations and arithmetic word-problems on understanding algebra using an RTI approach. The idea is that arithmetic is the foundation to learning algebra and conventional instruction causes children to misinterpret the equal sign as an operational symbol. Fluency in calculations provides a firm foundation in understanding arithmetic operational laws and generalisations which support prealgebraic thinking. Word-problems involve the use of symbolic representations (numerals and language), and this helps translate problem narratives into algebraic equations. Participants were 1,102 2nd Grade pupils from 127 classes across 25 schools. Children were first screened and divided into high, medium and low achievers. Then a Wechsler test of intelligence removed 92 children scoring below 9th percentile. 108 were further excluded (having moved or SEN). Teachers were randomly assigned to a calculation (386 pupils), word-problem (421 pupils) or business-as-usual-control group (295 pupils), stratified by school. Attrition was 9.5%. Both arithmetic calculations and arithmetic word-problems were carried out in 2 tiers. Tier 1-whole class teaching for 17 weeks (2 lessons per week; 40-45 mins per lesson) delivered by the researcher. In addition, intervention children also received Tier 2 (small group of 2-3 children) tutoring (3 times per week for 13 weeks). Outcomes were:

proximal calculations using researcher-developed instrument and distal calculations using commercial measures (the Wide Range Achievement Test (WRAT); proximal word problems_(using researcher-developed test) and distal word problems using commercial tests (KM-Revised Problem Solving and Iowa Test of Basic Skills). Prealgebraic knowledge was measured only at post-test using researcher-developed tests. Using only the results of the standardised tests (ITBS) which are not researcher-dependent and not intervention-related – ES for prealgebraic knowledge was 1.36 for word-problems versus control, and 1.32 versus calculations.

Al Otaiba et al. (2011) examined the use of assessment data to guide individualised instruction (RTI), in a teacher-level RCT, involving 14 schools, 23 treatment teachers (305 students) and 21 contrast teachers (251 students). The treatment used differentiated instruction in ongoing assessments of children's language and literacy skills. Teachers in the contrast condition received only a baseline professional development that included a researcher-delivered summer day-long workshop on individualised instruction. Students in treatment classrooms outperformed students in the contrast classrooms on reading skills, comprised of letter-word reading, decoding, alphabetic knowledge, and phonological awareness (0.52). Teachers in both conditions provided small group instruction, but teachers in the treatment condition provided significantly more individualised instruction.

Vadasy et al. (2013) looked at the longer term effectiveness of a standard protocol, Tier 2 supplemental vocabulary intervention for Kindergarten English learners (US Spanish-speakers) for 20 minutes per day for 20 weeks in small groups. The intervention as designed to develop root word vocabulary knowledge, and reinforce beginning word reading skills. There were originally 93 pupils in the treatment group and 92 in the control but scores were only obtained for 74 and 66 pupils respectively. The authors only computed ES for the positive outcomes - proximal reading vocabulary +0.23, distal reading vocabulary +0.29, and word reading +0.35.

Table 8.8 - Quality and impact detail: studies of RTI

Reference	Intervention	Smallest cell	Attrition	ES	NNTD-attrition	Quality
Piper and Korda 2011	**RTI**	**934 pupils**	**3%**	**0.79**	**709**	**3/4***
Fuchs et al. 2014	**RTI**	**295 pupils**	**10%**	**1.32**	**359**	**3***
Al Otaiba et al. 2011	**RTI**	**251 pupils**	**Unknown**	**0.52**	**-**	**3***
Vadasy et al. 2013	RTI tier 2	92 pupils	45	Work Reading 0.35 Early receptive vocabulary -0.09	0	2*
Jimenez et al. 2010	RTI	120 pupils	Not known	10 outcomes range from -0.04 to 0.68	-	2*
See et al. 2015	RTI	171 pupils	132	0.29	0	2*

Jimenez et al. (2010) undertook a study of a small group supplementary intervention based in the Canary Islands, and involving 241 children aged 5 to 8 at risk for reading (121 in intervention, 120 control). Attrition was not reported, and there was some initial imbalance. The intervention included small group reading comprehension. For the 10 tests reported the ES were 0.04, 0.68, 0.52, -0.03, -0.04, 0.14, 0.02, 0.06, 0.49, 0.00. Children who received the PREDEA curriculum had higher scores on the Early Grade Reading Assessment Test (EGRA) on initial sound identification, listening comprehension, letter sound knowledge and oral reading fluency compared to the control group.

See et al. (2015c) randomised (by school) all eligible at risk Year 6 pupils in 61 schools in England to receive RTI or not (30 treatment, 31 control). The pre- and post-test was the New Group Reading (NGRT) pre-test (a standardised test of literacy). After randomisation, 11 schools (three treatment and eight control schools) dropped out, reportedly due to organisational issues as a result of changes in leadership. In addition, one other control school conducted the post-test on the wrong year group of pupils. So valid data from only 49 schools was analysed (27 treatment and 22 control). Overall attrition was in excess of 25% meaning that the results of the trial must be treated as indicative only. For these pupils, RTI appears to have had a modest positive impact (+0.29). An analysis using only those pupils listed as eligible for free school meals produced an 'effect' size of +0.48.

The following reports are not cited in cited in Table 8.8 as they are weaker, some almost negligible as research, or because their design is not obviously appropriate to a causal claim.

Case et al. (2014) investigated the immediate and long-term effects of a Tier 2 intervention for beginning readers identified as having a high probability of reading failure using a randomised control trial in the US. 124 1 st Grade participants were randomly assigned either to a 25-session intervention targeting key reading components, including decoding, spelling, word recognition, fluency, and comprehension, or to a no-treatment control condition. There were short-term differences between the groups in terms of Decodable Word Fluency (ES=0.4), but these disappeared by the end of 2nd Grade.

A study by Graves et al. (2011) reported that RTI was particularly efficacious for pupils from disadvantaged backgrounds with learning difficulties, and was more effective for improving oral fluency than reading comprehension. All of the pupils involved were 'below' or 'far below' a basic level of literacy. This was a quasi-experimental study that compared small group intensive reading instruction (Tier 2) with a control group ('business as usual') involving 6th Graders with and without learning disabilities. The duration was 30 hours over 10 weeks.

Faggella-Luby and Wardwell (2011) examined the effects of the same Tier 2 intervention which randomly assigned 86 at-risk students in the 5th and 6th Grades (age 10-12) to three treatments – Story Structure (SS), Typical Practice (TP) and Sustained Silent Reading (SSR). Only 6th Grade students on SS and TP outperformed those in SSR in all three tests (standardised curriculum-based test, Strategy-Use test and Gates-MacGinitie Reading Comprehension). The impact on 5th Grade students was not clear. The Strategy-Use test assessed strategies that were taught only to students in the SS group, and is not a test of general comprehension or reading. So using this test may not be valid for comparison. Also, the study compared only post-test results without establishing whether the three groups were similar to start with. The small sample divided into three treatment groups and two Grade levels suggests that there were fewer than 20 in each group. This is too small for conclusive evidence.

Leroux et al. (2011) evaluated the intensive Tier 2 (small group) intervention and showed that there were 'significant' differences between treatment and comparison groups on two of three of the outcome measures. However, the difference was largely due to the continuing decline of the Tier 1 students in the comparison group, rather than real gains by the treatment group. The small sample of only 30 students across three Grade levels (Grade 6 to 8) from three middle schools is not large enough to provide convincing results. These students were identified as those with severe reading difficulties. The intervention may therefore help prevent decline in performance, but not offer 'catch-up' to normative 8th Grade reading levels.

Baker et al. (2014) looked at a number of literacy interventions, including RTI used with a cut-off comparing Tier 2 with everyone else receiving Tier 1 only. The treatment group achieved better SAT10 results.

Pullen et al. (2010) involved 224 US 1 st Grade children (age 6-7) - 98 identified as at-risk of reading disability and 126 not at risk, with the at risk pupils randomised to treatment or not. Experimental children were taught in the whole-class story book reading with direct instruction and also receive Tier 2 more intensive small group intervention which provides additional supplemental support. There are no pre-test results, and no report of attrition. The post test was a researcher-developed test of target words. There was a short-term advantage for treatment pupils, but control children made bigger progress from post to delayed post-test. This could be that the intervention was targeting words that were taught directly to the children, and once that was removed, no advantage was seen. In fact the children would have been better off not have the intensive extra support.

Harn et al. (2011) used the RTI tiered literacy intervention with 176 US 1 st Grade students at-risk of low attainment. They reported ES=0.4, but 33 pupils had missing scores, and the comparator was the previous cohort.

Clarke et al. (2014) examined the RTI Tier 2 maths intervention programme teaching whole numbers to children at risk in maths, using 89 low attaining 1 st Grade pupils individually randomised within 10 schools to RTI (44) or standard delivery (45). The intervention called Fusion incorporates explicit and systematic instructional principles of teaching. Children at risk of maths are taught in small groups of 5 and receive 60 lessons each lasting 30 minute over 20 weeks. Teachers received 3-hour training on content and pedagogical knowledge. On Curriculum-based and Early numeracy tests, the treatment group outperformed control (ES=0.14), and in the state test SAT ES=0.11. This study was well-conducted and well-reported, but is small.

Burns (2007) examined the effect of pre-teaching unknown words to 29 3 rd Grade children identified as learning disabled in basic reading skills to facilitate an instructional level within the standard curriculum, compared to 30 pupils who did not get the treatment. This was a RTI Tier 3 one-to one intervention. Treatment children outperformed control children in reading fluency (words read correctly per minute), with ES=1.47. However, this is a small study and the number of pupils in the control dropped to 19 cases.

Mattingly (2014) used a sample of 546 US Elementary schools of which 97 were known to be using RTI. The sample was reduced to 300 for propensity score matching. RTI schools had 1.8% increase in reading proficiency and showed no difference in maths. There is no report of attrition.

Bryant et al. (2008) looked at Tier 2 (small group) RTI impacts on maths, within a larger multi-tiered system based on regression discontinuity. Participants included 126 1st Graders and 140 2nd Graders who were not eligible and did not receive the intervention compared to 26 1st and 25 2nd Graders who were eligible and received intervention. The intervention was based on 18 weeks of 15 minute booster lessons. Attrition was around 20%. ES for 1st Grade was 0.04, and for 2nd Grade 0.19.

Case et al. (2014) investigated the immediate and long-term effects of a Tier 2 intervention for beginning readers identified as having a high probability of reading failure using a randomised control trial in the US. First-Grade participants (n = 123) were randomly assigned either to a 25-session intervention targeting key reading components, including decoding, spelling, word recognition, fluency, and comprehension, or to a no-treatment control condition. There were short-term differences between the groups in terms of Decodable Word Fluency (ES=0.4), but these disappeared by the end of 2nd Grade.

Oostdam et al. (2015) conducted two experiments on the effects of individualised and small-group guided oral reading interventions on the reading skills and reading attitude of poor readers in Grades 2-4 in the Netherlands. In the first, there 143 pupils from 8 schools (17 scores not presented), of which 43 were given continuous reading, 43 repeated reading (practice until fluent), and 40 were in the control. The intervention was one-to-one delivered by a TA. Using standardised reading tests the ES ranged from 0.21 to 0.45. The second study used the same approach but with 3 students per teaching group, using 84 in treatment and 55 in control. This was not so successful.

Berninger et al. (2006) reports on 4 studies to see if training in handwriting skills improves automatic handwriting and whether improvements in handwriting led to improvements in word reading, using Tier 1 (a supplementary instruction in general education) and 2 (an extended instruction for struggling students). The number of children in each study varied from 20 to 74 (for Study 4). Handwriting can improve, but does not transfer to word reading. Explicit instruction in the processes of composition led to more significant improvement.

Gilbert et al. (2013) used RTI with 212 struggling US 1st Grade readers (134 intervention, 78 control). Where pupils did not respond well 45 of the 134 were randomised to more intense treatment. The intensification made no difference, but the general approach produced better results (0.19).

Hearn (2014) used RTI with and without a particular differentiated approach, and evaluated it using convenience groups of 62 at-risk 2nd and 34 3rd Grade US students selected from four elementary schools. The attrition and impact are not clearly reported.

O'Connor et al. (2005) measured the effects of increasing levels of intervention in reading for a cohort of US children in Grades K through 3 to determine whether the severity of reading disability could be significantly reduced in the catchment schools. Tier I consisted of professional development for teachers of reading. Tier 2 consisted of small-group reading instruction 3 times per week, and Tier 3 of daily instruction delivered individually or in groups of two. A comparison of the reading achievement of third-Grade children who were at risk in kindergarten showed moderate to large differences favouring children in the tiered interventions in decoding, word identification, fluency, and reading comprehension.

Overall, the evidence is that RTI works, especially for literacy interventions with struggling readers. However, there is evidence elsewhere in this report suggesting that almost any coherent research-based approach conducted individually or in small groups can be effective. The precise protocol used may matter less than the tiered attention.

Callahan et al. (2015) is one of a few studies looking at differentiated instruction in English language for gifted students. In the US, 1,215 3rd Graders were randomised by classes, and treatment classes used two language arts units for gifted students. Outcomes were measured using the state assessments (the Iowa Test of Basic Skills), and the treatment classes performed better. There was no difference whether children were taught in pullout classes or in self-contained classes. Attrition is not reported. Nor were pre- and post-test scores published (the analysis was multivariate and contextualised). Due to the ceiling effect of the assessment there was no differentiation among the top scorers.

Schwartz et al. (2012) used a randomised experimental design to examine the relationship between teacher-student ratio and literacy learning outcomes for experienced intervention teachers working with the most at-risk first-Grade students. Eighty-five Reading Recovery teachers, working with 170 students, each taught in a 1:1 and a small-group instructional format with teacher-student ratios of 1:2, 1:3, or 1:5. Each teacher was randomly assigned to conduct a small group of 2, 3, or 5 students. They identified two first-Grade students who qualified for early intervention using Reading Recovery selection criteria and who were randomly assigned to either individual or small-group treatment conditions. Attrition across treatment combinations resulted in 30 pairs from teachers in the 1:2 condition, 23 pairs for teachers in the 1:3 condition, and 33 pairs for teachers in the 1:5 condition. The treatments lasted for 20 weeks, with daily 30-minute lessons. The students were assessed at pre-test and post-test with the six subtests of *An Observation Survey of Early Literacy Achievement* and the Slos-son Oral Reading Test—Revised (SORT-R). The 1:1 instruction yielded significantly higher outcomes than the combined small-group conditions on 8 of the 9 measures. The 1:1 condition resulted in significantly higher performance on eight of the nine outcome measures than the combined small-group treatments, the only exception being the Letter Identification measure, which reached ceiling levels by the post-test period. The effect sizes range from 0.6 for Text Reading Level to 0.19 for the Concepts About Print task. The small-group conditions did not differ significantly from one another. This suggests that individual attention is best.

8.5 Whole class teaching versus small class

Following OECD PISA 2012, there was concern among UK press and politicians about the results for England compared to Pacific Rim countries such as Singapore and coastal cities in China such as Shanghai. A junior education minister accompanied by experts visited Shanghai to study schools' success especially in maths. A key difference between these Pacific Rim cities and the UK was felt to be the proportion of time teachers spent on whole class direct instruction. Direct instruction is where the teacher works with the whole class in structured and purposeful ways, such as proposed by the National Literacy and Numeracy Strategies in England. The idea emerged from studies of teacher effectiveness where pupil performance was correlated with observed and reported teacher behaviour in class (Muijs and Reynolds 2011). The Routledge Handbook of Educational Effectiveness and Improvement claimed that "Achievement has been found to increase when most of the lesson is spent teaching the whole class, rather than work through worksheets or schedules on their own" (Reynolds et al. 2015, p.88). This explicit instruction has to be heavily interactive with pupils playing an active part in discussions, while remaining very structured, with clear objectives and summary at the end. The same genre of work suggests avoiding whole class lectures, increasing the time for whole-class interactions, reducing the time spent on individual and group work, and on interactions with only part of the class, and increasing both the subject and pedagogical knowledge of the teachers – ideally by employing specialist primary teachers (Miao and Reynolds 2015).

All of this sounds plausible, and is based on descriptions of teachers thought to be effective (as assessed by other means). But such correlational studies can be very misleading. The crucial question is whether these attributes of 'effective' teachers can be rolled out to others, leading to an improvement in their pupils' scores as well. Put another way, does intervening to make more teachers use whole-class interaction improve results? The National Literacy and Numeracy Strategies in England sought to do that, but observations suggested that traditional patterns of whole class interaction did not change much (Smith et al. 2004), or where they did teachers used more directive forms of teaching with little opportunities for pupils to explore and elaborate on their ideas (Hardman et al. 2003).

The concept of whole-class as opposed to small group instruction is based on the belief that instructional practices differ depending on whether teaching takes place in a homogeneous or heterogeneous whole-class (Ben-Ari and Kedem-Friedrich 2000). Early studies suggested that within-class ability grouping was more effective in raising attainment than traditional whole-class, self-contained teaching. A review by Slavin (1987) showed that students grouped according to the Joplin Plan (grouping by ability) outperformed those in the traditional, self-contained classrooms in 11 of the 14 studies. Provus (1960 found that students in within-Grade regroupings perform better than control students on the Iowa Test of Basic Skills (ITBS). Slavin reported that much of the growth was in the high ability groups (ES=0.79) than that of average (0.22) and low achievers (0.15). On the other hand, a comparison of 4 th Grade children in 5 regrouped classes and 5 self-contained classes found that control classes outperformed experimental classes on the ITBS in maths and across language and reading (Koontz 1961). However, most of these studies of within-class ability grouping and regrouping were methodologically flawed (curriculum effects, novelty, school and teacher effects). Evidently, participants were not randomly assigned to treatment conditions. These studies also did not include observational measures to identify the classroom dynamics. Other studies using observational data (e.g. Gerleman 1987) found that regardless of approaches used by teachers in the group work, the instructional practice of teachers mirrored whole-class teaching. And students in same-ability group did not engage in cooperative interactions, problem-solving or collaborate in completing assignments. Effectively, children worked individually but in the group. More recently, a review by Cheung and Slavin (2012) of effective reading programmes for English language learners in the US found successful approaches that were whole class, small group and one-to-one.

In this new review we found only three medium or high quality studies expressly addressing within-class grouping (Table 8.9). Both studies suggest that an element of small group activities is beneficial. Although the second study showed that whole class teaching was more effective compared to the 2-group active teaching and learning and 2-group control, the whole class teaching incorporated daily small group instruction with intensive remedial and enrichment activities. So it may not be the whole-class nor the small group interaction, but the occasional intensive enrichment and remedial group that is the driver for success.

Table 8.9 - Quality and impact summary: studies of class grouping

	Effective	Ineffective/unknown
Higher quality	2	1
Medium quality	0	0
Lower quality	1	0

Previous work, especially in the UK, has suggested that the deployment of teaching assistants in primary classrooms is both expensive and largely ineffective (e.g. Blatchford et al. 2012) – a finding that was reflected in the EEF Teaching and Learning Toolkit until very recently. However, there is some evidence here, and in other sections of this review, that it is the way in which TAs are deployed that is critical

Table 8.10 - Quality and impact detail: studies of class grouping

Reference	Intervention	Smallest cell	Attrition	ES	NNTD - attrition	Quality
Mason and Good 1993	**Within class grouping**	**3 schools, 570 pupils**	**Unknown**	**Whole class v 2 groups 0.3**	-	**3***
Gerber et al. 2014	**Teacher aides regular class v small class v regular class**	**26 schools (2070 pupils)**	**17%**	**Teacher aides 0 Small class (unclear)**	**0**	**3***
Rutt et al. 2014	**Catchup numeracy with TA**	**102 pupils**	**5%**	**Catchup 0.21 TA alone 0.27**	**16 22**	**3***

Rutt et al. (2014) compared a specific one to one teacher aide (TA) intervention for Year 6 catch-up with a generic use of TAs for one to one work, and a control. The smallest randomised group was 102 pupils. 18 of 336 pupils are missing. The ES for the catch-up intervention compared to the control was 0.21 but the ES for TAs alone using the same time was 0.27. This strongly suggests that it is individual attention that is beneficial and not any specific protocol.

Gerber et al. (2001) evaluated the effects of Project Star (a project that used teacher aides) on students' academic achievement. Participants were 6,300 children from

Kindergarten-Grade 3 in 79 US schools. There was some attrition and some new pupils entered. Full data was collected from 5,742 pupils in the first year (9% missing data) and by Grade 3 only 5,229 pupils remained due to attrition (17% missing). Pupils were randomised to either small class, regular class or regular class plus teacher aide. Compared to both whole class and whole class with teacher aides (TA), children in small classes appeared to do better in verbal tests. There were no significant differences between regular classes and those with TAs in the class on any test and on any Grade. In the long term TA pupils outperformed those in regular classes in verbal tests (ES = 0.2), but only in Grades1 and 2. By the 4th year, no differences were detected. The results suggest that small groups were more effective in improving verbal ability of children in the lower Grades, but no long- term effects could be discerned.

In another large-scale study involving 1,736 pupils from 9 schools Mason and Good (1993) compared two classroom organisations: whole-class instruction with pupils given enrichment and remediation in small groups and a 2-group active teaching and learning model where children were grouped within class by ability. A control 2-group was also introduced as comparison. Pupils were from 4th to 6th Grades from 81 classes. After matching, schools were randomly assigned to one of 3 conditions: 2-group model; whole-class and 2-group control (usual within-class ability grouping). Both ad hoc whole-class and the 2-group model incorporated the 16 elements of active maths teaching programme (Good et al.'s (1983). Teachers were also asked to incorporate the five components of quality teaching (actively assess student learning, classroom management, time on-task, reinforcement, peer tutoring and enrichment). Whole-class teachers used the 2-group model occasionally and the 2-group teachers used whole-class teaching occasionally. The difference between the two is that whole-class model emphasized daily formation of small groups for remedial and enrichment activities. Maths performance was measured using items taken by the district's curriculum objectives, selected by the researchers. There was no mention of attrition. Results suggest that whole-class group with remediation and enrichment in small groups outperformed the 2-group model (ES = +0.3) and the 2-group control. (ES = 0.3). However, there was no difference between the 2-group model and the 2-group control (ES = 0.03). The model that works best seems to be whole-class teaching with small group activities.

In a study conducted in Australia, Bourke (1986) looked at how class size might influence teachers' teaching practices and whether this in turn had an impact on pupils' maths performance. It is believed that teachers' teaching strategies may differ when using individualised instruction and whole class or small group instructions. The study involved 33 schools and an average of 2 Y5 teachers from each school who volunteered to take part (n = 63 teachers). Class sizes ranged from 12 to 33. Half had 25 or fewer. Children were aged 10-11. Each class was observed for 8-10 lessons over 12 weeks during maths. Teaching practices were measured by recording the frequency and type of interactions between teacher and students, questioning techniques, homework practices and classroom management of noise control. The author reported that none of the teacher variables were significantly related to class size, therefore they were not included in the multivariate analyses. However the author assumed that because teacher experience was a proxy for teacher quality, teacher's experience was included in the analyses. Controlling for student ability, class size and student achievement was negatively correlated (0.42). It was observed that teachers with smaller classes probed more frequently, had more homework completed, and tended to wait more often for answers from pupils. This study was given a zero rating because it is a correlational in design, so it is not possible to establish the direction of causation. Classes were not randomly allocated and there were no real comparison groups. Groups may differ at the outset and as the study found – ability are highly correlated with achievement. There was no baseline equivalence established, no clear report of sample size or attrition. It is also not clear how student ability and maths achievement were measured.

Whitburn (2001) argues for mixed ability grouping and challenges the practice of whole-class and same ability grouping in primary maths in the UK. This correlational study is based on over 14,000 pupils from four London boroughs. 3 cohorts in KS2 (Y3 and Y4) were tested between 1997 and 2000. Attrition ranged from 4% to 6%. Only a minority of schools have a policy of setting (200 children).

Majority of the children were taught in mixed-ability class groupings for maths (1000 children). In the first cohort, the average scores of children set by ability went down from 99.6 to 96.5, while pupils in mixed ability classes made gains from 100.1 to 100.6 (ES=0.23). Similar patterns exist for the 2 nd and 3 rd Cohorts with mixed ability children making bigger gains. Mixed ability grouping also benefitted different ability groups with biggest effects on low ability children. For Cohort 1 (ES = +0.02 for high ability; ES =+ 0.3 for middle ability; ES = +0.4 for low ability).

8.6 Individualised instruction

Individualised instruction, sometimes known as differentiated instruction, can take a number of forms (some of which are covered in other sections). Common to individualised instruction is where the instruction or activity is tailored to the individual needs of the learner. It is often employed as a strategy for children with special learning needs. A number of computer-related programmes also have elements of individualisation where the software determines the amounts and types of instruction for each child. A review by Slavin et al. (2011) of effective reading interventions for struggling readers which included only RCTs and quasi-experiments concluded one-to-one tutoring was effective, but a focus on improving classroom instruction was even better than one-to-one tutoring. Computer-assisted instruction generally had no benefit. A similar message emerges from a review for English language learners (Cheung and Slavin 2012). One-to-one tuition is effective, but all effective approaches tend to have extensive professional development, coaching, and cooperative learning.

Like most interventions, much research has been conducted on individualised instruction and almost all has suggested that children made improvements as a result. However, in many of these evaluations, it is often the case that the learner receives additional support, more lessons, more teaching and more attention. It is therefore, not clear if it is the individualised instruction or the additional lessons and individual attention that is driving up results. There are 4 large-studies all related and conducted by the same authors. The evidence is not strong because of unclear reporting of attrition, high attrition in one study and lack of demonstration of direct link between ISI and outcomes. These studies are summarised below.

Table 8.11 - Quality and impact summary: studies of Individualised instruction

	Effective	Ineffective/unknown
Higher quality	0	0
Medium quality	1	1
Lower quality	5	0

Table 8.2 - Quality and impact detail: studies of Individualised instruction

Reference	Intervention	Smallest cell	Attrition	ES	NNTD-attrition	Quality
Connor et al. 2011	Individualising Student Instruction	174 pupils	52 pupils	0.15	0	2*
Connor et al. 2009	Individualised instruction A2i software	230 pupils	Unknown	0.37	-	2*

Connor et al. (2009) randomised 10 elementary schools (461 1 st Grade) to receive individualised instruction via A2i software or not. ISI (Individualising Student Instruction) teachers received professional development training on how to individualise instruction in the classroom using the A2i Web-based software. The software uses an algorithm to work out the amount and types of instructions. Intervention was delivered by teachers to all the children in the classroom. Outcomes were assessed using the Woodcock-Johnson Test. Children's literacy skills were assessed using the Letter Word identification Test and Comprehension

Passage and the PPVT. Classroom observations and video recording of classroom instructions were also taken and coded to assess the type of instructions:

- Child Manage (CM) where child completed activities independently without teacher support
- Teacher and Child Together (TCM) where teacher was actively interacting with students.
- Whole class; small groups; individual or pairs
- Child focus or Meaning focus

In general, the results are not strongly linked to treatments or to classroom interaction patterns, but the more time children spent in TCM-MF instruction, the greater the growth in reading comprehension skill. Children who received 18 minutes more than the mean were predicted to perform better on reading comprehension (ES = 0.37) and letter word reading (ES=0.36). The reporting, including the precise number of pupils and whether these are the same schools as in Connor et al. (2010) and Connor et al. (2013), is not clear in many places.

In a follow-up paper, Connor et al. (2010) report on the results of 445 1st Grade pupils in the 10 schools. The more time that treatment group teachers spent using the A2i software, the less time students in their classroom spent in disruption and discipline events. Students in treatment classrooms spent significantly more time in instruction, more time in teacher/child-managed and child/peer-managed small groups, and more time working independently.

A later study by the same researchers (Connor et al. 2013) teachers of 468 st1 Grade students in 10 US elementary schools were trained to use Assessment to Instruction (A2i) software in their classes (Connor et al. 2013). The software recommended the amounts and types of instruction for each child, and teachers used the instructional materials from their regular curriculum and individualised the instruction for students. Teachers were randomly assigned to either reading or maths individualised instruction, but this allocation appears to have been made again every year meaning that the number of cases getting continuous A2i would be very small (around 29). 111 pupils dropped out by the third year (24% attrition) meaning that the results are not particularly trustworthy (even if there had been 234 pupils in the smallest group the NNTD would be 58, which is considerably less than 111). Pupils getting continuous A2i did better for Letter Word Identification and Reading Comprehension (Woodcock Johnson III) with ES=0.25 by third Grade.

The same authors (Connor et al. 2011) carried out another study, this time comparing students receiving individualised Student Instruction (ISI) with students doing group vocabulary instruction. 33 US 3rd Grade teachers (448 pupils) took part. Randomisation was at the teacher level and data was presented for 25 teachers and 396 pupils (174 control, 222 treatment). Results show that the approach may not be as effective for disadvantaged pupils.

The difficulty with assessing the effects of such an intervention like ISI is the multi-components involved. ISI has five components that work together to support teachers' reading instruction planning and implementation including: (1) Multiple dimensions conceptualisation of reading instruction (2) Student assessment and progress monitoring (feedback); (3) A2i web-based software; (4) Teacher training including online professional development resources, workshop, school, and classroom-based support; and (5) implementation in the classroom. Therefore, comparing children whose teachers have received additional support, training and resources with children whose teachers had none of these is not a fair comparison. A fairer comparison would be simply comparing children who received instructions tailored to their needs (in terms of the amount and types of instruction and activities) with those who had the regular instruction.

A large-scale study of City Connects, an individualised instruction programme that linked each child's strengths and needs to tailored and enrichment intervention, reported no impact for primary school children (age 5 to 11) on state standardised tests but strong positive effects for older children (An 2015). Positive results were reported for some report card Grades for Grade 4 and most report card scores for Grade 5 children. This study employed a propensity-score matching method to match treatment and control groups. The same paper reported another study using regression discontinuity and date of birth as cut-off suggested positive effects for 3rd and 5th Grade pupils' maths and reading (ES = +0.2 to 0.28) on the MCAS raw scores.

There were other much smaller and weaker studies but the results are difficult to discern. Lane et al. (2011) reported greater progress in writing for children taught self-regulated strategy on an individual basis, but writing quality was subjectively assessed using story quality elements and word count. Attrition was also high at 33%. Gelzheiser et al. (2011) studied an interactive one-to-one individualised programme was based on only 50 pupils, and groups were not matched at baseline. Testing was complex and reporting was poor – hard to make sense of what the results are. Another study using individualised instruction did not compare individualised instruction vs non-individualised instruction (Fyfe et al. 2014). It was a comparison of two different procedural approaches both using individualised instruction. Maths outcomes were assessed using researcher-developed test and the intervention was delivered by the experimenter making the results difficult to generalise to regular classroom situations. A randomised trial of individualised tutoring (Strayhorn and Bickel 2003) was not an evaluation of the effects of individualised tutoring. Rather it compared the effects of different amount of exposure to the programme. Not surprisingly children who had more sessions (45 minutes every 1.5 days) progressed faster than children who had fewer sessions (45 minutes every 8 days).

9. References

Aarnoutse, C. and Schellings, G. (2003) Learning reading strategies by triggering reading motivation, *Educational Studies*, 29 (4): 387-409

Adams, M. and Bruck, M. (1993) Word recognition: The interface of educational Policies and scientific research, *Reading and Writing: An interdisciplinary Journal,* 5, pp. 113-139

Adams, T. (2012) *Investigation of the effectiveness of the CompassLearning Math program on the mathematics success of urban students*. PhD. University of Wisconsin, USA

Adesope, O. O., et al. (2011). "Pedagogical Strategies for Teaching Literacy to ESL Immigrant Students: A Meta-Analysis." *British Journal of Educational Psychology* 81(4): 629-653.

Agarwal, P. Bain, P. Chamberlain, R. (2012) The Value of Applied Research: Retrieval Practice Improves Classroom Learning and Recommendations from a Teacher, a Principal, and a Scientist, *Educational Psychology Review*, 24 (3): 437-448

Al Otaiba, S., Connor, C., Folsom, J., Greulich, L., Meadows, J. and Li, Z. (2011) Assessment Data Informed Guidance to Individualize Kindergarten Reading Instruction: Findings from a Cluster Randomized Control Field Trial, *Elementary Schooling,* 111(4): 535-560

Alcoholado, C., Diaz, A., Tagle, A., Nussbaum, M. and Infante, C. (2016) Comparing the use of the interpersonal computer, personal computer and pen-and-paper when solving arithmetic exercises. *British Journal of Educational Technology*, 47(1): 91-105

Allsopp, D., Lovin, L., Green, G., & Savage-Davis, E. (2003) Why students with special needs have difficulty learning mathematics and what teachers can do to help. *Mathematics Teaching in the Middle School*, 8(6): 308-314

Altiparmak, K. and Ozdogan, E. (2010) A Study on the Teaching of the Concept of Negative Numbers. *International Journal of Mathematical Education in Science and Technology*, 41(1): 31-47

Alvarez-Marinelli, H., Blanco, M., Lara-Alecio, R., Irby, B., Tong, F. Stanley, K and Fan, Y (2016) Computer assisted English language learning in Costa

Rican elementary schools: an experimental study. *Computer Assisted Language Learning*, 29(1): 103-126

An, C. (2015) *Estimating the effectiveness of City Connects on middle school outcomes*, PhD. Boston College, USA

Andrews, R., Dan, H., Freeman, A., McGuinn, N., Robinson, A. and Zhu, D. (2005) *The effectiveness of different ICTs in the teaching and learning of English (written composition) 5–16*, Research Evidence in Education Library, London: EPPI-Centre, Social Science Research Unit, Institute of Education, University of London, http://eppi.ioe.ac.uk/EPPIWeb/home.aspx?&page=/reel/reviews.htm, accessed 26/3/06

Anghileri, J. (2006) *Teaching number sense* (2nd ed.) London: Continuum

Angrist J. and Lavy, V. (2002) New evidence on classroom computers and pupil learning, *The Economic Journal, 112,* pp. 735–765

Archambault, I., Pagani, L. and Fitzpatrick, C. (2013) Transactional associations between classroom engagement and relations with teachers from first through fourth grade. *Learning and Instruction*, 23: 1-9

Archer, K., Savage, R., Sanghera-Sidhu, S., Wood, E., Gottardo, A. and Chen, V. (2014) Examining the effectiveness of technology use in classrooms: A tertiary meta-analysis. *Computers & Education*, 78: 140-149

Arnold, A. (2010) *Exploring the Use of the Eight-Step Process in the Area of Third Grade Communication Arts*, PhD. Lindenwood University, USA.

Arnold, J., Kremer, K. and Mayer, J. (2014) Understanding Students' Experiments-What kind of support do they need in inquiry tasks? *International Journal of Science Education,* 36(16): 2719-2749

Baenen, N., Bernhole, A. Dulaney, C. and Banks, K. (1997) Reading Recovery: Long-term progress after three cohorts, *Journal of Education for Student s Placed at Risk*, 2, 2, 161

Baer, J. (2011) The impact of the Core Knowledge Curriculum on creativity, *Creativity Research Journal*, 15 (2-3): 297-300

Bai, Y., Mo, D., Zhang, L., Boswell, M., Rozelle, S. (2016) The impact of integrating ICT with teaching: Evidence from a randomized controlled trial in rural schools in China. *Computers and Education,* 96:1-14

Baines, E., Blatchford, P. and Chowne, A. (2007) Improving the effectiveness of collaborative group work in primary schools: effects on science attainment. *British Educational Research Journal,* 33(5): 663-680

Baker, D., Park, Y., Baker, S., Basaraba, D., Kame'enui, E. and Beck, C. (2012) Effects of a paired bilingual reading program and an English-only program on the reading performance of English learners in Grades 1-3. *Journal of School Psychology*, 50(6): 737-758

Baker, S., Gersten, R. and Lee, D. (2002) A synthesis of empirical research on teaching mathematics to low-achieving students. *The Elementary School Journal*, 103(1): 51-73

Baker, S., Smolkowski, K., Chaparro, E., Smith, J. and Fien, H. (2014) Using regression discontinuity to test the impact of a Tier 2 reading intervention in first grade, *Journal of Research on Educational Effectiveness*, 10.1080/19345747.2014.909548

Bakker, M., van den Heuvel-Panhuizen, M. and Robitzsch, A. (2015) Effects of playing mathematics computer games on primary school students' multiplicative reasoning ability. *Contemporary Educational Psychology*, 40:55-71

Bakosh, L. (2013) *Investigating the effects of a daily audio-guided mindfulness intervention for elementary school students and teachers*. PhD. Institute of Transpersonal Psychology, Sofia University, California

Bakosh, L., Snow, R., Tobias, J., Houlihan, J. and Barbosa-Leiker, C. (2016) Maximizing Mindful Learning: Mindful Awareness Intervention Improves Elementary School Students' Quarterly Grades. *Mindfulness*, 7(1): 59-67

Baroody, A., Purpura, D., Eiland, M. and Reid, E. (2015) The impact of highly and minimally guided discovery instruction on promoting the learning of reasoning strategies for basic add-1 and doubles combinations, *Early Childhood Research Quarterly*, 30 (1): 93–105

Baumer, S., Ferholt, B., Lecusay, R. (2005) Promoting narrative competence through adult-child joint pretense: Lessons from the Scandinavian educational practice of playworld. *Cognitive Development*, 20(4): 576-590

Bebell, D. and Pedulla, J. (2015) Quantitative Investigation into the Impacts of 1:1 iPads on Early Learners' ELA and Math Achievement. *Journal of Information Technology Education-Innovations in Practice*, 14: 191-215

Behrmann, L. and Souvignier, E. (2015) Effects of fit between teachers' instructional beliefs and didactical principles of reading programs. *European Journal of Psychology of Education,* 30(3): 295-312.

Ben-Ari, R. and Kedem-Friedrich, P. (2000) Restructuring heterogeneous classes for cognitive development: Social interactive perspective, *Instructional Science,* 28(2): 153-167.

Bennett, R. (2015) *The effect of math in focus: The Singapore Approach on elementary students' mathematics achievement*. PhD Thesis. Union University US, ProQuest Information & Learning.

Bentham, J., Davies, P. and Galbraith, D. (2015) Using a 'Literacy across the curriculum' intervention using self-regulation, Educational Review, 68, 1, 71-81

Berninger, V., Rutberg, J., Abbott, R., Garcia, N., Anderson-Youngstrom, M., Brooks, A. and Fulton, C. (2006) Tier 1 and Tier 2 early intervention for handwriting and composing. *Journal of School Psychology*, 44(1): 3-30

Bjorn, P. and. Leppanen, P. (2013) Accelerating decoding-related skills in poor readers learning a foreign language: a computer-based intervention. *Educational Psychology,* 33(6): 671-689.

Black, P. (2000) Research and the Development of Educational Assessment, *Oxford Review of Education*, 26 (3&4): 407-419

Black, P. and Wiliam, D. (1998) *Inside the black box: raising standards through classroom assessment,* London: GL Assessment

Blair, C. and Raver, C. (2014) Closing the Achievement Gap through Modification of Neurocognitive and Neuroendocrine Function: Results from a Cluster Randomized Controlled Trial of an Innovative Approach to the Education of Children in Kindergarten. *PLoS ONE* 9 (11)

Blalock, J. T. (2012) The impact of Singapore Math on student knowledge and enjoyment in mathematics. PhD Thesis, Louisiana Tech. University. US, *ProQuest Information & Learning*, 73: 1278-1278

Blatchford, P., Webster, R. and Russell, A. (2012) *Challenging the role and deployment of Teaching Assistants in mainstream schools*, Report to the Esmee Fairbairn Foundation, http://maximisingtas.co.uk/assets/content/edtareport-2.pdf.

Bliss, J., Askew, M. and Macrae, S. (1996) Effective teaching and learning: Scaffolding revisited. *Oxford Review of Education,* 22(1): 37-61

Blok, H., Oostdam, R., Otter, M., and Overmaat, M. (2002) Computer-assisted instruction in support of beginning reading instruction: a review, *Review of Educational Research*, 72, 1, 101-130

Boardman, A., Klinger, J., Buckley, P., Annamma, S. and Lasser, C. (2015) The efficacy of Collaborative Strategic Reading in middle school science and social studies classes. *Reading and Writing,* 28 (9): 1257-1283

Boden, M. and M. Boden (2007) Evolving spelling exercises to suit individual student needs. *Applied Soft Computing,* 7(1): 126-135.

Borman, K. M., Cotner, B., Lee, R., Boydston, T. and Lanehart, R. (2009) *Improving Elementary Science Instruction and Student Achievement: The Impact of a Professional Development Program, Society for Research on Educational Effectiveness.* Paper presented at the annual meeting of the Society for Research on Educational Effectiveness, March 1st-3rd, Crystal City, Virginia, USA

Bottino, R., Ott, M. and Benigno, V. (2009) Digital Mind Games: Experience-Based Reflections on Design and Interface Features Supporting the Development of Reasoning Skills. Proceedings of the 3rd European Conference on Games Based Learning: 53-61.

Bourke, S. (1986) How Smaller Is Better: Some Relationships between Class Size, Teaching Practices, and Student Achievement, *American Educational Research Journal,* 23(4): 558-571

Bowers, P.N., Kirby, J.R. and Deacon, S.H. (2010) The Effects of Morphological Instruction on Literacy Skills: A Systematic Review of the Literature. *Review of Educational Research* 80(2): 144-179.

Brackett, M. Rivers, S., Reyes, M. and Salovey, P. (2012) Enhancing academic performance and social and emotional competence with the RULER feeling words curriculum. *Learning and Individual Differences*, 22(2): 218-224

Bradshaw, C., Zmuda, J, Kellam S. and Ialongo N. (2009) Longitudinal Impact of Two Universal Preventive Interventions in First Grade on Educational Outcomes in High School. *Journal of Educational Psychology*, 101(4): 926-937.

Brooks, G. (2007) *What works for pupils with literacy difficulties? The effectiveness of intervention schemes*, London: DCSF Publications

Brooks, G., Cole, P., Davies, P., Davis, B., Frater, G., Harman, J. and Hutchison, D. (2002) *Keeping Up with the Children*, Evaluation for the Basic Skills Agency by the University of Sheffield and the National Foundation for Educational Research. London: Basic Skills Agency

Brooks, G., Harman, J. and Harman, M. (2003) *Catching Up at Key Stage 3: an evaluation of the Ruth Miskin [RML2] pilot project 2002/2003*, A report to the Department for Education and Skills, Sheffield: University of Sheffield

Brooks, G., Miles, J., Torgerson, C. and Torgerson, D. (2006) Is an intervention using computer software effective in literacy learning? A randomised controlled trial, *Educational Studies,* 32, 2, 133-43

Brown, G. (2004) *The efficacy of question-answering instruction for improving year 5 reading comprehension*, Unpublished PhD dissertation. University of Western Sydney (Sydney, Australia)

Brunstein, J. and Glaser, C. (2011) Testing a Path-Analytic Mediation Model of How Self-Regulated Writing Strategies Improve Fourth Graders' Composition Skills: A Randomized Controlled Trial. *Journal of Educational Psychology*, 103(4): 922-938.

Bryant, D. Bryant. B., Gersten, R., Scammacca, N. and Chavez, M. (2008) Mathematics Intervention for First- and Second-Grade Students With Mathematics Difficulties The Effects of Tier 2 Intervention Delivered as Booster Lessons. *Remedial and Special Education*, 29(1): 20-32.

Bullock, J. (2005) *Effects of the Accelerated Reader on read-ing performance of third, fourth, and fifth-grade students in one western Oregon elementary school*, University of Oregon; 0171 Advisor: Gerald Tindal. DAI, 66 (07A), 56-2529

Burger, K. (2015) Effective early childhood care and education: Successful approaches and didactic strategies for fostering child development. *European Early Childhood Education Research Journal,* 23(5): 743-760.

Burns, M. (2007) Reading at the instructional level with children identified as learning disabled: Potential implications for response-to-intervention. *School Psychology Quarterly,* 22(3): 297-313.

Burns, M.K., Petersen-Brown, S., Haegele, K., Rodriguez, M., Schmitt, B., Cooper, M., Clayton, K., Hutcheson, S., Conner, C., Hosp, J. and VanDerHeyden, A.M. (2016) Meta-Analysis of Academic Interventions Derived From Neuropsychological Data. *School Psychology Quarterly* 31(1): 28-42.

Caggiano, J. A. (2007) *Addressing the learning needs of struggling adolescent readers: The impact of a reading intervention program on students in a middle school setting*. Unpublished EdD dissertation. The College of William and Mary (Virginia)

Callahan, C., Moon, T., Oh, S., Azano, A. and Hailey, E. (2015) What Works in Gifted Education: Documenting the Effects of an Integrated Curricular/Instructional Model for Gifted Students. *American Educational Research Journal,* 52(1): 137-167.

Campbell, J. (2002) *An evaluation of a pilot intervention involving teaching philosophy to upper primary children in two primary schools, using the Philosophy for Children methodology*. PhD thesis. University of Dundee

Campbell, T., Oh, P., Maughn, M. and Zuwallack, R. (2015) A Review of Modeling Pedagogies: Pedagogical Functions, Discursive Acts, and Technology in Modeling Instruction. *Eurasia Journal of Mathematics Science and Technology Education*, 11(1): 159-176.

Campuzano, L., Dynarski, M., Agodini, R., and Rail, K. (2009) Effectiveness of reading and mathematics software products: Findings from two student cohorts. Washington, DC: U.S. Department of Education

Cantrell, S. C., Almasi, J.F., Carter, J.C., Rintamaa, M. and Madden, A. (2010) The Impact of a Strategy-Based Intervention on the Comprehension and Strategy Use of Struggling Adolescent Readers, *Journal of Educational Psychology*, Vol., 102, No. 2, pp. 257-280

Cantrell, S., Fullerton, J., Kane, T. and Staiger, D. (2008) National Board Certification and Teacher Effectiveness: Evidence from a Random Assignment Experiment. NBER Working Paper No. 14608, National Bureau of Economic Research.

Cappella, E., O'Connor, E., McCormick, M., Turbeville, A., Collins, A. and McClowry, S. (2015) Classwide efficacy of INSIGHTS: Observed Teacher Practices and Student Behaviors in Kindergarten and First Grade. *Elementary School Journal,* 116(2): 217-241.

Carlisle, J. F. (2010) Effects of Instruction in Morphological Awareness on Literacy Achievement: An Integrative Review *Reading Research Quarterly* 45(4): 464-487.

Carmon, Y. (2011) Assisting children's reading acquisition by concrete innovated toy-musical-notes technology. Inted2011: 5th International Technology, Education and Development Conference: 6341-6351. (Israel)

Carr, M., Taasoobshirazi, G., Stroud, R. and Royer, J. (2011) Combined fluency and cognitive strategies instruction improves mathematics achievement in early elementary school. *Contemporary Educational Psychology,* 36(4): 323-333.

Carvalho, C., Santos, J., Conboy, J. and Martins, D. (2014) Teachers' Feedback: Exploring Differences in Students' Perception, *Procedia- Social and Behavioural Sciences,* 159, 169-173

Case, L., Speece, D., Silverman, R., Schatschneider, C. Montanaro, E. and Ritchey, K. (2014). Immediate and Long-Term Effects of Tier 2 Reading Instruction for First-Grade Students With a High Probability of Reading Failure. *Journal of Research on Educational Effectiveness* 7(1): 28-53.

Castiglioni-Spalten, M. and Ehri, L. (2003) Phonemic awareness instruction: Contribution of articulatory segmentation to novice beginners' reading and spelling. *Scientific Studies of Reading,* 7(1): 25-52.

Cattle, J. and Howie, D. (2008) An evaluation of a school programme for the development of thinking skills through the CASE@KS1 approach. *International Journal of Science Education*, 30(2): 185-202.

Cena, J., Baker, D., Kame'enui, E., Baker, S., Park, Y and Smolkowski, K. (2013) The impact of a systematic and explicit vocabulary intervention in Spanish with Spanish-speaking English learners in first grade. *Reading and Writing*, 26(8): 1289-1316.

Chambers, B., Slavin, R., Madden, N., Abrami, P., Karanzalis, M. and Gifford, R. (2011) Small-group Computer-assisted Tutoring to Improve Reading Outcomes for Struggling First and Second Graders., *Elementary School Journal,* 111(4): 625-640.

Cheung, A. and Slavin, R. (2012) Effective Reading Programs for Spanish-Dominant English Language Learners (ELLs) in the Elementary Grades: A Synthesis of Research. *Review of Educational Research*, 82(4): 351-395.

Cheung, A. and Slavin, R. (2013) Effects of Educational Technology Applications on Reading Outcomes for Struggling Readers: A Best-Evidence Synthesis. *Reading Research Quarterly*, 48(3): 277-299.

Chiang, T., Yang, S. and Hwang, G-J. (2014) An Augmented Reality-based Mobile Learning System to Improve Students' Learning Achievements and Motivations in Natural Science Inquiry Activities. *Educational Technology & Society*, 17(4): 352-365.

Choi, J.I. (2013) The Effectiveness of Cognitive Scaffolding in an Elementary Mathematics Digital Textbook. *Educational Technology International* 14(1): 75-108.

Chou, P.-N., Chang, C-C. and Lu, P-F. (2015) Prezi versus Power Point: The effects of varied digital presentation tools on students' learning performance. *Computers & Education,* 91: 73-82. (Taiwan)

Clark, C. (2013) *Accelerated Reader and young people's reading. Findings from the National Literacy Trust's 2012 annual literacy survey on reading enjoyment, reading behaviour outside class and reading attitudes*, London: National Literacy Trust, http://www.literacytrust.org.uk/assets/0001/9353/AR_and_young_people_s_reading.pdf

Clarke, B., Doabler, C., Cary, M., Kosty, D., Baker, S., Fien, H. and Smolkowski, K. (2014) Preliminary Evaluation of a Tier 2 Mathematics Intervention for First-Grade Students: Using a Theory of Change to Guide Formative Evaluation Activities. *School Psychology Review*, 43(2): 160-178.

Clements, D. and Sarama, J. (2007) Effects of a preschool mathematics curriculum: Summative research on the Building Blocks project. *Journal for Research in Mathematics Education*, 38(2): 136-163.

Clements, D. and Sarama, J. (2008) Experimental evaluation of the effects of a research-based preschool mathematics curriculum. *American Educational Research Journal*, 45(2): 443-494.

Clements, D., Sarama, J., Spitler, M., Lange, A. and Wolfe, C. (2011) Mathematics Learned by Young Children in an Intervention Based on Learning Trajectories: A LargeScale Cluster Randomized Trial. *Journal for Research in Mathematics Education*, 42 (2): 127–166.

Clements, D.. Sarama, J., Farran, D., Lipsey, M., Hofer, K. and Bilbrey, C. (2011) An Examination of the Building Blocks Math Curriculum: Results of a Longitudinal Scale-Up Study. Paper presented at the Society for Research on Educational Effectiveness. Society for Research on Educational Effectiveness conference.

Codding, R., Chan-Ianetta, L., Palmer, M. and Lukito, G. (2009) Examining a Classwide Application of Cover Copy-Compare with and without goal setting to enhance mathematics fluency. *School Psychology Quarterly*, 24(3):173-185

Codding, R., Shiyko, M., Russo, M., Birch, S., Fanning, E. and Jaspen, D. (2007) Comparing mathematics interventions: Does initial level of fluency predict intervention effectiveness? *Journal of School Psychology,* 45(6): 603-617.

Coe, M., Hanita, M., Nishioka, V., Smiley, R. (2011) *An Investigation of the impact of the 6+1 Trait Writing Model on grade 5 student writing achievement:Final Report*. Washington DC: National Center for Education Evaluation and Regional Assistance, Institute of Education Sciences, US Department of Education

Coe, R., Aloisi, C., Higgins, S. and Major, L.E. (2014) *What makes great teaching? Review of the underpinning research*. London: Sutton Trust.

Cohen, M. and Johnson, H. (2012) Improving the acquisition and retention of science material by fifth grade students through the use of imagery interventions. *Instructional Science,* 40(6): 925-955.

Cohen, P.A., Kulik, J.A., Kulik, C.C. (1982). Educational Outcomes of Tutoring: A Meta-Analysis of Findings. *American Educational Research Journal*, 19(2), 237-248, http://www.dx.doi.org/10.3102/00028312019002237

Coladarci, T. and Gage, N. (1984) Effects of a Minimal Intervention on Teacher Behavior and Student Achievement. *American Educational Research Journal*, 21(3): 539-555.

Coles, J. (2012) *An evaluation of the teaching assistant led Switch-on literacy intervention*, Unpublished MA thesis, University of London Institute of Education

Colom, R., Moriyón, F., Magro, C. and Morilla, E. (2014) The Long-term Impact of Philosophy for Children: A Longitudinal Study (Preliminary Results).*Analytic Teaching and Philosophical Praxis*, *35*, 1

Concordia Online (2016) What is your teaching style? 5 effective teaching methods for your classroom. Posted 5 January 2013. http://education.cu-portland.edu/blog/teaching-strategies/5-types-of-classroom-teaching-styles/

Connor, C., Morrison, F., Fishman, B., Crowe, E., Al Otaiba, S. and Schatschneider, C. (2013) A Longitudinal Cluster-Randomized Controlled Study on the Accumulating Effects of Individualized Literacy Instruction on Students' Reading From First Through Third Grade. *Psychological Science,* 24(8): 1408-1419

Connor, C., Morrison, F., Fishman, B., Giuliani, S., Luck, M., Underwood, P., Bayraktar, A., Crowe, E. and Schatschneider, C. (2011) Testing the Impact of Child Characteristics x Instruction Interactions on Third Graders' Reading Comprehension by Differentiating Literacy Instruction. *Reading Research Quarterly*, 46(3): 189-221.

Connor, C., Piasta, S., Fishman, B., Glasney, S., Schatschneider, C., Crowe, E., Underwood, P. and Morrison, F. (2009) Individualizing Student Instruction Precisely: Effects of Child x Instruction Interactions on First Graders' Literacy Development. *Child Development,* 80(1): 77-100.

Connor, C., Ponitz, C., Phillips, B., Travis, Q., Glasney, S. and Morrison, F. (2010) First graders' literacy and self-regulation gains: The effect of individualizing student instruction. *Journal of School Psychology*, 48(5): 433-455

Cook, L. (2008) *Increasing middle grades math achievement through effective teaching practices.* PhD Thesis. Ann Arbor, Walden University. 3288765: 192.

Core Knowledge Foundation (2000) In Oklahoma City, a rigorous scientific study shows the positive equity effects of Core Knowledge, http://coreknowledge.org/CK/about/research/oklahoma_study_2000.htm, accessed April 24 2009

Cornoldi, C., Carretti, B., Drusi, S., and Tencati, C. (2015) Improving problem solving in primary school students: The effect of a training programme focusing on metacognition and working memory. *British Journal of Educational Psychology*, 85(3): 424-439.

Coughlan, S. (2013) Gove sets out 'core knowledge' curriculum plans. BBC News, Available from: http://www.bbc.co.uk/news/education-21346812 [Accessed 19 November 2015]

Courey, S., Balogh, E., Siker, J. and Paik, J. (2012) Academic music: music instruction to engage third grade students in learning basic fraction concepts. *Educational Studies in Mathematics,* 81(2): 251 278.

Cox, M., Abbott, C., Webb, M., Blakeley, B., Beauchamp, T. and Rhodes, V. (2003) *ICT and pedagogy, A review of the research literature,* ICT in Schools Research and Evaluation Series No. 18, Coventry/London: Becta/DfES, http://www.becta.org.uk/page_documents/research/ict_pedagogy_summary.pdf, accessed 10/2/05

Creemers, B. (1994) The effective classroom. London: Cassell.

Cunningham, M., Kerr, K., McEune, R., Smith, P. and Harris, S. (2004) *Laptops for Teachers, an Evaluation of the First Year of the Initiative,,* ICT in Schools Research and Evaluation Series No. 19. Coventry/London: Becta/DfES, http://www.becta.org.uk/page_documents/research/lft_evaluation.pdf, accessed 18/12/06

Darroch, B. (2009) Exemplary project: Singapore math: Action research on a curriculum change, student achievement, and teacher efficacy. Practical action research: A collection of articles (2nd ed.) R. A. Schmuck and R. A. Schmuck. Thousand Oaks, CA, US, Corwin Press: 96-96.

Dartnow, A., Borman, G. and Springfield, S. (2000) School reform through a highly specified curriculum: implementation and effects of the Core Knowledge Sequence, *The Elementary School Journal*, 101(2) 167-192.

De Corte, E., Verschaffel, L. and Van De Ven, A. (2001) Improving text comprehension strategies in upper primary school children: a design experiment, *British Journal of Educational Psychology*, Vol. 71, No.4, pp. 531-559

Decristan, J., Klieme, E., Kunter, M., Hochweber, J., Buttner, G., Fauth, B., Hondrich, A., Rieser, S., Hertel, S. and Hardy, I. (2015) Embedded Formative Assessment and Classroom Process Quality: How Do They Interact in Promoting Science Understanding? *American Educational Research Journal*, 52(6): 1133-1159.

Dennis, M., Sorrells, A. and Falcomata, T. (2016) Effects of Two Interventions on Solving Basic Fact Problems by Second Graders With Mathematics Learning Disabilities. *Learning Disability Quarterly*, 39(2): 95-112.

Department for Education and Employment (2000) Research into teacher effectiveness: A model of teacher effectiveness. Research Report No. 216 by Hay McBer. London: DfEE

DES (1988) *National Curriculum: Task Group on Assessment and Testing: A Report,* London: DES/Welsh Office.

Diamond, B., Maerten-Rivera, J., Rohrer, R. and Lee, O. (2014) Effectiveness of a Curricular an Professional Development Intervention at Improving Elementary Teachers' Science Content Knowledge and Student Achievement Outcomes: Year 1 Results. *Journal of Research in Science Teaching,* 51(5): 635-658.

Dina, D.G., Vicenza, C., Tania, D.M., Rosita, C.M., Daniela, F., Rosella, G. and Pierpaola, V. (2014). "The silent reading supported by adaptive learning technology: Influence in the children outcomes." Computers in Human Behavior.

Dion, E., Roux, C., Landry, D., Fuchs, D., Wehby, J. and Dupere, V. (2011) Improving Attention and Preventing Reading Difficulties among Low-Income First-Graders: A Randomized Study. *Prevention Science,* 12(1): 70-79.

Diperna, J., Lei, P., Bellinger, J. and Cheng, W. (2016) Effects of a universal positive classroom behaviour programme on student learning. *Psychology in the Schools,* 53(2): 189-203.

Doabler, C., Baker, S., Kosty, D. and Fien, H. (2015) Examining the association between explicit mathematics instruction and student mathematics achievement. *The Elementary School Journal,* 115(3): 304-333

Doabler, C., Nelson-Walker, N., Kosty, D., Baker, S., Smolkowski, K. and Fien, H. (2013) Explicit Instructional Interactions: Observed Stability and Predictive Validity during Early Literacy and Beginning Mathematics Instruction, Paper presented at the Fall 2013 Conference of the Society for Research on Educational Effectiveness, Washington, DC.

Doherr, E. (2000) *The demonstration of cognitive abilities central to cognitive behavioural therapy in young people: examining the influence of age and teaching method on degree of ability*, PhD thesis: University of East Anglia

Donker, A., de Boer, H., Kostons, D., Dignath van Ewijk, C. and van der Werf, M. (2014) Effectiveness of learning strategy instruction on academic performance: A meta-analysis. *Educational Research Review,* 11: 1-26.

Dorsett, R., Rienzo, C. and Rolfe, H. (2014) *Mind the gap: Evaluation report and executive summary.* London: Education Endowment Foundation.

Duke, J. (2011) *The Accelerated Reader Program in conjunction with best-practice reading instruction: The effects on elementary-school reading scores*. PhD. Capella University, USA.

Durkin, K. and Rittle-Johnson, B. (2012) The effectiveness of using incorrect examples to support learning about decimal magnitude. *Learning and Instruction*, 22(3): 206-214.

Dynarski, M, Agodini, R., Heaviside, S., Novak, T., Carey, N., Campuzano, L., Means, B., Murphy, R., Penuel, W., Javitz, H., Emery, D. and Sussex, W. (2007) Effectiveness of reading and mathematics software products: Findings from the first student cohort. Washington, DC: Institute of Education Sciences

Dyson, N., Jordan, N. and Glutting, J. (2013) A number sense intervention for low-income kindergartners at risk for mathematics difficulties. *Journal of Learning Disabilities,* 46(2): 166. (US)

Dyson, N., Jordan, N., Beliakoff, A. and Hassinger-Das, B. (2015) A Kindergarten Number-Sense Intervention With Contrasting Practice Conditions for Low-Achieving Children. *Journal for Research in Mathematics Education*, 46(3): 331-370

Ecalle, J., Kleinsz, N. and Magnan, A. (2013) Computer-assisted learning in young poor readers: The effect of grapho-syllabic training on the development of word reading and reading comprehension. *Computers in Human Behavior,* 29(4): 1368-1376.

Ecalle, J., Magnan, A. and Calmus, C. (2009) Lasting effects on literacy skills with a computer-assisted learning using syllabic units in low-progress readers. *Computers & Education*, 52(3): 554-561. (France)

Economist (2016) Teaching the Teachers, The Economist, 11/6/16. http://www.economist.com/news/briefing/21700385-great-teaching-has-long-been-seen-innate-skill-reformers-are-showing-best

Education Endowment Foundation (2015) *Education Endowment Foundation pupil premium toolkit*, http://educationendowmentfoundation.org.uk/uploads/pdf/Feedback_Toolkit_references.pdf

Ehri, L., Nunes, S., Stahl, S. and Willows, D. (2001) Systematic phonics instruction helps students learn to read: Evidence from the National Reading Panel's meta-analysis, *Review of Educational Research*, 71, 3, 393-447

Elisana, P., Eleni, T., Vasilis, G., Vasiliki, Z, Konstantina, K. (2011). "MUSIC AND MOVEMENT IN COMBINATION WITH MATHEMATICS: A NEW LEARNING PERSPECTIVE FOR FIRST GRADERS IN THE PRIMARY SCHOOL." 2011 4th International Conference of Education, Research and Innovation (Iceri): 4929-4934.

Ellis, V. (2013) An exploration of the impact of reform-based science instruction on second graders' academic achievement. Ann Arbor, The Florida State University. 3596492: 119.

Ennis, R. and Jolivette, K. (2014) Existing Research and Future Directions for Self-Regulated Strategy Development With Students With and At Risk for Emotional and Behavioral Disorders. *Journal of Special Education*, 48(1): 32-45.

Ercan, O. (2014) The effects of multimedia learning material on students' academic achievement and attitudes towards science courses. *Journal of Baltic Science Education,* 13(5): 608-621.

Facemire, N. (2000) *The effect of the accelerated reader on the reading comprehension of third graders*, MA dissertation. Salem-Teikyo University

Faggella-Luby, M. and Wardwell, M. (2011) RTI in a middle school: findings and practical implications of a tier 2 reading comprehension study. *Learning Disability Quarterly*, 34(1): 35-49

Fair, F., Haas, L., Gardosik, C., Johnson, D. , Price, D. and Leipnik, O. (2015) Socrates in the schools from Scotland to Texas: Replicating a study on the effects of a Philosophy for Children program. *Journal of Philosophy in Schools*, 2, 1

Fehr, C., Davison, M., Graves, M., Sales, G., Seipel, B. and Sekhran-Sharma (2012) The effects of individualized, online vocabulary instruction on picture vocabulary scores: an efficacy study. *Computer Assisted Language Learning*, 25(1): 87-102.

Fien, H., Baker, S., Santoro, L., and Chard, D. (2010) Promoting vocabulary development and knowledge of narrative texts through read aloud in first grade class-rooms. Paper presented at the annual meeting of the Society for Scientific Study of Reading, Berlin, Germany.

Fien, H., Santoro, L., Baker, S., Park, Y., Chard, D., Williams, S. and Haria, P. (2011) Enhancing Teacher Read Alouds With Small-Group Vocabulary Instruction for Students With Low Vocabulary in First Grade Classrooms. *School Psychology Review*, 40(2): 307-318.

Fößl, T., Ebner, M., Schön, S. and Holzinger, A. (2016) A Field Study of a Video Supported Seamless Learning-Setting with Elementary Learners. *Journal of Educational Technology & Society*, 19(1): 321-336.

Foster, I. (2001) The principal's role as instructional leader: Assessing academic performance among African -American elementary -school students in a higher order thinking skills program. Ann Arbor, Northern Illinois University. 3023684: 154.

Fuchs D, Fuchs L, Thompson A, Al Otaiba S, Yen L, Yang N, Braun M, O'Connor R. (2002b) Exploring the importance of reading programs for kindergartners with disabilities in mainstream classrooms. *Exceptional Children*. 68: 295-311.

Fuchs, D., Fuchs, L., Mathes, P. and Simmons, D. (1997) Peer-Assisted Learning Strategies: making classrooms more responsive to diversity. *American Educational Research Journal,* 34(1): 174-206

Fuchs, L. and Fuchs, D. (1986) Effects of Systematic Formative Evaluation: A Meta-Analysis, *Exceptional Children*, 53: 199-208.

Fuchs, L. S., Fuchs, D. and Karns, K. (2001) Enhancing kindergartners' mathematical development: Effects of peer-assisted learning strategies *Elementary School Journal* 101(5): 495-510.

Fuchs, L., Fuchs, D., Yazdian, L. and Powell, S. (2002) Enhancing first-grade children's mathematical development with Peer-Assisted Learning Strategies. *School Psychology Review*, 31(4): 569-583

Fuchs, L., Malone, A., Schumacher, R., Namkung, J., Hamlett, C., Jordan, N., Siegler, R., Gersten, R. and Changas, P. (2016) Supported Self-Explaining During Fraction Intervention. *Journal of Educational Psychology*, 108(4): 493-508.

Fuchs, L., Powell, S., Cirino, P., Schumacher, R., Marrin, S., Hamlett, C., Fuchs, D., Compton, D. and Changas, P. (2014) Does Calculation or Word-Problem Instruction Provide a Stronger Route to Prealgebraic Knowledge? *Journal of Educational Psychology*, 106(4): 990-1006.

Fung, D. (2014) Promoting critical thinking through effective group work: A teaching intervention for Hong Kong primary school students. *International Journal of Educational Research*, 66: 45-62. (Hong Kong)

Fyfe, E., DeCaro, M. and Rittle-Johnson, B. (2014) An alternative time for telling: When conceptual instruction prior to problem solving improves mathematical knowledge. *British Journal of Educational Psychology*, 84(3): 502-519.

Gage, N. (1985) Hard Gains in Soft Sciences: The Case of Pedagogy. Bloomington: Phi Delta Kappa.

Gallagher, H. A., Woodworth, K, McCaffrey, T., Park, C.J., Wang, H, (2014). Impact Evaluation of National Writing Project Professional Development Program, Society for Research on Educational Effectiveness.

Galton, M., et al. (1999). "Changes in Patterns of Teacher Interaction in Primary Classrooms: 1976-96." British Educational Research Journal 25(1): 23-37.

Galuschka, K., Ise, E., Krick, K. and Schulte-Körne, G. (2014) Effectiveness of treatment approaches for children and adolescents with reading disabilities: a meta-analysis of randomized controlled trials, *PLoS One*, 26, 9, doi: 10.1371/journal.pone.0089900

Gamo, S., Sander, E. and Richard, J.F. (2010). "Transfer of strategy use by semantic recoding in arithmetic problem solving." Learning and Instruction 20(5): 400-410.

Garelick, B. (2006) Miracle Math: A Successful Program from Singapore Tests the Limits of School Reform in the Suburbs. *Education Next,* 6(4): 38-45.

Gelzheiser, L.M., Scanlon, D., Vellutino, F., Hallgren-Flynn, L and Schatschneider, C. (2011) Effects of the interactive strategies approach-extended: A Responsive and Comprehensive Intervention for Intermediate-Grade Struggling Readers. *Elementary School Journal* 112(2): 280-306.

Gerber, S.B., Finn, J.D., Chilles, C.M. and Byd-Zaharias, J. (2001) Teacher aides and students' academic achievement. *Educational Evaluation and Policy Analysis* 23(2): 123-143.

Gerleman, S. L. (1987) An observational study of small-group instruction in fourth-grade mathematics classrooms. *Elementary School Journal*, 88(1): 3-28.

Gersten, R., Chard, D., Jayanthi, M., Baker, S., Morphy, P. and Flojo, J. (2009) Mathematics instruction for students with learning disabilities: A meta-analysis of instructional components. *Review of Educational Research*, 79, 1202–1242. doi:10.3102/0034654309334431

Gersten, R., Dimino, J., Jayanthi, M., Newman-Gonchar, N., Taylor, M. (2013) Impact of the Teacher Study Group Professional Development Program on Student Vocabulary and Observed Teaching Practice: A Replication in First Grade Classrooms, SREE Spring 2013 Conference, https://www.sree.org/conferences/2013s/program/downloads/abstracts/878_2.pdf

Gilbert, J.K., Compton, D.L., Fuchs, D., Fuch, L.S., Bouton, B., Barquero, L.A. and Cho, E. (2013) Efficacy of a First-Grade Responsiveness-to-Intervention

Prevention Model for Struggling Readers. *Reading Research Quarterly* 48(2): 135-154.

Glaser, C. and Brunstein, J.C. (2007) Improving fourth-grade students' composition skills: Effects of strategy instruction and self-regulation procedures. *Journal of Educational Psychology* 99(2): 297-310.

Glenberg, A., Willford, J, Gibson. B., Goldberg, A. and Zhu, X. (2012) Improving Reading to Improve Math. *Scientific Studies of Reading,* 16(4): 316-340.

Gollwitzer, A., Oettingen, G., Kirby, T.A., Duckworth, A.L. and Mayer, D. (2011). "Mental contrasting facilitates academic performance in school children." Motivation and Emotion 35(4): 403-412.

Good, R., Simmons, D., and Smith, S. (1998), "Effective academic interventions in the United States: Evaluating and enhancing the acquisition of early reading skills." *School Psychology Review*, vol. 27, pp. 45-56.

Good, T. L., Grouws, D. A., and Ebmeier, H. (1983) *Active mathematics teaching*. New York: Longman.

Goodman, G. (1999) *The Reading Renaissance/Accelerated Reader Program*, Pinal County school-to-work evaluation report, Tucson, AZ: Creative Research, Inc. (ERIC Document Reproduction Service No. ED427299)

Goodwin, A. P. and S. Ahn (2013) A Meta-Analysis of Morphological Interventions in English: Effects on Literacy Outcomes for School-Age Children. *Scientific Studies of Reading* 17(4): 257-285.

Goolsbee, A. and Guryan, J. (2005) The impact of internet subsidies for public schools, *Review of Economics and Statistics,* 88, 2, 36-347

Gorard, S. (2002) Political control: A way forward for educational research?, *British Journal of Educational Studies*, 50 (3): 378-389

Gorard, S. (2013) *Research Design: Robust approaches for the social sciences*, London: SAGE

Gorard, S. (2015) A proposal for judging the trustworthiness of research findings, ResearchED January 2015, http://www.workingoutwhatworks.com/en-GB/Magazine/2015/1/Trustworthiness_of_research

Gorard, S. (2015) Rethinking "quantitative" methods and the development of new researchers, *Review of Education*, 3, 1, 72-96, doi: 10.1002/rev3.3041

Gorard, S. and Gorard, J. (2015) What to do instead of significance testing? Calculating the 'number of counterfactual cases needed to disturb a finding', *International Journal of Social Research Methodology*, 19, 4, 481-489

Gorard, S. and See BH (2013) *Do parental involvement interventions increase attainment? A review of the evidence*, London, The Nuffield Foundation,http://www.nuffieldfoundation.org/sites/default/files/files/Do_parental_involvement_interventions_increase_attainment1.pdf

Gorard, S., See, BH and Davies, P. (2012) *The impact of attitudes and aspirations on educational attainment and participation*, York: Joseph Rowntree Foundation, 103 pages, http://www.jrf.org.uk/publications/aspirations-educational-attainment-participation

Gorard, S., Siddiqui, N. and B.H. See (2015a) Philosophy for Children: Evaluation report and executive summary. London: Education Endowment Foundation

Gorard, S., Siddiqui, N. and See, B.H. (2015b) An evaluation of the 'Switch-on-Reading' literacy catch-up programme. *British Educational Research Journal,* 41(4): 596-612.

Gorard, S., Siddiqui, N. and See, B.H. (2016) An evaluation of Fresh Start as a catch-up intervention: a trial conducted by teachers. *Educational Studies*, 42(1): 98-113

Graham, S., Harris, K.R. and Santangelo, T. (2015) Research-Based Writing Practices and the Common Core Meta-analysis and Meta-synthesis. *Elementary School Journal* 115(4): 498-522.

Graham, S., McKeown, D. Kiuhara, S. and Harris, K.R. (2012) A Meta-Analysis of Writing Instruction for Students in the Elementary Grades. *Journal of Educational Psychology* 104(4): 879-896.

Graves, A., Brandon, R., Duesbery, L. McIntosh, A. and Pyle, N. (2011). The Effects of Tier 2 Literacy Instruction in Sixth Grade: Toward the Development of a Response-to-Intervention Model in Middle School, *Learning Disability Quarterly*, 34: 1, 73-86 (full paper not available, analysis based on abstracts).

Greek-speaking children: Can training of phonological memory contribute to reading development? *European Journal of Psychology of Education*, 17 (1): 63-73

Greenfader, C. M., Brouillette, L and Farkas, G. (2015). "Effect of a Performing Arts Program on the Oral Language Skills of Young English Learners." Reading Research Quarterly 50(2): 185-203.

Greenleaf, C. and Petrosino, A. (2008) Response to Slavin, Cheung, Groff and Lake, *Reading Research Quarterly*, 43, 4, 349-354

Griffin, C. C. and A. K. Jitendra (2009). "Word Problem-Solving Instruction in Inclusive Third-Grade Mathematics Classrooms." Journal of Educational Research 102(3): 187-201.

Griggs, J., Speight, S. and Javiera, C.F. (2016) *Ashford Teaching Alliance Research Champion: Evaluation report and executive summary*. London: Education Endowment Foundation.

Guthrie, J.T., McRae, A., Coddington, C.S. Lutz Klauda, S., Wigfield, A. and Barbosa, P. (2009) Impacts of comprehensive reading instruction on diverse outcomes oflLow- and high-achieving readers, *Journal of Learning Disabilities*, Vol. 42, No. 3, pp. 195-214

Hairrell, A., Rupley, W.H., Edmonds, M., Larsen, R., Simmons, D., Wilson, V., Byrns, G. and Vaughn, S. (2011). "Examining the Impact of Teacher Quality on Fourth-Grade Students' Comprehension and Content-Area Achievement." Reading & Writing Quarterly 27(3): 239-260.

Hanley, P., Slavin, R. and Elliott, L. (2015) *Thinking, doing and talking science. Evaluation report and summary*. London: Education Endowment Foundation.

Hardiman, M., Rinne, L. and Yarmolinskaya, J. (2014). "The Effects of Arts Integration on Long-Term Retention of Academic Content." Mind, Brain, and Education 8(3): 144-148.

Hardman, F., Smith, F. and Wall, K. (2003). "'Interactive Whole Class Teaching' in the National Literacy Strategy." *Cambridge Journal of Education* 33(2): 197-215

Harn, B.A, Chard, D.J., Biancarosa, G. and Kameènui, E.J. (2011) Coordinating instructional supports to accelerate at-risk first-grade readers' performance: An Essential Mechanism for Effective RTI. *Elementary School Journal* 112(2): 332-355.

Harris, R, and Ratcliffe, M. (2005) Socio-scientific issues and the quality of exploratory talk –what can be learned from schools involved in a 'collapsed day'project? *The Curriculum Journal*, 16(4): 439-453.

Hastie, P.A., Rudisill, M.E. and Wadsworth, D.D. (2013). "Providing students with voice and choice: lessons from intervention research on autonomy-supportive climates in physical education." Sport Education and Society 18(1): 38-56.

Hasty, E. J. (2010). The effects of a high quality teaching professional development program on fourth grade student achievement. Ann Arbor, Walden University. 3413603: 207.

Hattie, J, and Timperley, H. (2007) The power of feedback, *Review of Educational Research*, 77 (1): 81-112

Hattie, J. (1992) What works in Special Education Presentation to the Special Education Conference, May, 1992, http://www.education.auckland.ac.nz/webdav/site/education/shared/hattie/docs/special-education.pdf

Haywood, S., Griggs, J., Lloyd, C., Morris, S., Kiss, Z. and Skipp, A. (2015) Act, Sing and Play: Evaluation report and executive summary. London: Education Endowment Foundation

Hazelton, M. and Brearley, D. (2008) Singapore Math: Challenging and Relevant Curriculum for the Gifted Learner. *Understanding Our Gifted*, 21(1): 10-12.

Hearn, E. S. (2014). Investigation of differences in star reading scores for second- and third-grade students who received differentiated reading instruction. Ann Arbor, Liberty University. 3631480: 127.

Heller. J., Daehler, K., Wong, N., Shinohara, M. and Matric, L. (2012) Differential effects of three professional development models on teacher knowledge and student achievement in elementary science, *Journal of Research in Science Teaching*, 49(3): 333-362

Hiebert, J. and Wearne, D. (1993) Instructional Tasks, Classroom Discourse, and Students' Learning in Second-Grade Arithmetic. *American Educational Research Journal*, 30(2): 393-425.

Hier, B. O. and Ecker,t,T.L.(2014) Evaluating Elementary-Aged Students' Abilities to Generalize and Maintain Fluency Gains of a Performance Feedback Writing Intervention. *School Psychology Quarterly* 29(4): 488-502.

Hirashima, T., Yokoyama, T., Okamoto, M. and Takeuchi, A. (2007). Learning by Problem-Posing as Sentence-Integration and Experimental Use. Artificial Intelligence in Education. R. Luckin, K. R. Koedinger and J. Greer. 158: 254-261.

Hirsch, D. (2007) *Chicken and Egg: child poverty and educational inequalities,* London: Campaign to End Child Poverty, http://www.endchildpoverty.org.uk/index.html, accessed 14/9/07

Hirsch, E. (1987) *Cultural literacy: what every American needs to know*, New York: Vintage

Holliman, A.J. and Hurry, J. (2013) The effects of Reading Recovery on children's literacy progress and special educational needs status: a three-year follow-up study. *Educational Psychology* 33(6): 719-733.

Hong, Y. (2012). Teacher matters: Re-examining the effects of grade-3 test-based retention policy. Ann Arbor, University of Toronto (Canada). NR97346: 222.

Hopfenbeck, T. and Stobart, G. (2015) Large scale implementation of assessment for learning, *Assessment in Education*, 22, (1):1-2

Horsfall, S. and Santa, C. (1994) *Project CRISS: Validation report for the program effectiveness panel*. Unpublished manuscript. In WWC (2010) *Project CRISS® (CReating Independence through Student-owned Strategies).* What Works Clearinghouse Intervention Report. Washington: US Department of Education, Institute of Education Sciences

House of Commons Education and Skills Committee (2005) *Teaching Children to Read: Eighth report of session 2004-05:* http://www.publications.parliament.uk/pa/cm200405/cmselect/cmeduski/121/121.pdf

Houtveen, T. and W. van de Grift (2012). "Improving Reading Achievements of Struggling Learners." School Effectiveness and School Improvement 23(1): 71-93.

Huang, H.-M. E. and K. G. Witz (2011). "Developing children's conceptual understanding of area measurement A curriculum and teaching experiment." Learning and Instruction 21(1): 1-13.

IAPC (2002) IAPC research: experimentation and qualitative information, in Trickey, S. and Topping, K.J. (2004) Philosophy for children: a systematic review, *Research Papers in Education*, 19, 3, 365-380

Integrated Social-Emotional Learning and Literacy Intervention: Impacts After 1 School Year, *Journal of Consulting and Clinical Psychology*, 78 (6): 829-842

Interactive Inc. (2002) *An efficacy study of READ 180, a print and electronic adaptive intervention program: Grades 4 and above*. New York, NY: Scholastic Inc. Evaluated in WWC (2009) *READ 180*. What Works Clearinghouse Intervention Report. Washington: US Department of Education, Institute of Education Sciences

Iverson, S. and Tunmer, W. (1993) Phonological processing skills and the Reading Recovery program, *Journal of Educational Psychology*, 85, 1, 112-126, Updated December 2015, What Works Clearinghouse.

Jaciw, A., Hegseth, W., Lin, L., Toby, M., Newman, D., Ma, B.and Zacamy, J. (2016) Assessing Impacts of Math in Focus, a Singapore Math Program, *Journal of Research on Educational Effectiveness,* DOI: 10.1080/19345747.2016.1164777

James-Burdumy, S., Mansfield, W., Deke, J., Carey, N., Lugo-Gil, J., Hershey, A., Douglas, A., Gersten, R., Newman-Gouchar, R., Dimino, J. and Faddis, B. (2009) *Effectiveness of selected supplemental reading comprehension interventions: impacts on a first cohort of fifth-grade students* (NCEE 2009-4032). Washington, DC: National Center for Educational Evaluation and Regional Assistance, Institute of Education Sciences, U.S. Department of Education

Jerrim, J. and Vignoles, A. (2015) The causal effect of East Asian 'Mastery' methods of English children's mathematics. Department of Quantitative Social Science Working Paper No. 15-05.

Jimenez, J.E. Rodriguez, C., Crespo, P., Gonzalez, D., Artiles, C. and Alfonso, M. (2010) Implementation of Response to Intervention (RtI) Model in Spain: An example of a collaboration between Canarian universities and the department of education of the Canary Islands. *Psicothema*, 22(4): 935-942

Johnson, R. and Howard, C. (2003) The effects of the accelerated reader program on the reading comprehension of pupils in grades 3, 4, and 5,*The Reading Matrix*, Vol. 3, No. 3, pp. p. 87-96

Johnston, R. , McGeown, S., and Watson, J. (2012) Long-term effects of synthetic versus analytic phonics teaching on the reading and spelling ability of 10 year old boys and girls, *Reading and Writing*, 25, 6, 1365-1384

Johnston, R. and Watson, J. (2004) Accelerating the development of reading, spelling and phonemic awareness skills in initial readers, *Reading and Writing: An Interdisciplinary Journal*, 17, 4, 327-57

Jones, S., Brown, J., Hoglund, W. and Aber, J. (2010) A School-Randomized Clinical Trial of an

Jonsson, A., Lundahl, C.and Holmgren, A. (2015) Evaluating a large-scale implementation of Assessment for Learning in Sweden, *Assessment in Education*, 22, 1, 104-121

Joseph, L. M. and Eveleigh, E.L. (2011) A Review of the Effects of Self-Monitoring on Reading Performance of Students With Disabilities. *Journal of Special Education* 45(1): 43-53.

Jun, S.W., Ramirez, G., & Cumming, A. (2010). Tutoring Adolescents in Literacy: A Meta-Analysis. *Journal of Education*, 45(2) 219-238. http://mje.mcgill.ca/article/view/4770/6491

Kamps, D., Abbott, M., Greenwood, C., Wills, H., Veerkamp, M. and Kaufman, J. (2008) Effects of Small Group Reading Instruction and Curriculum Differences for Students Most at Risk in Kindergarten Two-Year Results for Secondary- and Tertiary-Level Interventions, *Journal of Learning Disabilities,* 41 (2): 101-114

Karpicke, J., Blunt, J., Smith, M. and Karpicke, S. (2014) Retrieval-based learning: The need for guided retrieval in elementary school children. *Journal of Applied Research in Memory and Cognition,* 3(3): 198-206.

Keehn, S. (2003). "The effect of instruction and practice through readers theatre on young readers' oral reading fluency." Reading Research and Instruction 42(4): 40-61.

Kelly, P., Gomez-Bellenge, F-X and Chen, J. (2008) Learner outcomes for English language learner low readers in an early intervention. *Tesol Quarterly* 42(2): 235-260.

Kerins, M., Trotter, D. and Schoenbrodt, L. (2010) Effects of a Tier 2 intervention on literacy measures: Lessons learned, *Child Language Teaching & Therapy*, 26 (3): 287-302

Khan, M. and Gorard, S. (2012) A randomised controlled trial of the use of a piece of commercial software for the acquisition of reading skills, *Educational Review*, 64, 1, 21-36

Khodami, N. and M. Hariri (2013) Comparing the Efficacy of Planning Training with Metacognitive Training on Improving the Educational Performance of the Iranian Elementary d-graders With Math Learning Disability. 3rd World Conference on Psychology, Counseling and Guidance, Wcpcg-2012. H. Uzunboylu and M. Demirok. 84: 24-28.

Kim, J., Samson, J., Fitzgerald, R. and Hartry, A. (2010) A randomized experiment of a mixed-methods literacy intervention for struggling readers in grades 4-6: effects on word reading efficiency, reading comprehension and vocabulary, and oral reading fluency, *Reading and Writing: An Interdisciplinary Journal, 23* (1): 1109-1129.

Kim, K., VanTassel-Baska, J., Bracken, B., Feng, A., Stambaugh, T. and Bland, L. (2012) Project Clarion: Three Years of Science Instruction in Title I Schools among K-Third Grade Students, *Research in Science Education,* 42 (5): 813-829

Kim, P. (2006) Effects of 3D virtual reality of plate tectonics on fifth grade students' achievement and attitude toward science, *Interactive Learning Environments*, 14 (1): 25-34

Kim, W. (2012) The Effects of Self-Regulation on Science Vocabulary Acquisition of English Language Learners With Learning Difficulties, *Remedial and Special Education,* 34 (4): 225-236

King, B., and Kasim, A. (2015) *Evaluation of Rapid Phonics*, Education Endowment Foundation: London, https://educationendowmentfoundation.org.uk/uploads/pdf/Rapid_Phonics_(Final).pdf

Kini, T. and Podolsky, A. (2016) Does Teaching Experience Increase Teacher Effectiveness? A Review of the Research, Learning Policy Institute, https://learningpolicyinstitute.org/wp-content/uploads/2016/06/Teaching_Experience_Report_June_2016.pdf

Klinger, J., Vaughn, S., Arguelles, M. and Hughes, S. (2004) Collaborative Strategic Reading: Real World Lessons From Classroom Teachers. *Remedial and Special Education*, 25(53): 291-302

Klingner, J., Vaughn, S. and Schumm, J. (1998) Collaborative strategic reading during social studies in heterogeneous fourth-grade classrooms. *The Elementary School Journal,* 99(1): 3-20

Kluger, A., and DeNisi, A. (1998) Feedback interventions: Towards the understanding of a double-edge sword. *Current Directions in Psychological Science,* 7: 67–72

Koontz, W. F. (1961) A study of achievement as a function of homogeneous grouping. *Journal of Experimental Education,* 30(2): 249-253.

Krashen, S. (2007) Accelerated Reader: Once again, evidence still lacking. *Knowledge Quest 36 September/October*, Available at: http://www.ala.org/aasl/aaslpubsandjournals/knowledgequest/kqwebarchives/v36/361/361krashen

Kukkonen, J., Karkkainen, S., Dillon, P. and Keinonen, T. (2014) The Effects of Scaffolded Simulation Based Inquiry Learning on Fifth-Graders' Representations of the Greenhouse Effect, *International Journal of Science Education,* 36 (3): 406-424

Lane, K., Harris, K., Graham, S., Driscoll, S., Sandmel, K., Morphy, P., Hebert, M., House, E. and Schatschneider, C. (2011) Self-Regulated Strategy Development at Tier 2 for Second-Grade Students With Writing and Behavioral Difficulties: A Randomized Controlled Trial, *Journal of Research on Educational Effectiveness*, 4 (4): 322-353

Lanes, D., Perkins, D., Whatmuff, T., Tarokh, H. and Vincent, R. (2005) *A survey of Leicester City Schools using the RML1 and RML2 literacy programme*, Leicester: Leicester City LEA (mimeograph)

Lang, L., Schoen, R., LaVenia, M., Oberlin, M. (2014) Mathematics Formative Assessment System--Common Core State Standards: A Randomized Field

Trial in Kindergarten and First Grade, Society for Research on Educational Effectiveness. SREE Spring Conference, 6th-8th March 2014, Washington D.C. Available from: http://files.eric.ed.gov/fulltext/ED562773.pdf [Accessed 20th June 2016]

Larrain, A., Howe, C., Cerda, J. (2014) Argumentation in whole-class teaching and science learning. Psykhe: *Revista de la Escuela de Psicología*, 23(2): 1-15.

Lee, E. and Moore, P. (2004) Helping struggling readers comprehend information texts, Paper presented at the International Association of School Librarianship conference, June 2004, Dublin, Ireland.

Lee, O., Buxton, C., Lewis, S. and LeRoy, K. (2006) Science inquiry and student diversity: Enhanced abilities and continuing difficulties after an instructional intervention, *Journal of Research in Science Teaching*, 43 (7): 607-636

Lei, J., and Zhao, Y. (2005) Technology uses and pupil achievement: A longitudinal study, *Computers and Education*, 49, pp. 284–296

Leroux, A., Vaughn, S., Roberts, G. and Fletcher, J. (2011) *Findings from a Three-Year Treatment within a Response to Intervention Framework for Students in Grades 6 with Reading Difficulties*, Paper presented at the Society for Research on Educational Effectiveness Conference, (no details about place and date of conference) http://www.eric.ed.gov/PDFS/ED518866.pdf.

Lesaux, N. and Siegel, L. (2003) The development of reading in children who speak English as a second language, *Developmental Psychology,* 39 (6): 1005-1019.

Li, Q. and Ma, X. (2010) A meta-analysis of the effects of computer technology on school students' mathematics learning. *Educational Psychology Review*, 22, 215–243

Linares, L., Rosbruch, N., Stern, M., Edwards, M., Walker, G., Abikoff, H. and Alvir, J. (2005) Developing cognitive-social-emotional competencies to enhance academic learning, *Psychology in the Schools,* 42 (4): 405-417

Lipko-Speed, A., Dunlosky, J. and Rawson, K. (2014) Does testing with feedback help grade-school children learn key concepts in science? *Journal of Applied Research in Memory and Cognition*, 3 (3): 171-176

Lipman, M., Sharp, A. and Oscanyon, F. (1980) *Philosophy in the classroom: Appendix B*, Philadelphia: Temple University Press

Lipowski, S., Pyc, M., Dunlosky, P. and Rawson, K. (2014) Science achievement of English language learners in urban elementary schools: Results of a first-year professional development intervention, *Journal of Research in Science Teaching*, 45 (1): 31-52

Lloyd, C., Morris, S., Edovald, T., Skipp, A., Kiss, Z., & Haywood, S. (2015) *Durham Shared Maths Project: Evaluation report and executive summary*. London: Education Endowment Foundation

Lorch, R., Lorch, E., Freer, B., Dunlap, E., Hodell, E. and Calderhead, W. (2014) Using Valid and Invalid Experimental Designs to Teach the Control of Variables Strategy in Higher and Lower Achieving Classrooms, *Journal of Educational Psychology,* 106 (1): 18-35

Losinski, M., Cuenca-Carlino, Y., Zablocki, M. and Teagarden, J. (2014) Examining the Efficacy of Self Regulated Strategy Development for Students with Emotional or Behavioral Disorders: A Meta-Analysis, *Behavioural Disorders,* 40 (1): 52-67

Lubliner, S. and Smetana, L. (2005) The effects of comprehensive vocabulary instruction on title I students' metacognitive word-learning skills and reading comprehension, *Journal of Literacy Researc*h, 37 (2): 163-200

Lysakowski, R., and Walberg, H. (1982) Instructional effects of cues, participation, and corrective feedback: A quantitative synthesis. *American Educational Research Journal*, 19: 559–578

Lysenko, L. and Abrami, P. (2014) Promoting reading comprehension with the use of technology, *Computers & Education*, 75: 162-172

Macedo-Rouet, M., Braasch, J., Britt, M. and Rouet, J. (2013) Teaching Fourth and Fifth Graders to Evaluate Information Sources During Text Comprehension, *Cognition and Instruction*, 31 (2): 204-226

Mackley, T. A. (2000). Direct instruction of subject-matter content and cognitive skills associated with the Ohio fourth -grade proficiency test. Ann Arbor, The Ohio State University. 9971598: 133.

Manchester Institute of Education (2016) *Promoting alternative thinking strategies. Evaluation report and executive summary*. London: Education Endowment Foundation

Maridaki-Kassotaki, K. (2002) The relation between phonological memory skills and reading ability in
Marulis, L. and Neuman, S. (2010) The Effects of Vocabulary Intervention on Young Children's Word Learning: A Meta-Analysis, *Review of Educational Research*, 80 (3): 300-335
Marulis, L. and Neuman, S. (2013) How Vocabulary Interventions Affect Young Children at Risk: A Meta Analytic Review, *Journal of Research on Educational Effectiveness*, 6 (3): 223-262
Marzano, R.J. (2003) What works in schools: Tanslating research into action. Alexandria, VA: Association for Supervision and Curriculum Development.
Marzano, R.J., Pickering, D.J. and Pollock, J.E. (2001) Classroom instruction that works: Research-based strategies for increasing student achievement.
Mashburn, A., et al. (2016). "The Impacts of a Scalable Intervention on the Language and Literacy Development of Rural Pre-Kindergartners." Applied Developmental Science 20(1): 61-78.
Mason, D. and Good, T. (1993) Effects of Two-Group and Whole-Class Teaching on Regrouped Elementary Students' Mathematics Achievement. *American Educational Research Journal,* 30(2): 328-360.
Mason, L., Davison, M., Hammer, C., Miller, C. and Glutting, J. (2013) Knowledge, writing, and language outcomes for a reading comprehension and writing intervention, *Reading and Writing*, 26 (7): 1133-1158
Mathes, P. G., & Babyak, A. E. (2001) The effects of Peer-Assisted Literacy Strategies for first-grade readers with and without additional mini-skills lessons. *Learning Disabilities Research & Practice,* 16(1): 28–44.
Mathes, P., Denton, C., Fletcher, J., Anthony, J., Francis, D. and Schatschneider, C. (2005) The effects of theoretically different instruction and student characteristics on the skills of struggling readers, *Reading Research Quarterly*, 40 (2): 148-182
Mathes, P., Torgesen, J., and Allor, J.H. (2001) The effects of peer-assisted literacy strategies for first-Grade Readers with and without additional computer-assisted instruction in phonological awareness, *American Educational Research Journal,* 38 (2): 371-410

Mathis, D. (1996). *The Effect of the Accelerated Reader Program on Reading Comprehension*, US Department of Education, http://files.eric.ed.gov/fulltext/ED398555.pdf

Matsumura, L., Garnier, H. and Spybrook, J. (2013) Literacy coaching to improve student reading achievement: A multi-level mediation model, *Learning and Instruction*, 25: 35-48

Mattingly, A. (2014) *The Effects of Response to Intervention on Elementary School Academic Achievement and Learning Disability Identification,* PhD. North Carolina State University, USA.

May, H., Gray, A., Gillespie, J., Sirinides, P., Sam, C., Goldsworthy, H., Armijo, M. and Tognatta, N. (2013) *Evaluation of the i3 scale-up of Reading Recovery*, University of Delaware

May, H., Gray, A., Sirinides, P., Goldsworthy, H., Armijo, M., Sam, C. Gillespie, J. and Tognatta, N. (2015) Year one results from the multisite randomized evaluation of the i3 scale-up of Reading Recovery, American Educational Research Journal, 52, 3, 547-581

McArthur, G., Eve, P., Jones, K., Banales, E., Kohnen, S., Anandakumar, T., Larsen, L., Marinus, E., Wang, HC and Castles, A. (2012) Phonics training for English-speaking poor readers, *Cochrane Database of Systematic Reviews*, 12, doi: 10.1002/14651858.CD009115.pub2

McCutcheon, D., Green, L., Abbott, R. and Sanders, E. (2009) Further evidence for teacher knowledge: supporting struggling readers in grades three through five. *Reading and Writing*, 22: 401-423

McEldoon, K., Durkin, K. and Rittle-Johnson, B. (2013) Is self-explanation worth the time? A comparison to additional practice, *British Journal of Educational Psychology,* 83 (4) 615-632 2013

McGinty, A., Breit-Smith, A., Fan, X., Justice, L. and Kaderavek, J. (2011) Does intensity matter? Preschoolers' print knowledge development within a classroom-based intervention, *Early Childhood Research Quarterly,* 26 (3): 255-267

McMaster, K. L., Fuchs, D., Fuchs, L. S., & Compton, D. L. (2005). Responding to nonresponders: An experimental field trial of identification and intervention methods. *Exceptional Children,* 71(4), 445–463.

McNally, S. (2014) Hampshire Hundreds, Evaluation report. London: EEF. Available fromhttps://educationendowmentfoundation.org.uk/evaluation/projects/hampshire-hundreds/ [Accessed 28th June 2016]

Menon, S. and Hiebert, E. (2005) A comparison of first graders' reading with little books or literature-base basal anthologies, *Reading Research Quarterly,* 40 (1): 12-38

Mercer, N., Wegerif R. and Dawes, L. (1999) Children's talk and the development of reasoning in the classroom, *British Educational Research Journal*, 25(1): 95-111

Merrell, C., and Kasim, A. (2015) *Evaluation of Butterfly Phonics*, Education Endowment Foundation: London, http://www.realaction.org.uk/wp-content/uploads/2014/07/Butterfly_Phonics_Final-EEF-report.pdf

Meyer, B., Wijekumar, K., Middlemiss, W. Higgley, K., Lei, P.W., Meier, K. and Spielvogel, J. (2010) Web-based tutoring of the structure with or without elaborated feedback or choice for fifth and seventh grade readers, *Reading Research Quarterly,* 45(1): 62-92

Miao, Z. and Reynolds, D. (2015) Effectiveness of mathematics teaching: the truth about China and England, BERA Blog, Available from: https://www.bera.ac.uk/blog/effectiveness-of-mathematics-teaching the-truth-about-china-and-england [Accessed 16th June 2016]

Miller, D. and Robertson, D. (2011) Educational benefits of using game consoles in a primary classroom: A randomised controlled trial. *British Journal of Educational Technology*, 42, 850–864.

Mononen, R. and Aunio, P. (2014) A Mathematics intervention for low-performing Finnish second graders: findings from a pilot study, *European Journal of Special Needs Education*, 29 (4): 457-473

Moore, W., Hammond, L. and Fetherston, T. (2014) Analysis of the Use of Explicit Instruction Techniques to Improve Word Learning from Story Book Read-Alouds, *Australian Journal of Learning Difficulties,* 19(2): 153-172

Morales, K. (2013) *The effectiveness of the Smart Board® in increasing the mathematical achievement and motivation of first grade students,* PhD Thesis. St John's University

Moran, A., Swanson, A., Gerber, M. and Fung, W. (2014) The Effects of Paraphrasing Interventions on Problem-Solving Accuracy for Children at Risk for Math Disabilities, *Learning Disabilities Research and Practice,* 29 (3): 97-105

Moriyón, F. and Tudela, E. (2004): What we know about Research in Philosophy with children. Retrieved from https://philoenfant.org/2015/10/30/resume-de-103-recherches-en-philosophie-pour-les-enfants/ June 25 2016

Morris, D., Tyner, B., and Perney, J. (2000) Early steps: Replicating the effects of a first-grade reading intervention program, *Journal of Educational Psychology,* 92 (4): 681-93

Muijs, D. and Reynolds, D. (2011) Effective Teaching, London: SAGE

Muthukrishna, N. (2013). "Raising the quality of primary level mathematics teaching and learning in schools in American Samoa: A model for South Africa." Perspectives in Education 31(3): 122-138.

National Literacy Trust (2010) Are children's literacy skills improving or getting worse, http://www.literacytrust.org.uk/about/faqs/filter/about%20literacy%20in%20the%20uk#q713, accessed July 2010

Newman, D., Finney, P.B., Bell, S. Turner, H., Jaciw, A.P., Zacamy, J.L. and Gould, L.F. (2012). Evaluation of the Effectiveness of the Alabama Math, Science, and Technology Initiative (AMSTI). Final Report. NCEE 2012-4008, National Center for Education Evaluation and Regional Assistance.

Nichols, J. (2013) *Accelerated Reader and its effect on fifth-grade students' reading comprehension (*Doctoral dissertation, Liberty University)

Nunes, T., Bryant, P., Barros, R., and Sylva, K. (2012) The relative importance of two different mathematical abilities to mathematical achievement. *British Journal of Educational Psychology*, 82, 136–156

NYC Department for Education (2012) The NYC Core Knowledge Early Literacy Pilot, Available from: http://www.coreknowledge.org/mimik/mimik_uploads/documents/712/CK%20Early%20Literacy%20Pilot%203%2012%2012.pdf [Accessed 26th June 2016].

O'Connor, E.E., Cappella, E., McCormick, M.P. and McClowry, S.G. (2014) An Examination of the Efficacy of INSIGHTS in Enhancing the Academic and Behavioral Development of Children in Early Grades. *Journal of Educational Psychology* 106(4): 1156-1169.

O'Connor, M., Arnott, W., McIntosh, B. and Dodd, B. (2009) Phonological awareness and language intervention in preschoolers from low socio-economic backgrounds: A longitudinal investigation. *British Journal of Developmental Psychology* 27: 767-782.

O'Connor, R.E., HRTY, K.R. and Fulmer, D. (2005). Tiers of Intervention in Kindergarten Through Third Grade. Journal of *Learning Disabilities* 38(6): 532-538.

OFSTED (2004) *ICT in schools: the impact of government initiatives*, School Portraits Eggbuckland Community College, London: Ofsted, www.ofsted.gov.uk/publications/index.cfm?fuseaction=pubs.displayfile&id=3704&type=pdf, accessed 26/3/06

OFSTED (2010) *Reading by six: How the best schools do it*, London: OFSTED

Oostdam, R., Blok, H. and Boendermaker, C. (2015) Effects of individualised and small-group guided oral reading interventions on reading skills and reading attitude of poor readers in grades 2-4, *Research Papers in Education,* 30 (4): 427-450

Ouston, J. (1998) *The school effectiveness and improvement movement: a reflection on its contribution to the development of good schools*, presented at ESRC Redefining Education Management seminar, Open University, 4/6/98

Paris, A. H. and S. G. Paris (2007) Teaching narrative comprehension strategies to first graders. *Cognition and Instruction,* 25(1): 1-44.

Park, S. J. (2013) Do Highly Qualified Teachers Use More Effective Instructional Practices than other Teachers: The Mediating Effect of Instructional Practices, Society for Research on Educational Effectiveness Conference, 7th-9th March, Washington D.C. Available from http://files.eric.ed.gov/fulltext/ED563054.pdf [Accessed 28th June 2016].

Paul, T., VanderZee, D., Rue, T. and Swanson, S. (1996) Impact of the Accelerated Reader technology-based literacy program on overall academic achievement and school attendance. Paper presented at the National Reading Research

Centre Conference on *Literacy and Technology for the 21st Century* (Atlanta, GA, October 4, 1996)

Pavonetti, L., Brimmer, K. and Cipielewski, J. (2000) Accelerated Reader [R]: What Are the Lasting Effects on the Reading Habits of Middle School Students Exposed to Accelerated Reader [R] in Elementary Grades? Paper presented at the Annual Meeting of *the National Reading Conference* (50th, Scottsdale, AZ, November29-December 2, 2000)

Peak, J. and Dewalt, M. (1994) Reading Achievement: Effects of Computerized Reading Management and Enrichment, *ERS Spectrum*, 12(1), 31-34

Pelgrum, W. (2001) Obstacles to the integration of ICT in education: results from a worldwide educational assessment, *Computers and Education*, 37, pp. 163-178

Pennucci, A., & Lemon, M. (2014) Updated inventory of evidence- and research-based practices: Washington's K–12 Learning Assistance Program. (Doc. No. 14-09-2201). Olympia: Washington State Institute for Public Policy. Retrieved from: http://www.wsipp.wa.gov/ReportFile/1568/Wsipp_Updated-Inventory-of-Evidence-and-ResearchBased-Practices-Washingtons-K-8209-12-Learning-Assistance-Program_Report.pdf

Pesco, D. and Devlin, C. (2015) The effects of explicit instruction on French-speaking kindergarteners' understanding of stories. *Child Language Teaching & Therapy*, 31(2): 195-206.

Phelan, J., Choi, K., Vendlinkski, T., Baker, E. and Herman, J. (2011) Differential Improvement in Student Understanding of Mathematical Principles Following Formative Assessment Intervention. *Journal of Educational Research*, 104(5): 330-339.

Phillips, B.M. Clancy-Menchetti, J. and Lonigan, C.J. (2008) Successful Phonological Awareness Instruction With Preschool Children Lessons From the Classroom. *Topics in Early Childhood Special Education* 28(1): 3-17.

Pikulski, J. and Chard, D. (2005) Fluency: Bridge between decoding and comprehension, *The Reading Teacher*, 58, 6, 510-519

Pilli, O. and Aksu, M. (2013) The effects of computer-assisted instruction on the achievement, attitudes and retention of fourth grade mathematics students in North Cyprus. *Computers & Education*, 62: 62-71.

Pinnell, G., DeFord, D. and Lyons, C. (1988) *Reading Recovery: Early intervention for at-risk first graders*, Educational Research Service Monograph, Arlington, VA: Educational Research Service.

Pinnell, G., Lyons, C., DeFord, D., Bryk, A. and Seltzer, M. (1994) Comparing instructional models for the literacy education of high risk first graders, *Reading Research Quarterly*, 29, 1, 8-39

Piper, B. and Korda, M. (2011) Early Grade Reading Assessment (EGRA) Plus: Liberia. Program Evaluation Report, RTI International.

Pittard, V, Bannister, P and Dunn, J (2003) *The big pICTure: The impact of ICT on attainment, motivation and learning*, London: DfES, http://www.dfes.gov.uk/research/data/uploadfiles/ThebigpICTure.pdf, accessed 22/11/05

Potocki, A., Ecalle, J. and Magnan, A. (2013) Effects of computer-assisted comprehension training in less skilled comprehenders in second grade: A one-year follow-up study. *Computers & Education,* 63: 131-140.

Potocki, A., Ecalle, J. and Magnan, A. (2015) Computerized comprehension training for whom and under which conditions is it efficient? *Journal of Computer Assisted Learning,* 31(2): 162-175.

Powell, T. (2014) *A comparative analysis of the Singapore math curriculum and the everyday mathematics curriculum on fifth grade achievement in a large northeastern urban public school district,* PhD. Seton Hall University, USA.

Principato, K. (2010) *A Quantitative Study of the Added-Value of Co-Teaching Models Implemented in the Fourth Grade Classes of a Suburban New Jersey School District*, PhD. Temple University, USA.

Provus, M. M. (1960) Ability grouping in mathematics. *Elementary School Journal,* 60: 391-398.

Puhalla, E. (2011) Enhancing the Vocabulary Knowledge of First-Grade Children With Supplemental Booster Instruction. *Remedial and Special Education,* 32(6): 471-481.

Pullen, P., Tuckwiller, E., Konold, T., Maynard, K. and Coyne, M. (2010) A Tiered Intervention Model for Early Vocabulary Instruction: The Effects of Tiered Instruction for Young Students at Risk for Reading Disability. *Learning Disabilities Research and Practice,* 25(3): 110-123.

Puma, M., Tarkow, A. and Puma, A. (2007) *The Challenge of Improving Children's Writing Ability: A Randomised Evaluation of Writing Wings*, Washington DC: Institute of Education Sciences, US Department of Education

Puzio, K. and G. T. Colby (2013) Cooperative Learning and Literacy: A Meta-Analytic Review. *Journal of Research on Educational Effectiveness* 6(4): 339-360.

Reynolds, D., Teddlie, C., Chapman, C. and Springfield, S. (2015) Effective school processes, p.77 in Chapman, C., Muijs, D., Reynolds, D., Sammons, P. and Teddlie, C. (Eds.) The Routledge Handbook of Educational Effectiveness and Improvement, London: Routledge

Reznitskaya, A., Glina, M., Carolan, B., Michaud, O., Rogers, J. and Sequeria, L. (2012) Examining transfer effects from dialogic discussions to new tasks and contexts. *Contemporary Educational Psychology*, 37(4): 288-306.

Rienzo, C., Rolfe, H. and Wilkinson, D. (2015) Changing mindsets: Evaluation report and executive summary. London: Education Endowment Foundation.

Rimm-Kaufman, S., Larsen, R., Baroody, A., Curby, T., Merritt, E., Abry, T., Thomas, J. and Ko, M. (2014) Efficacy of the Responsive Classroom Approach: Results From a 3-Year, Longitudinal Randomized Controlled Trial, *American Educational Research Journal,* 51(3): 567-603.

Ripley, D. (2015) *An Examination of Flipped Instructional Method on Sixth Graders' Mathematics Learning: Utilizing Propensity Score Matching,* PhD. University of Nevada, USA.

Ritter, M., Park, J., Saxon, T. and Colson, K. (2013) A Phonologically Based Intervention for School-Age Children With Language Impairment: Implications for Reading Achievement. *Journal of Literacy Research,* 45(4): 356-385.

Rosas, R., Nussbaum, M., Cumsille, P., Marianov, V., Correa, M., Flores, P., Grau, V., Lagos, F., Lopez, X., Lopez, V., Rodriguez, P. and Salinas, M. (2003) Beyond Nintendo: design and assessment of educational video games for first and second grade students. *Computers & Education*, 40(1): 71-94.

Rose, D. and Dalton, B. (2002) Using technology to individualize reading instruction, pp. 257-274 in C. Block, L. Gambrell and M. Pressley (Eds.)

Improving comprehension instruction: Rethinking research, theory, and classroom practice, San Francisco: Jossey Bass Publishers

Ross, S., Nunnery, J. and Goldfeder, E. (2004) A randomized experiment on the effects of Accelerated Reader/Reading Renaissance in an urban school district: Preliminary evalua-tion report. Memphis, TN: The University of Memphis, *Centre for Research in Educational Policy*

Rouse, C., and Krueger, A. (2004) Putting computerized instruction to the test: A randomised evaluation of a "scientifically-based" reading program, *Economics of Education Review*, 23, pp. 323–338

Rudd, P. and Wade, P. (2006) *Evaluation of Renaissance Learning Mathematics and Reading Programs in UK Specialist and Feeder Schools*, (Final Report), Slough, UK: National Foundation for Educational Research, Available online: http://www.nfer.ac.uk/publications/SRY01/SRY01_home.cfm

Runfola, M., Etopio, E., Hamlen, K., and Rozendal, M. (2012) Effect of Music Instruction on Preschoolers' Music Achievement and Emergent Literacy Achievement. *Bulletin of the Council for Research in Music Education*, 192: 7-27.

Rutt, S., Easton, C. and Stacey, O. (2014) *Catch-up numeracy. Evaluation report and executive summary.* London: Education Endowment Foundation.

Ryder, J., Tunmer, W. and Greaney, K. (2008) Explicit instruction in phonemic awareness and phonemically based decoding skills as an intervention strategy for struggling readers in whole language classrooms, *Reading and Writing,* 21(4): 349-369.

Sainsbury, M., Whetton, C., Keith, M. and Schagen, I. (1998) Fallback in attainment on transfer at age 11: evidence from the Summer Literacy Schools evaluation. *Educational Research*, Vol. 40, No. 1, pp. 73-81

Sarama, J., Clements, D., Wolfe, C. and Spitler, M. (2012) Longitudinal Evaluation of a Scale-Up Model for Teaching Mathematics With Trajectories and Technologies. *Journal of Research on Educational Effectiveness,* 5(2): 105-135.

Scheerens, J. (1992) Effective schooling: Research, theory and practice. London: Cassell.

Scheerens, J. (1999) School effectiveness in developed and developing countries: A review of the research evidence. web.worldbank.org/archive/website00237/WEB/DOC/JAAP699.DOC

Scholastic Research (2008) *Desert Sands unified school district, CA*. New York, NY: Scholastic Inc.

Schünemann, N., Sporer, N. and Brunstein, J. (2013) Integrating self-regulation in whole-class reciprocalteaching: A moderator–mediator analysis of incremental effects on fifth graders' reading comprehension. *Contemporary Educational Psychology,* 38(4): 289-305.

Schwartz, R. (2005) Literacy learning of at-risk first-grade students in the Reading Recovery early intervention, *Journal of Educational Psychology*, 97, N2, 257-26

Schwartz, R., Schmitt, M. and Lose, M. (2012) Effects of teacher-student ratio in response to intervention approaches, *The Elementary School Journal,* 112 (4): 547-567.

Scott, L. (1999) *The Accelerated Reader program, reading achievement, and attitudes of students with learning disabilities,* Unpublished doctoral dissertation, Georgia State University, Atlanta (ERIC Document Reproduction Service No. ED 434431)

See, B.H. and Kokotsaki, D. (2016) Impact of arts education on children's learning and wider outcomes. *Review of Education*. DOI: 10.1002/rev3.3070

See, B.H., Gorard, S. and Siddiqui, N (2015a) Anglican Schools Partnership: Effective feedback. Evaluation report and executive summary. London: Education Endowment Foundation

See, B.H., Gorard, S. and Siddiqui, N. (2015b) *Word and World Reading: Evaluation report and executive summary*. London: Education Endowment Foundation

See, B.H., Gorard, S. and Siddiqui, N. (2015c) Best practice in conducting RCTs: Lessons learnt form an independent evaluation of the Response-to-Intervention programme. *Studies in Educational Evaluation*, 47: 83-92.

See, B.H., Gorard, S. and Siddiqui, N. (2016) Teachers' use of research evidence in practice: a pilot study of feedback to enhance learning. *Educational Research,* 58(1): 56-72

Serin, O. (2011) The effects of the computer-based instruction on the achievement and problem solving skills of the science and technology students, *The Turkish Online Journal of Educational Technology,* 10(1): 183-201

Shamir, A., Tzuriel, D. and Rozen, M. (2006) Peer mediation - The effects of program intervention, maths level, and verbal ability on mediation style and improvement in maths problem solving, *School Psychology International,* 27 (2): 209-231

Shannon, D. M., Twale, D.J. and Moore, M.S. (1998). "TA Teaching Effectiveness: The Impact of Training and eaching Experience." The Journal of Higher Education 69(4): 440-466.

Shannon, L., Styers, M., Wilkerson, S., and Peery, E. (2015) Computer-assisted learning in elementary reading: A randomized control trial, *Computers in the Schools,* 32, 1, 20–34, doi: 10.1080/07380569.2014.969159

Shapiro, L. and Solity, J. (2008) Delivering Phonological and Phonics Training within Whole-Class Teaching, *British Journal of Educational Psychology,* 78(4): 597-620.

Shayer, M. and Adhami, M. (2010) Realizing the cognitive potential of children 5-7 with a mathematics focus: Post-test and long-term effects of a 2-year intervention. *British Journal of Educational Psychology* 80(3): 363-379.

Shin, M. and Bryant, D. (2015) Fraction Interventions for Students Struggling to Learn Mathematics: A

Siddiqui, N., Gorard, S. and See, BH (2015) Accelerated Reader as a literacy catch-up intervention during the primary to secondary school transition phase, *Educational Review,* 68, 2, 139-154

Silverstein, G., Frechtling, J. and Miyoaka, A. (2000) *Evaluation of the use of technology in Illinois public schools: Final report* (prepared for Research Division, Illinois State Board of Education), Rockville, MD: Westat

Simmons, D., Kame'enui, E., Harn, B., Coyne, M., Stoolmiller, M., Edwards, L., Santoro, L., Smith, S.,

Siraj-Blatchford, I. and Taggart, B. (2014) Exploring Effective Pedagogy in Primary Schools: Evidence from Research. London: Pearson.

Siraj-Blatchford, I., Shepherd, D., Melhuish, E., Taggart, B., Sammons, P. and Sylva, K (2011) *Effective pedagogical strategies in English and mathematics*

in Key Stage 2: A study of Year 5 classroom practice from the EPPSE 3-16 longitudinal study. DfE Research Report DFE-RR129. London: DfE
Sivin-Kachala, J., and Bialo, E. (2000) *2000 research report on the effectiveness of technology in schools* (7th ed.), Washington DC: Software and Information Industry
Skiba, R., Casey, A., and Center, B. (1985–1986) Nonaversive procedures in the treatment of classroom behavior problems, *Journal of Special Education,* 19: 459–481
Skipp, A. and Tanner, E. (2016) *The Visible Classroom.* Evaluation report and executive summary. London: Education Endowment Foundation.
Slavin, R. and Lake, C. (2008) Effective programs in elementary mathematics: A best-evidence synthesis, *Review of Educational Research,* 78, 427–515.
Slavin, R. E. (1987) Ability grouping and student achievement in elementary schools: A best-evidence synthesis. *Review of Educational Research*, 57(3): 293-336.
Slavin, R., Lake, C., Chambers, B., Cheung, A. and Davis, S. (2009) Effective reading programmes for the elementary grades: A best evidence synthesis, *Review of Educational Research,* 79, 4, 1391-1466.
Slavin, R., Lake, C., Davis, S. and Madden, N. (2011) Effective programs for struggling readers: A best evidence synthesis, *Educational Research Review,* 6 (1): 1-26
Smith, E. and Gorard, S. (2005) 'They don't give us our marks': the role of formative feedback in student progress, *Assessment in Education*, 12(1): 21-38
Smith, F., Hardman, F., Wall., K. and Mroz, M. (2004) Interactive Whole Class Teaching in the National Literacy and Numeracy Strategies. *British Educational Research Journal,* 30(3): 395-411.
Soboleski, P. (2011) *Fast ForWord: An Investigation of the Effectiveness of Computer-Assisted Reading Intervention,* PhD. Bowling Green State University, USA.
Sontag, C. and Stoeger, H. (2015) Can highly intelligent and high-achieving students benefit from training in self-regulated learning in a regular classroom context. *Learning and Individual Differences* 41: 43-53.

Speight, s., Callahan, M., Griggs, J. and Javiera, C.F. (2016) Rochdale research into practice: evaluation report and executive summary. London: Education Endowment Foundation

Sprague, K., Hamilton, J., Coffey, D., Loadman, W., Lomax, R., Moore, R., Faddis, B. and Beam, M. (2010) *Using randomized clinical trials to determine the impact of reading intervention on struggling adolescent readers: reports of Research from five nationally funded striving readers grants.* Papers presented at the Society for Research on Educational Effectiveness Conference, (no details about place and date of conference) https://www.sree.org/conferences/2010/program/abstracts/208.pdf

Stanford, A. (2014) *The effects of teacher's teaching style and experience on elemenrary students' mathematical achievement,* PhD. Liberty University, USA. Available from: http://digitalcommons.liberty.edu/doctoral/909/ [Accessed 15th June 2016]

Stein, M. L., Berends, M., Fuchs, D., McMaster, K., Sáenz, L., Yen, L., & Compton, D. L. (2008). Scaling up an early reading program: Relationships among teacher support, fidelity of implementation, and student performance across different sites and years. *Educational Evaluation and Policy Analysis*, 30(4): 368–388.

Sterling, D. (2010) *Effects of Differentiated and ACTIVboard Instruction on Third and Fifth Grade Students' Academic Performance*, PhD. Walden University, USA.

Strambler, M. and McKown, C. (2013) Promoting Student Engagement Through Evidence-Based Action Research With Teachers, *Journal of Educational and Psychological Consultation*, 23 (2): 87-114

Strayhorn, J. and Bickel, D. (2003) A randomized trial of individual tutoring for elementary school children with reading and behavior difficulties, *Psychological Reports,* 92, 427-444

Stringfield, S., Dartnow, A., Borman, G.. and Rachuba, L. (2000) *National evaluation of Core Knowledge Sequence implementation Final Report. Report No. 49*. Baltimore: CRESPA, John Hopkins University

Styles, B., Clarkson, R. and Fowler, K. (2014) Rhythm for Reading: Evaluation report and executive summary. London: Education Endowment Foundation

Swanson, H. L. and Sachse-Lee, C. (2000) A meta-analysis of single-subject-design intervention research for students with LD. *Journal of Learning Disabilities* 33(2): 114-136.

Tanner, E., Brown, A., Day, N., Kotecha, M., Low, N., Morrell, G., Turczuk, O., Brown, V., Collingwood, A., Chowdry, H., Greaves, E., Harrison, C., Johnson, G. and Purdon, S. (2011) *Evaluation of Every Child a Reader*, London: NatCen

Tchoshanov, M. (2011) Relationship between teacher knowledge of concepts and connections, teaching practice, and student achievement in middle grades mathematics, *Educational Studies in Mathematics*, 76(2): 141-164.

The Guardian (2012) US idea of 'cultural literacy' and key facts child should know arrives in UK. http://www.theguardian.com/education/2012/oct/15/hirsch-core-knowledge-curriculum-review. Accessed 28 October 2015

The Rose Report (2016) I*ndependent review of the teaching of early reading*. London: DfES

Thomas, C., Beck, T. and Kaufman, N. (2007) Attributes of effective and efficient kindergarten reading intervention: An examination of instructional time and design specificity, *Journal of Learning Disabilities*, 40 (4): 331-47

Tok, Ş., & Mazı, A. (2015) The effect of Stories for Thinking on reading and listening comprehension: a case study in Turkey, *Research in Education*, 93(1), 1-18

Tong, F., Irby, B., Lara-Alecio, R., Guerrero, C., Fan, Y. and Huerta, M. (2014) A Randomized Study of a Literacy-Integrated Science Intervention for Low-Socio-economic Status Middle School Students: Findings from first-year implementation, *International Journal of Science Education*, 36 (12): 2083-2109

Topping, K. (2014) *What kids are reading: The book reading habits of students in British Schools 2014*: An Independent Study, Renaissance Learning Inc.: United Kingdom

Topping, K. J., & Trickey, S. (2007). Collaborative philosophical inquiry for schoolchildren: Cognitive gains at 2-year follow-up. *British Journal of Educational Psychology*, *77*, 4, 787-796

Torgerson C. and Zhu D. (2003) *A systematic review and meta-analysis of the effectiveness of ICT on literacy learning in English, 5-16,* Research Evidence in Education Library. London: EPPI-Centre, Social Science Research Unit, Institute of Education, University of London

Torgerson, C., Brooks, G. and Hall, J. (2006) *A Systematic Review of the Research Literature on the Use of Phonics in the Teaching of Reading and Spelling*, London: DfES, Research Report 711, https://czone.eastsussex.gov.uk/sites/gtp/library/core/english/Documents/phonics/A%20Systematic%20Review%20of%20the%20Research%20Literature%20on%20the%20Use%20of%20Phonics%20in%20the%20Teaching%20of%20Reading%20and%20Spelling.pdf

Torgerson, D., Torgerson, C., Ainsworth, H., Buckley, H., Heaps, C., Hewitt, C. and Mitchell, N. (2014b) Improving writing quality. Evaluation report and executive summary. London: Education Endowment Foundation.

Torgerson, D., Torgerson, C., Mitchell, N., Buckley, H., Ainsworth, H., Heaps, C. and Jefferson, L. (2014) *Grammar for writing: Evaluation report and executive summary*. London: Education Endowment Foundation.

Trickey, S. and Topping, K. (2004) Philosophy for children: a systematic review, *Research Papers in Education*, 19(3): 365-380

Troia, G. (2004) Migrant students with limited English proficiency - Can fast ForWord Language™ make a difference in their language skills and academic achievement? *Remedial and Special Education,* 25 (6): 353-366

Truckenmiller, A., Eckert, T., Codding, R. and Petscher, Y. (2014) Evaluating the impact of feedback on elementary aged students' fluency growth in written expression: A randomized controlled trial, *Journal of School Psychology,* 52 (6): 531-548

Tseng, C-M. (2014) *The effects of the science writing heuristic (SWH) approach versus traditional instruction on yearly critical thinking gain scores in grade 5-8 classrooms,* PhD. University of Iowa, USA.

Vadasy, P. and Sanders, E. (2008) Repeated reading intervention: Outcomes and interactions with readers' skills and classroom instruction. *Journal of Educational Psychology,* 100(2): 272-290.

Vadasy, P. and Sanders, E. (2011) Efficacy of Supplemental Phonics-Based Instruction for Low-Skilled First Graders: How Language Minority Status and Pretest Characteristics Moderate Treatment Response. *Scientific Studies of Reading,* 15(6): 471-497.

Vadasy, P., Nelson, J. and Sanders, E. (2013) Longer Term Effects of a Tier 2 Kindergarten Vocabulary Intervention for English Learners. *Remedial and Special Education,* 34(2): 91-101.

Vadasy, P., Sanders, E., and Abbott, R. (2008) Effects of supplemental early reading intervention at 2-year follow up: Reading skill growth patterns and predictors, *Scientific Studies of Reading*, 12(1): 51-89.

Van der Kooy-Hofland, V., Bus, A. and Roskos, K. (2012) Effects of a brief but intensive remedial computer intervention in a sub-sample of kindergartners with early literacy delays, *Reading and Writing,* 25(7): 1479-1497.

Van Keer, H. (2004) Fostering reading comprehension in fifth grade by explicit instruction in reading strategies and peer tutoring, *British Journal of Educational Psychology,* 74: 37-70.

Van Luit, J. (2009) Nonverbal learning disabilities and arithmetic problems: the effectiveness of an explicit verbal instruction model, In: Scruggs, T. and Mastropieri, M. (eds.) *Policy and Practice.* Bradford: Emerald Group Publishing Ltd, pp. 265-289.

Vaughn, S., Mathes, P., Linan-Thompson, S., Cirino, P., Carlson, C., Pollard-Durodola, S., Cardenas-Hagan, E. and Francis, D. (2006) Effectiveness of an English intervention for first-grade English language learners at risk for reading problems, *Elementary School Journal,* 107(2): 153-180.

Vaughn, S., Wexler, J., Leroux, A., Roberts, G., Denton, C., Barth, A. and Fletcher, J. (2012) Effects of Intensive Reading Intervention for Eighth-Grade Students With Persistently Inadequate Response to Intervention, *Journal of Learning Disabilities,* 45 (6): 515-525

Vernon-Feagans, L., Bratsch-Hines, M., Varghese, C., Bean, A. Hedrick, A. (2015) The Targeted Reading Intervention: Face-to-Face vs. Webcam Literacy Coaching of Classroom Teachers. *Learning Disabilities Research and Practice*, 30(3): 135-147.

Vollands, S., Topping, K. and Evans, R. (1996) *Experimental evaluation of computer assisted self-assessment of reading comprehension: Effects on reading achievement and attitude*, ERIC Document, ED 408 567

Vollands, S., Topping, K. and Evans, R. (1999) Computerized self-assessment of reading comprehension with the Accelerated Reader: action research, *Reading and Writing Quarterly*, 15, 3,197–211

Waller, L. (2013) *Math intervention teachers' pedagogical content knowledge and student achievement*. PhD Thesis. Eastern Kentucky University, USA.

Wanzek, J. and Vaughn, S. (2007) Research-based implications from extensive early reading interventions, *School Psychology Review,* 36(4): 541-561.

Wanzek, J., Vaughn, S., Scammacca, N., Metz, K., Murray, C., Roberts, G., and Danielson, L. (2013) Extensive Reading Interventions for Students With Reading Difficulties After Grade 3, *Review of Educational Research*, 83(2): 163-195.

Wanzek, J., Wexler, J., Vaughn, S. and Ciullo, S. (2010) Reading interventions for struggling readers in the upper elementary grades: a synthesis of 20 years of research, *Reading and Writing*, 23(8): 889-912.

Waxman, H., Lin, M., and Michko, G. (2003) *A meta-analysis of the effectiveness of teaching and learning with technology on pupil outcomes*, North Central Regional Educational Laboratory Web site: http://www.ncrel.org/tech/effects2/waxman.pdf, accessed 28/2/06

Wells, N., Myers, B., Todd, L., Barale, K., Gaolach, B., Ferenz, G., Aitken, M., Henderson, C., Tse, C., Pattison, K., Taylor, C., Connerly, L., Carson, J., Gensemer, A., Franz, N. and Falk, E. (2015) The Effects of School Gardens on Children's Science Knowledge: A randomized controlled trial of low-income elementary schools, *International Journal of Science Education*, 37(17): 2858-2878.

What Works Clearing House (2008) *Accelerated Reader: WWC intervention report*, IES, http://ies.ed.gov/ncee/wwc/interventionreport.aspx?sid=12

What Works Clearinghouse (2009) *Singapore Math*. Washington: US Dept of Education, Institute of Education Sciences.

What Works Clearinghouse (2010) *Quick Review of the Report "Effectiveness of Selected Supplemental Reading Comprehension Interventions: Impacts on a*

First Cohort of Fifth-Grade Students". Princeton: Institute of Education Sciences.

What Works Clearinhoouse (2010) Sound partners, Washington: US Dept of Education, Institute of Education Sciences.

What Works Clearinghouse (2015) *Primary mathematics intervention report: Singapore Math*. Washington: US Dept of Education, Institute of Education Sciences.

What Works Clearinghouse (2013) Reading Recovery, http://ies.ed.gov/ncee/wwc/interventionreport.aspx?sid=420

Wheldall, K. (2000) Does Rainbow Repeated Reading add value to an intensive literacy intervention programme for low-progress readers? An experimental evaluation, *Educational Review*, Vol. 52, No. 1, pp. 29-36

Whitburn, J. (2001) Effective Classroom Organisation in Primary Schools: Mathematics, *Oxford Review of Education*, 27(3): 411-428

White, B. and Frederiksen, J. (1998) Inquiry, modelling and meta-cognition: making science accessible to all students. *Cognition and Instruction,* 16 (1): 3-118

White, D. and Robertson, L. (2015) Implementing assistive technologies: A study on co-learning in the Canadian elementary school context, *Computers in Human Behavior*, 51: 1268-1275.

White, R., Williams, I. and Haslem, M. (2005) *Performance of District 23 students participating in Scholastic READ 180*. Washington, DC: Policy Studies Associates. Evaluated in WWC (2009) *READ 180.* What Works Clearinghouse Intervention Report. Washington: US Department of Education, Institute of Education Sciences

Whitehurst-Hall, J. (1999) *The impact of the Core Knowledge Curriculum on the achievement of seventh and eighth grade students,* PhD. University of Georgia, USA.

Wijekumar, K., Meyer, B., Lei, P-W., Lin, Y-C., Johnson, L., Spielvogel, J., Shurmatz, K., Ray, M. and Cook, M. (2014) Multisite Randomized Controlled Trial Examining Intelligent Tutoring of Structure Strategy for Fifth-Grade Readers, *Journal of Research on Educational Effectiveness*, 7(4): 331-357.

Williams, J., Pollini, S., Nubla-Kung, A., Snyder, A., Garcia, A., Ordynans, J. and Atkins, J. (2014) An Intervention to Improve Comprehension of Cause/Effect Through Expository Text Structure Instruction, *Journal of Educational Psychology*, 106(1): 1-17.

Williams, S. (1993) *Evaluating the effects of philosophical enquiry in a secondary school*, The Village Community School Philosophy for Children Project

Wise, J., Sevcik, R., Morris, R., Lovett, M. and Wolf, M. (2007) The growth of phonological awareness by children with reading disabilities: A result of semantic knowledge or knowledge of grapheme-phoneme correspondences? *Scientific Studies of Reading*, 11(2): 151-164.

Wolf, M. and Katzir-Cohen, T. (2001) Reading fluency and its intervention, *Scientific Studies of Reading*, 5, 3, 211-239

Wong, N.-Y., Lam, C., Sun, X. and Chan, M. (2009) From exploring the middle zone to constructing a bridge: Experimenting in the spiral Bianshi mathematics curriculum, *International Journal o Science and Mathematics Education*, 7(2): 363-382.

Woods, D.E. (2007) *An investigation of the effects of a middle school reading intervention on school dropout rates*. Unpublished doctoral dissertation. Virginia Polytechnic Institute and State University (Blacksburg)

Worth, J., Sizmur, J., Ager, R. and Styles, B. (2015) Improving numeracy and literacy. Evaluation report and summary. London: Education Endowment Foundation.

WWC (2009) *READ 180. What Works Clearinghouse Intervention Report*. Washington: US Department of Education, Institute of Education Sciences

WWC (2010) *Project CRISS (Creating Indepence through Student-owned Strategies)*. Washington: US Dept of Education, Institute of Education Sciences.

WWC (2012) Peer-Assisted Learning/Literacy Strategies. Washington: US Dept of Education, Institute of Education Sciences. Retrieved from http://ies.ed.gov/ncee/wwc/interventionreport.aspx?sid=619

WWC (2013) Elementary School Mathematics intervention report: Peer-Assisted Learning Strategies. Washington: US Dept of Education, Institute of

Education Sciences. Retrieved from http://ies.ed.gov/ncee/wwc/interventionreport.aspx?sid=619

Wyse, D. and Goswami, U. (2008) *Synthetic phonics and the teaching of reading, British Educational Research Journal*, 34. 6, 691-710

Xue, Y. and Meisels, S. (2004) Early Literacy Instruction and Learning in Kindergarten: Evidence from th Early Childhood Longitudinal Study: Kindergarten Class of 1998-1999, *American Educational Research Journal*, 41(1): 191-229.

Ysseldyke, J., Spicuzza, R., Kosciolek, S. and Boys, C. (2003) Effects of a learning information system on mathematics achievement and classroom structure, *Journal of Educational Research,* 96(3): 163-173.

Zacharia, Z., Lazaridou, C. and Avraamidou, L. (2016) The use of mobile devices as means of data collection in supporting elementary school students' conceptual understanding about plants, *International Journal of Science Education,* 38(4): 596-620.

Zeng-Wei, H., et al. (2016) Authoring Robot-Assisted Instructional Materials for Improving Learning Performance and Motivation in EFL Classrooms. *Journal of Educational Technology & Society* 19(1): 337-349.

Zenner, C., Herrnleben-Kurz, S. and Walach, H. (2014) Mindfulness-based interventions in schools – a systematic review and meta-analysis, *Frontiers in Psychology*, 5, Article 603.

Zhang, Y. and Zhou, X. (2016) Building Knowledge Structures by Testing Helps Children With Mathematical Learning Difficulty, *Journal of Learning Disabilities*, 49(2): 166-175.

Zhang, Z. G. and Schumm, J. (2000) Exploring effects of the keyword method on limited English Proficient students' vocabulary recall and comprehension, *Reading Research and Instruction,* 39(3): 202-221.

Zhou, J. and Urhahne, D. (2013) Teacher judgment, student motivation, and the mediating effect of attributions, *European Journal of Psychology of Education,* 28(2): 275-295.

Printed in Great Britain
by Amazon